Neuropolitics

Edited by

Sandra Buckley

Michael Hardt

Brian Massumi

THEORY OUT OF BOUNDS

Neuropolitics

Thinking, Culture, Speed

William E. Connolly

Theory Out of Bounds   *Volume 23*

University of Minnesota Press

Minneapolis • London

An earlier version of chapter 4 first appeared as "Brain Waves, Transcendental Fields, and Techniques of Thought," *Radical Philosophy* 94 (March/April 1999); reprinted with permission.
An earlier version of chapter 7 appeared as "Speed, Concentric Cultures, and Cosmopolitanism," *Political Theory* 28 (October 2000): 519–618; copyright 2000 Sage Periodicals Press; reprinted with permission of Sage Periodicals Press.

Published by the University of Minnesota Press
111 Third Avenue South, Suite 290
Minneapolis, MN 55401-2520
http://www.upress.umn.edu

LIBRARY OF CONGRESS CATALOGING-IN-PUBLICATION DATA
Connolly, William E.
Neuropolitics : thinking, culture, speed / William E. Connolly.
p.   cm. — (Theory out of bounds ; v. 23)
Includes bibliographical references and index.
ISBN 0-8166-4021-1 (hc : alk. paper) — ISBN 0-8166-4022-X (pbk. :
alk. paper)
1. Thought and thinking.   2. Culture—Philosophy.   3. Speed—Social
aspects.   4. Mind and body—Social aspects.   I. Title.   II. Series.
B105.T54 C66 2002
128—dc21
2002000858

Printed in the United States of America on acid-free paper

The University of Minnesota
is an equal-opportunity educator and employer.

12 11 10 09 08 07   10 9 8 7 6 5 4 3

For David and Debbie

In fact, an important and pervasive shift is beginning to take place in cognitive science under the very influence of its own research. This shift requires that we move away from the idea of a world as independent and extrinsic to the idea of a world as inseparable from the structure of these processes of self-modification.

—Francisco J. Varela, Evan Thompson, and Eleanor Rosch, *The Embodied Mind: Cognitive Science and Human Experience*

Neurons that fire together wire together.

—Gerald M. Edelman and Giulio Tononi, *A Universe of Consciousness: How Matter Becomes Imagination*

Out of damp and gloomy days, out of solitude, out of loveless words directed at us, *conclusions* grow up in us like fungus: one morning they are there, we know not how, and they gaze upon us. Woe to the thinker who is not the gardener but only the soil of the plants that grow up in him!

—Friedrich Nietzsche, *Daybreak*

Hostility to art is also hostility to the new, the unforeseen.

—Robert Bresson, *Notes on the Cinematographer*

However, nobody has yet determined the limits of the body's capabilities.

—Spinoza, *The Ethics*

Contents

Preface

THE AMBULANCE DRIVER arrived in the middle of the night. He told the two teens their parents had been in a car accident. Their mom was injured but would survive. Their dad was dying. The driver would take them to the hospital. Their mother had asked him to do so, as they wheeled her into the emergency room. They departed immediately, forgetting the two young kids sound asleep in the house.

When they arrived their mother was in bad shape. The doctors would not allow her to see her husband. But they could. He had fallen into a coma. His body was entangled in tubes and instruments. Other relatives soon arrived in small groups. His grandfather pulled the boy aside. He said it was now time for him to become a man and support the family. The sixteen-year-old wondered whether these words were well timed. His dad was still breathing in the next room, for god's sake, albeit with technical help.

Pluma was permitted to visit Bill two days later. Her concussion had improved. She looked down at her husband and said, "Hi, Bill, I'm okay." He puckered his lips and made a smacking sound. Some people began to wonder whether the announcement of his impending death was premature.

He sank into a deeper coma. It lasted about a month and a half. Then, slowly, he began to crawl out. One hot summer night, fairly late on, the former navy private informed his son that they were prisoners on a battleship. With grim authority he ordered the boy to grab the prison nurse when she arrived, lock her in the closet, and make a run for it with him. The boy tried to reason with the private. He said, "Look, this is a hospital, and everybody here is helping you." No response. Eventually the boy said, "If we were actually on a boat in the middle of the ocean, Dad, there would be no place to run." The private stared coldly at him, the way you would look at a coward in the middle of a war.

The boy decided not to join the enemy ranks. Not immediately, at least. So he worked with his dad on the plan. Keep the maniac talking and conspiring. It was not a great idea. The pressure built up as the plan progressed. He finally said, "Dad, your pelvis is broken and you can barely walk, let alone make a run for it with me. (I may have to make that run alone...)"

"You hold on to me, boy, and we'll run together."

"Okay."

A plan sealed in solidarity. That night, when the nurse walked into the room, the boy took two quick steps toward her. Then, just before tossing the guard into the closet, he glanced back at his dad with that sideways look they had shared many times when plots hatched against "the girls" were about to falter. The two fell into laughter. The scheme collapsed into itself for another night. The nurse was pleased they were having such a good time.

The prisoner made a break for it alone two nights later. They eventually found the escapee limping around the hospital grounds with a wastebasket full of belongings. Nobody knew how the commando had made it down the hall, several flights of stairs, out the door, and past the parking lot into a wooded area. The adventure, however, made him a favorite of the staff. People now shared stories about his daily exploits, of which there were many. But the family was also obliged to have someone on hand all night, every night. Or else they would put bars around the paranoid's bed during the late-night shifts. He would, in effect, find himself on a prison ship.

It was summer and school was out. The boy thus found himself in a good position to watch his dad climb up a few plateaus of disposition, perception, memory, and judgment over the next several weeks. The thirty-six-year-old man was eventually released. After another year of recovery, he returned to the auto factory. For the first time in his life, he loved the work. A little brain damage goes a long way on the assembly line. His short-term memory was shot; his higher intellectual capacities were curtailed. But he retained a strong sense of self, he had a sweet disposition, and he often gave sound advice during the next decades to his children, stepchildren, and grandchildren when they wondered what to do with their lives.

My curiosity about relays between brain activity and cultural life arrived the honest way. I can now offer a decent account of which of my father's brain nodules were badly damaged, which regained limited capacity, and which functioned well. Certainly his hippocampus—the delicate brain nodule involved in laying down new memories—never made it all the way back. Otherwise the house would not have been perpetually overstocked with milk and short on bread.

From time to time I have looked into brain research only to move away. It seemed too sucked into a reductive model of science and unappreciative of the need to enter into communication with phenomenological experience. A few years ago I took another look. It turned out that exciting things were happening and that political questions I had been exploring over the past two decades could profit from attention to research into brain-body-culture relations.

This study explores the intersections of thinking, technique, ethical judgment, cultural pluralism, speed, and cosmopolitanism. It is a continuation of two recent studies, *The Ethos of Pluralization* and *Why I Am Not a Secularist*. More than those books, however, it folds insights from neuroscience and film, respectively, into its explorations. And it engages the issues of speed and time more actively. By *neuropolitics* I do not mean that politics is reducible to genetically wired brain processes or that scientific observation of body/brain activity captures the actual experience of those observed. Reactions in cultural theory against such reductions are well taken, as we shall see in later pages. But, unfortunately, those very reactions often issue in arid conceptions of thinking, language, culture, ethics, and politics. To escape the curse of reductive biology, many cultural theorists reduce body-politics to studies of how the body is *represented* in cultural politics. They do not appreciate the *compositional* dimension of body-brain-culture relays. By *neuropolitics*, then, I mean the politics through which cultural life mixes into the composition of body/brain processes. And vice versa. The new neuroscience, while needing augmentation from cultural theory, encourages students of culture to attend to the layered character of thinking; it also alerts us to the critical significance of *technique* in thinking, ethics, and politics.

As I have followed this trail it has become clear that attention to cinema can also inform these explorations. The words, sounds, images, and rhythms through which films prompt a synthesis of experience by viewers simulate the way multimedia techniques and (what I call) micropolitics work in other venues. Film analysis helps us to discern multimedia techniques at work in organizing perceptual experience, consolidating habits, composing ethical dispositions, and spurring new thoughts into being. Technique provides a medium through which cultures and brains infuse each other. Hand gestures, for instance, do not merely accompany speech.

There is evidence that early in life such gestures help to activate speech capacity; later they serve as invaluable aids and triggers to adult talk. The idea is to draw neuroscience, film theory, and political theory into communication to examine the role technique plays in thinking, ethics, and politics. Some films, as we shall see, also challenge linear conceptions of time, encouraging us to address the ethical and political implications of adopting a nonlinear conception.

I am indebted to many people for this book. My mother and father first. They taught by doing: make the most of what the contingencies of life offer. Their deaths render more palpable the multiple ways in which memory enters perception, thinking, judgment, and action. Recollection forms merely its surface; waves of memory subsist below recollection. I honor my parents in my dreams, these days. My children teach me too. David and Debbie help me, among many other things, to be alert to the rapid pace of life and to the productive possibilities accompanying its risks. They enliven me by their ways of being.

A Fellowship at the National Humanities Centre at Australian National University in the spring of 1999 allowed me to consolidate this study. Several scholars at ANU and the University of Sydney, most notably Anne Curthoys, John Docker, Paul Patton, Duncan Ivison, Moira Gatens, Ann Kaplan, and Barry Hindess, read and discussed several chapters. Mike Shapiro showed me how pertinent the study of film is to the issues that grip both of us. I have also presented early drafts of chapters as papers at a symposium between Charles Taylor and me on secularism at the Center for the Critical Analysis of Contemporary Culture at Rutgers; the Conference on Obscene Powers at Southampton, England; a symposium on secularism and religion at Bellagio, Italy; a symposium on anthropology and secularism at City University of New York; the Institute for Philosophy and Public Policy at the University of Maryland; a couple of meetings of the American Political Science Association (APSA); and a theme panel on my work at a meeting of the International Studies Association. In each case, comments and suggestions by other participants have proved very helpful. Talal Asad, Ben Corson, David Campbell, Tom Dumm, Bonnie Honig, Lauren Berlant, Steve Johnston, Kara Shaw, Mort Schoolman, Michael Warner, Stephen White, and Linda Zerilli have read sections of the manuscript and offered valuable comments.

The Johns Hopkins University is a stimulating place for intellectual life in general and political theory in particular. Conversations with Dick Flathman regularly prompt my thinking. And discussions with graduate students in theory seminars have proved critical. I mention Jacquie Best, Jason Frank, Davide Panagia, Paul Saurette, Kathy Trevenen, Nick Tampio, Blake Ethridge, John

Tambornino, Kam Shapiro, Lars Tonder, Paulina Ochoa, Smita Rahman, Andrew Ross, and Matt Moore as particularly compelling interlocutors. Kathy Trevenen doubled as a reader of the penultimate draft, helping me to refine the final version. Wendy Brown, a political theorist, Paul Patton, a philosopher, and Zachary Mainen, a neuroscientist, read an early draft of the entire manuscript. I am particularly grateful for their thoughtful comments and proposals, most of which have wound their way into the final result. Thanks, finally, to Jane Bennett. The seminars we have taught together at Hopkins find considerable expression in this book. Her work informs me, and, one hopes, her mode of being nudges the composition of my soul a bit closer to the sensibility I embrace in theory.

O N E

The Body/Brain/Culture Network

Neuroscience and Thinking

MY FIRST MISSION in this study is to explore the critical role that technique and discipline play in thinking, ethics, and politics, and to do so in a way that accentuates the creative and compositional dimensions of thinking. By the *creative dimension* I mean the opaque process by which new ideas, concepts, and judgments bubble into being; by the *compositional dimension* I mean the way in which thinking helps to shape and consolidate brain connections, corporeal dispositions, habits, and sensibilities. Some theories, themselves products of arduous thought, ironically depreciate the activity in which the theorists are invested: they reduce thinking to cognition, or situate it in a wide band of transcendental regulations that curtail its inventiveness, or contract it into a bland intellectualism that neglects its affective sources, somatic entanglements, and effects. But the inventive and compositional dimensions of thinking are essential to freedom of the self and to cultivation of generosity in ethics and politics. Thinking participates in that uncertain process by which new possibilities are ushered into being. One invention may be a new identity that jostles the roster of established constituencies as it struggles to find space. Another may be a thought-imbued disposition, incorporated into the sensibility of an individual or folded into the ethos of engagement between constituencies.

The first objective, then, is to address complex relays in thinking among technique, composition, and creativity. The second is to explore the new cultural pluralism, within and across territorial states, that beckons on the horizon of contemporary possibility. The assignment is to rework several representations of culture, ethics, and politics in the light of the exploration into the layered character of thinking. And to rework extant images of thinking in the light of this engagement with body-brain-culture relations. My wager is that we can best pursue such an agenda by dipping into three tributaries:

1. A minor tradition of reflection upon nature, memory, thinking, the layering of culture, and an ethics of cultivation advanced at various times by theorists such as Lucretius, Spinoza, Friedrich Nietzsche, Henri Bergson, William James, Sigmund Freud, Stuart Hampshire, Gilles Deleuze, Isabelle Stengers, and Ilya Prigogine

2. The new neuroscience of culture/brain/body relations, which comes into its own when placed into conversation with the first tradition, advanced by researchers such as Antonio Damasio, Joseph LeDoux, V. S. Ramachandran, and Francisco Varela

3. Contemporary cinema techniques that heighten our powers of perception; alert us to complex relays among affect, thinking, technique, and ethics; teach us how to apply pertinent techniques to ourselves; and reveal things about the constitution of time that might otherwise remain hidden

I pull these streams together to rework some established images of thought, culture, time, and possibility. My interest is not to predict the probability of the vision I support, but to make its possibility shine more brightly. The terms of the assignment expose a problem. I am neither a neuroscientist nor a student of film. My task is to enter into conversation with neuroscience and film in the interest of advancing cultural theory. I seek to draw sustenance from them to reflect upon perception, thinking, and time in politics.

Each issue engaged, no matter how removed it seems at first, is hitched to an agenda to advance a political pluralism appropriate to the acceleration of speed, compression of distance, and multidimensional diversity marking contemporary life. By *multidimensional diversity* I mean not just those contentious sects within Christianity that helped to motivate the invention of public secularism. Multidimensional pluralism covers multiple zones of diversity—in gender practice, sensual affiliation, conjugal form, ethnic identification, source of morality, language, and religious/ metaphysical orientation. By the *compression of distance* I mean the contraction of the time it takes to move people, management techniques, capital, products, labor, armies, weapons, ideas, books, newspapers, images, diseases, grievances, and aspirations across large stretches of territory.

You will have noticed neuroscience on the list of topics to address. Because it is, the following question is often posed to me these days, particularly by friends: "But, Bill, doesn't that venture drive you to the very reductionism (or scientism, phrenology, sociobiology, genetic determinism, behaviorism, eliminative materialism, barefoot empiricism, depreciation of language, etc.) you have heretofore fought against?" I don't think so. My sense is that in their laudable attempt to ward off one type of reductionism too many cultural theorists fall into another: they lapse into a reductionism that ignores how biology is mixed into thinking and culture and how other aspects of nature are folded into both.

Every theory of culture bears an implicit relation to biology and biological theory. The more cultural theorists try to avoid this gritty terrain, the more they either implicitly recapitulate one of two classical conceptions of nature that have long contended for primacy in Euro-American life or levitate toward a disembodied model of thinking, culture, and ethics that is difficult to sustain. By *classical conceptions of nature* I mean, first and roughly, the rich theo-teleological tradition that is inaugurated by Aristotle, finds expression in one side of Augustine, becomes consolidated in Aquinas, is reconfigured into a necessary subjective presumption in Kant's philosophical revolution, becomes reenergized by Hegel, and now finds more muted and variable expression in the work of Maurice Merleau-Ponty, Alasdair MacIntyre, Martha Nussbaum, and Charles Taylor. I mean, second, the lawlike model of science that sets itself against the first tradition, unfolds in Copernicus and Galileo after a desperate struggle with the Catholic Church, becomes perfected by Kepler and Newton, is transfigured into a necessary regulative ideal of scientific knowledge by Kant, and continues in *some* contemporary versions of quantum mechanics, relativity, neuroscience, and evolutionary theory. When cultural theory invokes the first tradition, it slips into a model of essentially embodied selves attuned to thick universals or an intrinsic purpose. When it supposes the second, it often either retreats toward a disembodied conception of cultural life or crawls into the black hole of sociobiology.

Perhaps the existing pool of alternatives is too small. At any rate, I am inspired by the dissenting discourse on nature noted above. It is when the new neuroscience is put into conversation with this tradition, and both are augmented by insights from contemporary cinema, that things become interesting. Indeed, some participants in the new neuroscience, as we shall see, are moving in this direction under their own steam.

I contend neither that conceptions of thinking and culture can simply be *derived* from a particular conception of nature nor that the minor tradition inspiring me has been definitively established. In fact, it is unwise to extrapolate with serene confidence from any domain of inquiry to another. Such jumps in the past helped to create the reductionism that has shadowed the human sciences since the time of Hobbes. But every image of nature does set conditions and restraints that must be negotiated somehow to support a specific conception of culture. Today competition between the two prevailing images of nature is still so authoritative, at least in cultural theory, that it thwarts exploration into the complex relations among thinking, culture, brains, and bodies.

Isabelle Stengers, a philosopher of science, indicates how developments within the natural sciences themselves create new possibilities of thought about the nature of science. She contends that these developments, generated by experiences of dissonance between the regulative ideal of scientific knowledge and processes that seem to deviate from it, open a door to new experimentation in cultural theory too. But she also knows that contemporary guardians of determinism, reductionism, and the sufficiency of lawlike knowledge work diligently to delegitimate such efforts, even though the ideals they endorse themselves contain a powerful dose of speculation. These guardians police deviations from the established ideal of knowledge almost as diligently as Cardinal Bellarmine and Pope Urban VIII guarded the Vatican view of the cosmos against Galileo and his telescope. Here, though, is Stengers on the opening and the possibility:

> At both the macroscopic and microscopic levels the sciences of nature are thus liberated from a narrow conception of objective reality, which believes it must in principle deny novelty and diversity in the name of an unchanging universal law.... They are from now on open to unpredictability, no longer viewed in terms of imperfect knowledge, or of insufficient control. Thus, they are open to a dialogue with a nature that cannot be dominated by a theoretical gaze, but must be explored with an open world to which we belong, in whose construction we participate.[1]

It is not *whether* practitioners committed to different regulative ideals of knowledge come to terms with anomalies, small fluctuations with big effects, and limits to the human ability to specify initial conditions precisely, but *how* they do.

Some put their money on a determinist regulative ideal, whereas others project an element of unpredictability and historical development into the most complex systems of nature. I join Nietzsche, Prigogine, and Stengers, for reasons to be reviewed in chapter 3, in pursuing the second agenda.

"A dialogue with a nature that cannot be dominated by a theoretical gaze"—the hardest nut to crack in pursuing that dialogue, at least in cultural theory, is the place of neuroscience in the study of body/brain/culture relations. Cultural theorists are wary of forging the connection, with good historical reasons. The previous history of contact fostered a deadly reductionism.[2] But changes in neuroscience make the case for renewing the conversation more compelling. Many contemporary neuroscientists (Damasio, LeDoux, and Varela are exemplary here) have already opened the door from their side. They have read William James, Sigmund Freud, and Maurice Merleau-Ponty more carefully than most of us have consulted work in their field. And it is well to remember that leading cultural theorists of the nineteenth and early twentieth centuries such as Henri Bergson, James, Merleau-Ponty, and Freud paid close attention to the biological theories of their day. It might be wise for us to do the same. So let me start by summarizing three recent case studies.

1. Ms. Jones is very intelligent and is also excellent at learning new facts. So her hippocampus, the brain nodule that launches the network for laying down new memories, is in fine shape. But she exudes a positive attitude toward life, never ruffled by new experiences of danger, betrayal, or abuse. "We were to learn that this very same attitude pervaded all areas of her life. She made friends easily, formed romantic attachments without difficulty, and had often been taken advantage of by those she trusted. . . . It was as if negative emotions such as fear and anger had been removed from her affective vocabulary, allowing the positive emotions to dominate her life."[3] And, indeed, when tests were run to gauge her ability to discriminate between dangerous and benign situations according to conventional signs, she failed them miserably.

2. Mrs. Dodd recently had a stroke and lost the use of her left hand. She is quite capable of recognizing people, speaking, and making everyday judgments in most situations. But she also

insists that she can use her left hand normally when she in fact cannot. She is questioned: "Can you use your right hand?" "Yes..." "Can you use your left hand?" Yes..." "Can you clap?" "Yes." "Will you clap for me now?" "Yes." "Are you clapping?" "Yes, I'm clapping."[4] Whatever experiment is run with Mrs. Dodd she either insists that she is accomplishing the feat in question when she is not or explains her failure to do so by reference to some annoying interference (her arm is tired after being pestered by the doctors, she slipped up this particular time, and so on).

3. Philip lost his left arm several years ago after an accident. He, like many others with severed limbs, has been plagued by severe "phantom pain" in that arm, a pain that cannot be relieved because there is no arm to which it is attached. Working on the hunch that the pain is bound up with messages transmitted to the brain of paralysis in the lost arm, V. S. Ramachandran developed a "mirror box" that allows Philip, when peering into it, to see an image in which both of his arms appear to be functioning. When asked to move his right and left arms simultaneously, he moves his right arm and the mirror image makes it appear that both arms are moving. "Oh, my God! Oh, my God, doctor! This is unbelievable.... My left arm is plugged in again. It's as if I'm in the past.... I can feel my elbow moving, my wrist moving. It's all moving again."[5] Philip and some other patients have been able to reduce or relieve phantom arm pain by using the mirror box to simulate movement in their lost limb.

Before pursuing possible implications of these three examples for cultural theory, let's consider common objections that seek to cut off precisely this exploration. One charge is that these are individual cases, whereas cultural theory deals with collective relations and intersubjective processes. There is something to the objection, but its import is easily overstated. Some neuroscientists, as we shall see in later chapters, construct experiments that play up the intersubjective character of thinking and judgment introduced here. More fundamentally, it is not only pertinent to see that life is culturally constituted, it is also important to come to terms with the *layered* character of culture itself. Although cultural theorists do have things to teach neuroscientists, some research by the latter can teach us a thing or two about the layered character of culture. It can show us how the inwardization of culture, replete with resistances and ambivalences, is installed at several levels of being, with each level both interacting with the others and marked by different speeds, capacities, and degrees of linguistic sophistication. These examples help in this respect, doing so in ways that leave open the Freudian interpretation of culture as a possibility without automatically treating it as the only way to come to terms with the layering of culture. To explore these issues, of course, is sometimes to draw these findings into a perspective that is not entirely that of the neuroscientists themselves.

A related objection is that the exploration of damage to body/brain processes undercuts appreciation of how denial, repression, ambivalence, displacement, and sublimation occur in the absence of such injuries. The researchers in question, however, do not deny this. Rather, they alert cultural theorists to the need to attend to work in neuroscience as they advance such interpretations; they show how such interpretations in the absence of that awareness can treat denial as the only issue when other things are involved; and, as we shall see in chapters 4 and 5, they suggest the pertinence of a wider range of techniques to thinking, judgment, and ethics than are often sanctioned in cultural theory in general or psychoanalytic theory in particular.

A final objection is the most substantial: that sophisticated observation of brain physicochemical activity may *correlate* with phenomenological experiences of thinking, desiring, dreaming, judging, and so on, but it cannot capture the shape and quality of those experiences. This objection is so important it deserves to be transfigured into a grounding theme of this study: to date, and into the foreseeable future, there is a gap between third-person observations of brain/body activity, however sophisticated they have become in recent neuroscience, and phenomenological experience correlated with those observations. The question is not how to eliminate the discrepancy but how to respond to it. One response is to treat it as a sign that mind and body are different substances, as in the mind/body dualism of Descartes and, in a different way, of Kant. Alternatively, it might be treated as a sign that humans, as embodied, thinking beings, form two irreducible perspectives on themselves. Spinoza introduced this view, treating thought and extension as two aspects of the same substance rather than two kinds of stuff from which the universe is composed. I adopt a modified version of Spinoza's "parallelism," to be developed in chapter 4.

In my judgment, neither that thesis nor those contending against it have been proved. But a modified Spinozism can marshal points in its favor.[6] First, it expresses the understanding of those who contend that human life evolved from lower forms without divine intervention, and it does so without reducing human experience to third-person accounts of it. Second, it encourages cultural theorists to explore accumulating evidence of significant correlations between the observation of body/brain processes and the lived experience of thinking. Third, it encourages us to come to terms actively with a variety of *techniques*—many of which already operate in everyday life—that can stimulate changes in thinking without adopting a reductionist image of thought in doing so. Fourth, it allows us to explore how thinking itself can sometimes modify the microcomposition of body/brain processes, as a new pattern of thinking becomes infused into body/brain processes. For, as Gerald Edelman and Giulio Tonino, two leading neuroscientists, put the point pithily, "Neurons that fire together wire together."[7] The version of parallelism adopted here encourages exploration of opaque, ubiquitous relations between technique and thinking without reducing the experience of thinking itself to a series of observational states. It appreciates the complexity of thinking while encouraging us to deploy technique to become more thoughtful.[8] Technique is part of culture, and thinking is neurocultural.

With these provisos in mind, let's explore the three cases summarized above. A brain scan of Ms. Jones by Antonio Damasio revealed that "both amygdalae, the one in the left and the one in the right temporal lobes, were almost entirely calcified."[9] The amygdala is a speedy, crude little brain nodule that communicates with higher, slower brain regions, triggering feelings of fear, caution, and anxiety in response to specific encounters. It does not itself express those feelings, but relays messages to bodily centers where they are felt. The amygdala is apparently not activated when feelings of pleasure and joy emerge.

The case of Ms. Jones already indicates something about the layered complexity of thinking, feeling, and judgment. It suggests that cultural learning is inscribed to some degree in memory traces of the amygdala, even if that brain nodule is itself simple in linguistic complexity and even though more refined brain regions must be engaged before complex interpretations of its crude, affectively imbued memory arise. The tests given to Ms. Jones did consist of conventional cues. Ms. Jones's case also illustrates how much of perception and thinking is prior to consciousness, even without introducing a repression hypothesis to make that point. Several brain nodules of different speed and capacity of cultural organization are linked together and to several body zones by a series of relays and feedback loops. They operate together to give texture to memory, perception, thinking, and judgment.

The case also opens questions about the constitutive role of affect in thought and judgment. As neuroscience pulls away from computer models of the brain widely accepted in the 1970s, the significance of affect also moves front and center. It is still an uncertain domain. What role does affective memory play in the movement of thought and judgment? If the movement of affect has a quirky element, is that quirkiness transmitted to the mobility of thought itself? What would it be like to think without affect? (Ms. Jones does not do that; she lacks anxiety and fear, not happiness, joy, and positive anticipation.) What about laughter as a manifestation of surplus affect? Can it, when triggered by side perceptions at odds with the dominant drift of perception and interpretation, interrupt the flow of thought and open a window of creativity in it? The idea, once more, is not to derive the logic of cultural activity from neuroscience. It is to pursue *conversations* between cultural theory and neuroscience.

In the case of Mrs. Dodd, a key question is why the strategy of denial is so powerful. Is this because, as some psychologists have argued, the patient retreats into denial after experiencing such a numbing injury? Or is it because, as some neuroscientists have argued, the damage to the right hemisphere that makes the left arm immovable also creates "perceptual neglect" of the patient's left side? Neither theory quite does the job, according to V. S. Ramachandran, although his experimentally informed speculations incorporate some elements from both. Mrs. Dodd does have damage to the right hemisphere, and experiments do show that the left side is neglected in her perceptual experience. But she also answers pointed questions in a way that suggests a subdued sense that she is covering up something. When asked, for instance, whether she had tied her shoelace the day before (she had not), she replied emphatically, "I tied the shoelace *with both hands*," in a way that is at least consonant with the denial hypothesis. But one of the things impaired in Mrs. Dodd "is the manner in which the brain deals with a discrepancy in sensory inputs about the body image."[10]

Ramachandran suggests that the observable damage to the right hemisphere does more than cause perceptual neglect of the left arm. It does that. But it also inhibits the production of disconcerting evidence that could counter attempts on the left side to preserve the body image intact before the injury occurred. That is, damage to the right hemisphere leaves the left hemisphere more free to resist evidence that confirms the inability to move the arm. Again, it is not that rationalization never occurs without right hemisphere damage, but that right hemisphere damage both exacerbates it and gives the conformist left hemisphere hegemony in interpretation. Ramachandran says:

> What we have observed in Betty and the other patients...supports the idea
> that the left hemisphere is conformist, largely indifferent to discrepancies,
> whereas the right hemisphere is the opposite: highly sensitive to perturbation.
> But our experiments only provide circumstantial evidence for this theory.
> We needed direct proof.[11]

I don't know whether Ramachandran is right. But one way to test his interpretation is to use technologies such as functional magnetic resonance and positron emission topography, which have been widely available for only about a decade. In one series of tests on clients who have normal capacity in all brain regions, a discrepancy between performance and body image makes the right hemisphere "light up." But of course this does not happen in those with right hemisphere damage, lending support to Ramachandran's conjecture that damage to the right hemisphere not only disables left arm movement but also gives theory-spinning, identity-protecting activity on the left side free rein in protecting the image of bodily integrity. Such tests, in general, enable researchers to record the flow of connections between zones making up the brain/body network.

These explorations, and others like them, further support the idea that thinking is a complex, layered activity, with each layer contributing something to an ensemble of dissonant relays and feedback loops between numerous centers. These loops include many different bodily sites sending signals about the state of the body to the brain.

The first two examples, taken together, suggest the insufficiency of what might be called intellectualist and deliberationist models of thinking that retain so much credibility in philosophy and the human sciences. Attempts to give singular priority to the highest and conceptually most sophisticated brain nodules in thinking and judgment may encourage those invested in these theories to underestimate the importance of body image, unconscious motor memory, and thought-imbued affect.

The third case, the man whose phantom pain is relieved by the mirror technique, is perhaps the most fascinating. Ramachandran shows how psychological models of phantom pain are inadequate to explain the phenomenon, but he does so in a way that retains a place for imagination and illusion both in the production of intense, stubborn pain and in its relief. His initial move is to review the brain's map of bodily zones in the homunculus, a small complex located near the top of the cerebral cortex. It receives messages about body states in different zones of the body and registers them on an arc-shaped surface.

The "sensory homunculus," as it is now called, forms a greatly distorted representation of the body on the surface of the brain, with the parts that are particularly important taking up disproportionately large areas. For example, the area involved with the lips or with the fingers takes up as much space as the area involved with the entire trunk of the body..., presumably because your lips and fingers are highly sensitive to touch...whereas your trunk is considerably less sensitive, requiring less cortical space. For the most part the map is orderly though upside down. However...upon close examination you will see that the face is not near the neck, where it should be, but is below the hand. The genitals, instead of being between the thighs, are located below the foot.[12]

I will let the reader work out Ramachandran's playful theory of the foot fetish. But consider his account of phantom pain in the hand. When the limb is lost, no message can be sent by the limb to its corresponding site on the brain map. Nor can one be received by the limb from the brain. But when Ramachandran touched a couple of spots on the patient's cheek, he found that the amputee now felt the touch on both his cheek *and* his phantom hand, whereas people with intact hands do not feel the touch at the second site. They feel it only on the cheek, where the touch is applied. Somehow, hand feeling can migrate to sensory fibers on the face among people who have lost their hands. A creative move by the brain below the conscious recognition and willful control of the agents involved, you might say. But it can be tough for amputees who smile or grimace a lot. This migration of sensory feeling on the surface of the homunculus is borne out with other patients, according to Ramachandran, both in their stated responses to touch and temperature change and through measurements of brain activity in the zones in question.

The brain sometimes remaps itself when it loses messages from a lost limb, so feelings previously linked to one bodily site move to another spot on the map close to the original site. Spinoza and Merleau-Ponty would say that the brain recomposes itself to retain a coherent body image under new conditions. Speaking of another patient with phantom pain, Ramachandran says now "every time Tom smiles or moves his face and lips, the impulses activate the 'hand' area of his cortex, creating the illusion that his hand is still there."[13] This is a dramatic instance of what I am calling the compositional dimension of body/brain/culture activity.

How does such remapping occur? It still remains uncertain, but Ramachandran's best surmise is that there is a redundancy of connections between the "hand" and the brain, and that the secondary route becomes activated when the primary connection to the real hand is lost. The arousal of the secondary pattern suggests how each neural pattern is nested in a larger complex. "Far from signaling a specific location on the skin, each neuron in the map is in a state of dynamic equilibrium with other adjacent neurons; its significance depends strongly on what other neurons in the vicinity are doing."[14]

How does a phantom limb become entangled in a feeling of intense pain? A good bet is that confused signals are sent to the brain site from the newly activated area; the brain misinterprets the mess as a signal of pain, so that the amputee now experiences pain in an absent limb. Moreover, since no countermessages are sent by the limb itself (because it is not there), the pain is intensified through a series of feedback loops not subject to self-correction. The more you tighten your jaw muscles while the dentist works on a tooth, the more sharply you feel pain in that area.

We have traveled some distance from a theory of denial anchored in the view that the trauma of limb loss creates a semblance of pain that talk therapy might relieve. But, still, some concept of denial is invoked in describing how the brain works below the level of intellectual attention to preserve an earlier body image. And therapy in an expanded sense is relevant here too. In the case in question, specific tactics are purposely applied by others, or the actors themselves, to body/brain relays below conscious regulation. Doing so promotes modest brain remapping.

The most brilliant innovation in this respect is Ramachandran's introduction of the mirror box to reduce phantom pain. It is still uncertain how long such relief lasts, and it does not work for all patients. But in those for whom it does work it seems likely that a modest recomposition of brain connections is accomplished through a movement in one limb and a mirror image that makes the missing limb *appear* to move also. Ramachandran uses this occasion to enunciate some reservations about computer models of the brain:

> Popularized by artificial intelligence researchers, the idea that the brain behaves like a computer, with each nodule performing a highly specialized job and sending its output to the next nodule is widely believed. . . . But my experiments . . . have taught me that this is not how the brain works. Its connections are extraordinarily labile and dynamic. Perceptions emerge as a result of reverberations of signals between different levels of the sensory hierarchy, indeed even across different senses. The fact that visual input can eliminate the spasm of a nonexistent arm and then erase the associated memory of pain vividly illustrates how extensive and profound these interactions are.[15]

Ramachandran's experiments with phantom pain suggest how variable in speed and complexity different levels of the brain/body network are.

They suggest as well how sensory experiences such as visual image, sound, smell, and movement interact in mapping brain patterns. Finally, they suggest that in domains where direct intellectual reconfiguration is insufficient ("I now accept the loss of my limb, so I should stop feeling pain") an ensemble of techniques or tactics applied to regions below direct intellectual control can sometimes reorganize predispositions to perception, feeling, and judgment. These experiments in brain rewiring by tactical means invite a return to forgotten questions about how cultural ritual, discipline and arts of self-cultivation infiltrate into patterns of thinking, identity, and ethical sensibility.

They also invite attention to the interplay of sound, rhythm, movement, and image in the films we watch in dark theaters. For films, too, communicate affective energies to us, some of which pass below intellectual attention while still influencing emotions, judgments, and actions. These considerations encourage us to augment intellectualist models of thinking and culture with a perspective that appreciates the dense interweaving of genetic endowment, image, movement, sound, rhythm, smell, touch, technique, trauma, exercise, thinking, and sensibility. Thinking is implicated in body/brain/culture networks that extend well beyond the skin of the thinker.

A Touch of Vertigo

If you are interested in the relationship between technique, feeling, perception, and thought, film might provide a strategic site of exploration. Films both apply techniques to us to mobilize affect and teach us about how such techniques work outside the celluloid world. In this study I draw upon several films to explore the role of affect in the mobility of thought, the role of memory traces in faith and judgment, the intimate relation between technique and thinking, and the nonlinear character of time.

Consider, by way of a first example, *Vertigo*, a film I have seen three times over a span of twenty-five years. It can be engaged in several ways, and my engagement has shifted each time I have viewed it. Laura Mulvey, for instance, examines how the gaze that governs the film is male. Tania Modleski contends that the male gaze is both there and "severely disturbed" as the film carries the characters through a series of dizzying experiences.[16] Another interpretation, taking off from Modleski's account, might ask how fantasy, illusion, and disturbance circulate between male and female characters as the film advances. My interest is touched by these concerns, but it focuses on the techniques by which the film induces effects on the infraconscious perception of viewers. The question is what cinematic tactics can teach us about the cultural stimuli to thought and thoughtlessness, the layering of perception, and the role of affect in perception and thought. These insights, once developed, can inform the reflective techniques we apply to ourselves to stimulate thought, to complicate judgment, or to refine ethical sensibility. So an interest in thinking about thought governs my exploration of film technique. That interest does not distinguish me from others, for it is often present in film interpretation. It does shift the focus, however, from appraising the ideological politics, narrative form, and cultural message to exploring the relations between narrative flow and specific techniques of delivery. To keep my mind on that issue, I select films that have touched me in some way or other, often in ways that surprised me, and sometimes in ways that disturbed me. In none of the selections is my *first* impulse to reach for an ideological gun and start firing—even though there are things in the politics of the films I would criticize.

In *Vertigo*, director Alfred Hitchcock carries us to the point where John "Scottie" Ferguson, the retired detective who gets dizzy at high places, is recovering. His recovery is slow because a year ago he saw Madeleine—the eerily beautiful woman whose husband hired him to follow her because she was communing with a dead woman—jump to her death from a mission bell tower. He did not chase her to the top before she jumped because an attack of vertigo stopped him in his tracks on the way up. He is now haunted by a mixture of guilt, love for the dead woman, and a strange sense that she may still be alive. We hope he recovers from the last folly. But we too may have an uncanny sense that she is alive. Why? Is it entirely because we participate in the feminine mystique in which Scottie is caught? I doubt that such an explanation suffices. There is an additional element. When she falls, we are located in the same line of vision as Scottie, whose vertigo agitates his vision as he stares down at the falling body. We are agitated too by the intensity of the drama, which is accentuated by the musical score accompanying it. The body, as it drops head first, looks less like a live body falling than it should. Besides, the scream precedes the falling body in a way that is at odds with the probable timing of a person who has jumped. When I saw (and heard) the film a second time after many years, knowing the plot but not recalling its details, it seemed to me that Hitchcock at that moment fell below the technical virtuosity normally marking his films. But I now think, after a third viewing, that he inserted in both Scottie and us a side perception unavailable for conscious attention while the unnerving action was under way. We absorb an infraconscious perception that later infuses an eerie undertone of doubt into recollections of Madeleine's fall to death. That doubt could be explained away, of course, as due to our desire that this beautiful woman be alive. Such an expla-

nation, while pertinent, may not suffice, partly because not everyone who participates in the nagging doubt about Madeleine's death is deeply invested in the particular
ideal of femininity infecting Scottie. But they may still be haunted by an infraconscious perception that disrupts their first impression of a fall they have seen with
their own two eyes. And so is Scottie. For just as we share his line of vision, he
shares ours.

The layered memory of the scene becomes fodder for dreams
and daydreams. The result might be a new and surprising line of thought or an obsessive course of action not fully comprehensible to the one overtaken by it. So
Johnneo—as his other and practical girlfriend Midge sometimes calls him—finds
himself searching the San Francisco streets for Madeleine a year after he has recov-
ered enough from her loss to get up and around. One day he meets Judy, a working-
class woman with darker hair and a coarser style who nonetheless looks strikingly
like Madeleine.

The infraconscious memory of a body that does not fall precisely
like a live body makes a contribution to both Scottie's search for Madeleine and his
later obsession with the woman who looks strangely like her. It may infect the viewers too, drawing us into Scottie's improbable search more than we otherwise might
be. Hitchcock displays the layered character of perception, memory, and judgment
in the ways he works upon us. Often enough he invites us to think about what he
does and how he does it.

After Scottie concludes that Judy is really Madeleine, he insists
that they change their plans for dinner and drive to a restaurant that happens to be
on the same road he and Madeleine had taken to the mission. If she is Madeleine,
she is implicated in murder. By this point we know she is Madeleine (Hitchcock had
to fight to get this point past the producer). We feel her anxiety level rise as they
drive to the mission again. As we do, Hitchcock does more supplemental work on
our anxieties. The scene flashes from a take in which the car is going down the right
side of the road to one in which Scottie is driving on the left side. There is a short
cut, and we then return to the car running faster down the left side of the road, with
the white dividing line dimly discernible through the rear window. The eye takes in
more than it registers explicitly, as I will show in the next chapter. The first time I
saw this scene, I was engrossed in the intense feelings it engendered. I did not form
an explicit image of the car in the left lane, but an implicit awareness of it surely
formed part of the subtext agitating me: in San Francisco, driving on the left side of
the road is apt to cause a head-on collision. This side perception was not exactly a
repressed perception: it never made it to the conscious level to be repressed.

Something in my second viewing of the film enabled me to convert the side perception into a conscious image. It *was* a second viewing after all, and I was reading Bergson at the time on how the influx of sensory material must be *subtracted* to enable action-oriented perception. I was stunned. On yet a subsequent viewing, with three other people, we observed the lane switch together. Here Hitchcock does to us what Scottie does to Madeleine, and what she had previously done to him. He infects us with a touch of vertigo. A little vertigo is indispensable to creative thinking, while a lot can freeze you into a zombie, as Scottie found out for a year after Madeleine's apparent death.

A Lacanian reading of this story could be given. To abbreviate: Madeleine embodies the fantasy of the impossible woman for Scottie, and he is doomed to pursue that fantasy wherever it takes him.[17] He can thus step to the edge of the precipice in the mission tower without getting dizzy only after Madeleine has jumped to her death. Such an interpretation is plausible, but it does not *exhaust* the one I would offer. Its parameters are sometimes presented as too complete and closed, leaving little room for experimental thought and action to stretch the possibilities of being it acknowledges. There are other elements in the film — two of which we have reviewed — that call into question not so much what Scottie does as the inevitability of his doing it. Consummate narratives invest theory, explanation, and interpretation with more certainty and sufficiency than they warrant. They express the hubris of theory in a world too complexly intermeshed to fit the strictures of either lawlike explanation or deep interpretation.

I shall argue later that it is precisely at the nodal points where the fundamental assumptions of contending theories differ that we should strive for reciprocal modesty. Interpretations presented as both authoritative and final close down experimentation with new possibilities of being and action before the experiments have a chance to get off the ground. And inordinate confidence in the explanatory sufficiency of a particular narrative often goes hand in hand with the tendency to mute the significance of technique in film and life. The importance of technique to perception, thinking, judgment, and action becomes accentuated if we acknowledge that we still don't know with assurance everything we can do or become.

Interesting things might happen if you place film technique into contact with your own perceptual experience, and both of these in turn with engagements with perception and thinking in contemporary neuroscience and cultural theory. Attention to one forum allows you to address questions to the others. Or test things enacted in them. Some findings in cultural theory and neuroscience, initially implausible to many, might become available to a wider audience through this or that film.

Spellbound

Film was, after all, the preeminent medium through which Freudian theory became infused into popular culture in the United States during the 1940s and 1950s. You might draw upon film techniques to trigger creativity in your own thinking or to cultivate some noble potentiality in your sensibility.

We will examine in chapter 5 how and why Freud shies away from the "pagan" techniques that figure prominently in film today. But Ramachandran, Bergson, and Hitchcock, unconstrained by Freud's restrictions in *this* domain, could have a field day together. All three might concur with Robert Bresson, the film director, when he says, "Hostility to art is also hostility to the new, the unforeseen."[18] And, perhaps, with a corollary: Hostility to art and the new finds expression in doctrines that set stringent limits in advance on experimentation in cultural theory and technique in cultural life.

The Layering of Culture

Today many cultural and political theorists act as if ethics and politics do, could, or should consist of deliberation alone. They are deliberative democrats. Critical theorists often contest that view, but many of them then treat subliminal influences as if they were reducible to modes of manipulation or behavioral management to be overcome in a rational or deliberative society. Here the world of ritual, artistry, technique, and micropolitics often becomes equated with "magic," "primitivism," "paganism," or "the aestheticization of politics."[19] Others affirm the latter processes by talking about the "constructed character" of desire, identity, and culture; but then some limit the materials of social construction to sophisticated linguistic performances that are relevant but insufficient to the phenomena. Some constructivists, you might say, do not make their constructivism deep or layered enough, paying too little attention to how lower layers become sedimented. But if constructivism remains thin and untextured, and no third way is consolidated between it and the flat realism it challenges, the stage is set for a forceful return to the other side of a too-simple statement of alternatives. Others examine the role of tactics and discipline in identity and culture but then leave both out of thinking, morality, or reason, doing so to retain the purity of one or all these activities. Others yet acknowledge these elements but then act as if they do their real work only in the private realm where "religion" and "the life world" are said to flourish. Still others acknowledge the insufficiency of the foregoing images but enclose thinking, culture, and ethical cultivation in a theo-teleological doctrine, fearing that the world would fall apart if the embodied, layered character of thinking and culture were not contained in a teleological frame. They defend a layered, organic conception of thinking, identity, and culture, even as they insist that the accelerated pace of contemporary life pulls people away from attunement to intrinsic purpose. In doing so, they may discourage cultural theorists who seek to deepen appreciation of the layered character of thought and culture but hesitate to throw their weight behind a theo-teleological perspective by doing so.[20]

I draw things from several of these traditions. For example, I would probably choose constructivism over realism *if* the choices were reduced to those two. And I think participants in the theo-teleological tradition are wise to link their readings of corporeo-cultural life to an ethic of cultivation over a morality of command. It is just that I don't endorse, as will become clear, the social ideal to which they typically attach that ethic. I am not in a position to prove my alternative definitively, but neither are they. They have, in a sense, had things easy, defending themselves mostly against the twin alternatives of biological reductionism and insufficiently layered models of culture. We might enliven the terms of debate by introducing another party more actively into the conversation: a perspective that addresses the layered character of being without endorsing finalism, that taps into creative possibilities residing in the dissonances between layers of culture, and that locates promise as well as danger for cultural pluralism in the acceleration of pace in contemporary life. According to the tradition mined here, too many perspectives disparage the layering of thinking, ethics, and culture; the distinctive roles technique, discipline, and cultivation play in them; or both.

What, more closely, is the conjunction between thinking and culture? Culture is constituted in part by the perceptions, beliefs, and concepts in it. Thought enters into, in Hegel's terms, the subjective and intersubjective dimensions of culture. Here tension, dissonance, and discrepancy can arise not only between the beliefs of one constituency and those of others, but between dispositional tendencies and explicit beliefs in the same constituency. Much about the ambivalence, conflict, and mobility of culture is lodged in the latter dimension. But such an image, while relevant, is still insufficient to the layered complexity of thinking and culture. First, it fails to gauge how sedimented "memory traces"—as intensive thought fragments in a self or culture—can affect thinking and judgment without themselves being articulable, and how the application of subtle techniques sometimes affects the shape and intensity of such traces. We leave such an exploration for a later chapter, in the interest of pursuing here another dimension of culture.

Cultural ideas and beliefs are organized, consolidated, and constrained in what, following Hegel, can be called the objective dimension of institutional life.[21] *Objektivat*, in German, means that which "stands over," as well as that which is "detached." The first sense is the most pertinent. The objective dimension of culture not only enters into subjective and intersubjective life, it recoils back upon subjective dispositions and intersubjective understandings, providing things to be inwardized by them, or limiting their possibilities of realization, or setting barriers to be acted upon. It is easy to see how subjective desires, judgments, demands, and anxieties can be at odds with the layered matrix of cultural understandings. You might think yourself innocent of a crime because your image of responsibility deviates from that expressed in prevailing judicial practice. So the intersubjective stands over the subjective, even while being woven into it.

There is more yet to the objective element. Ideationally infused practices such as those associated with energy sources, architectural forms, incentive systems, dietary regimes, practices of property, dictionaries, the treatment of disease, work processes, police modes of arrest and violence, investment and saving instruments, corporeal skills, and punishment have nonideational elements woven into them. True, anthracite, merely a black rock in some contexts, becomes a crucial energy resource in a different ideational setting. But the shift from rock to energy resource is not *only* ideational. Try burning gravel in a potbellied stove to heat up your cabin. And anthracite is not ideational about itself. When anthracite becomes a key source of energy instead of, say, wood, oil, or nuclear power, the institutional complex into which it is inserted exerts distinctive effects upon the speed, curvature, and limits of cultural life. Try burning anthracite to power a jet plane.

The objective dimension of culture, finally, includes specific ways in which one materialized institution meshes with, grates on, or collides with others, engendering complex meshworks of dependence and interdependence that recoil back upon individual desires, constituency pursuits, ethical injunctions, and state agendas. The objective dimension of culture, again, is not isolable from the intersubjective; culture would collapse into a heap without the ideational element. But layered materializations of culture nonetheless recoil back upon life as arrangements to inwardize, resources to deploy, limits to encounter, barriers to modify, and gridlocks to suffer.

Take marriage and family. They find expression through ambivalent habits of affection, obligation, and responsibility mobilized, condensed, and constrained in institutional life. Do you want to get married, sharing at least a minimal understanding with others of marriage as a long-term bond between two adults with rights and obligations attached to it? It helps if a church or state sanctions the idea, houses a ceremony, attaches inheritance rights to it, provides assurances of support for the progeny in case of death; if the type of relationship you seek is represented in routine ways in TV dramas and films; if the family you seek to build is consonant with the job prospects available to you and your spouse and the means of conception sanctioned by the state; if the military supports it; if your neighbors and family fold it into routine practices of friendship, sociality, holiday celebration, inheritance, and club memberships; if insurance companies recognize it in spousal benefit packages; if teachers and administrators treat your child as the product of a legitimate marriage or birth procedure; if the laws of reproduction and divorce correspond to your judgment about the nature of the bond. These institutional conditions of realization carry constraints with them that stand over and against some ideas you and others may invest in the idea of marriage, as people often find when their conjugal aspirations stretch coded materializations in the domains of religion, ethnicity, gender, age, work, class, or status. Do you seek a divorce? Time to run through the same litany.

The objective institutions that preexist us become infused to variable degrees into dispositions, perceptions, beliefs, and resistances we share and contest with others. If thinking helps to compose culture, the objective dimension of culture helps to compose thinking, making the relays and feedback loops that connect bodies, brains, and culture exceedingly dense. As you attend to the complex relays joining bodies, brains, and culture, the hubris invested in tight models of explanation and consummate narratives of interpretation becomes vivid.

Techniques of the self and micropolitics are critical to an expansive ethos of pluralism, as well as to more closed regimes at odds with such an ethos. They intervene at innumerable points "in between": between subliminal attachment and explicit belief; between implicit memory and explicit aspirations; between shared beliefs in one domain and those in others; between new dispositions surging into being and linguistic practices imperfectly congruent with them; between constituency aspirations to new rights and laws or traditions that forbid them; between legally sanctioned norms and counterpresumptions entrenched in family, school, neighborhood, work, or military practice; between the organization of work and aspirations at odds with it; between corporate codes and patterns of gossip, rumor, and scandal that enforce or subvert them; between energy sources mixed into economic life and collective desires for a cleaner and more self-sustaining economy. By *relational techniques of the self* I mean choreographed mixtures of word, gesture, image, sound, rhythm, smell, and touch that help to define the sensibility in which your perception, thinking, identity, beliefs, and judgment are set. Relational techniques of the self are typically applied at some of the above flash points. By *micropolitics* I mean such techniques organized and deployed collectively by professional associations, mass-media talk shows, TV and film dramas, military training, work processes, neighborhood gangs, church meetings, school assemblies, sports events, charitable organizations, commercial advertising, child rearing, judicial practice, and police routines. It is not that every institution is exhausted by micropolitics, but that the micropolitical dimension of each is potent because of the critical functions the institution performs in organizing attachments, consumption possibilities, work routines, faith practices, child rearing, education, investment, security, and punishment.

Micropolitics operates below the threshold of large legislative acts and executive initiatives, even as it ranges widely and sets conditions of possibility for these more visible actions. Technique and micropolitics form connective links joining practices of memory, perception, thinking, judgment, institutional design, and political ethos. They do not form the only links. Far from it. Market, antimarket practices (such as oligopolies, monopolies, and command systems), state decrees, and interstate agreements also play critical roles. I focus on these interstitial media for three reasons: first, because they play a critical role below the threshold of political visibility inside every domain of life, including the four institutional complexes just listed; second, because they are underappreciated by intellectualists entranced by unlayered images of thinking, thin conceptions of culture, and deliberative conceptions of democracy; third, because those who do address them often join a thick image of culture to a mandatory vision of national or civilizational unity inimical to the diversity needed during a time when the pace of life has accelerated and territorial distance has become compressed.

TWO

The Color of Perception

Formatting Perception

IN AN INTRIGUING ESSAY, Samuel Weber discusses the effects of television on perception. He notes a difference, recorded in ordinary language, between perceiving things in everyday life and "watching television." The latter locution expresses awareness of how television news programs relay perceptions to us already organized by other people, institutions, and instruments. Television predigests what we watch. In this it is like photography and film, but

> what distinguishes television from these other media is its power to combine such separation with the presentness associated with sense perception. What television transmits is not so much *images*, as is almost always argued. It does not transmit representations but rather the *semblance of presentation as such*, understood as the power not just to see and to hear but *to place before us*. Television thus serves as a surrogate for the body in that it allows for a certain sense-perception to take place; but it does this in a way that no body can, for its perception takes place in more than one place at a time.[1]

Television compresses two places of perception into one; it therefore is often unclear how much of the presentation is shaped by the medium and how much by the events "covered." We are aware of this, as the locution "watching television" reveals. But we easily forget it while watching TV. The long-term effect of this combination, it is said, is the generation of skepticism and cynicism about public media, even as viewers remain vulnerable to media manipulation of experience. That may be why, Weber thinks, many people prefer sporting events and soap operas to news broadcasts and talk shows. These programs present people in contests, neighborhoods, hospitals, and police departments getting on with the loves, corruption, generosities, and disasters of everyday life, as they were before so much experience was compressed into that fateful relation between the screen and the viewer's eyeballs.

I concur in the common preference for soaps and sporting events over talk shows. I also think that the very difference between television and everyday perception Weber notes encourages people to ignore another connection between these two practices. For action-oriented perceptions in everyday life are also subjected to a process of formatting that enables them to be perceptions. In both TV-mediated settings and action-oriented situations, a host of sensory material must be reduced and processed by a technocultural apparatus to render perception possible. The problem is that the veneer of objectivity that television commentators typically present when they report the news merges with the cynicism of viewers about the prior organization of TV images to forestall popular thinking about the complexity of perception per se. Television could be a preeminent medium through which to explore the formatting of perception. It could be a medium that both displays its complexity and teaches us how to work upon the processes that precede and enable perception.

Consider soaps and sitcoms, along merely one dimension. As a soap proceeds daily for weeks, the viewer moves back and forth effortlessly across several sub–story lines, with significant delays between specific scenes that stitch a particular line together. A new scene might be informed by what occurred several scenes before. In proceeding across interruptions from one scene to another, the viewer does not normally subject the previous scenes to explicit recollection. They form an implicit background, allowing the plot to unfold effortlessly. The past is folded into current perception as virtual memory, enabling the story line or the joke to proceed. That is, the past operates on the present below the threshold of explicit memory. Soaps and sitcoms can bring this constitutive feature of perception sharply into view precisely because we "watch" a set of movements occurring elsewhere rather than move ourselves within these settings.

TV could teach a lot about how perception works. It, however, does not live up to its potential. Part of the reason is that its news programs and talk shows are dominated by talking heads who purport to report things as they are, even as they sometimes expose "bias" in other shows or politicians. The cumulative result of this combination is that simple objectivity is set up as the gold standard of perception, while critics accuse each other of failing to live up to it. This game of mutual recrimination set against a simple standard of objectivity, in turn, fosters the public cynicism that many TV talking heads purport to resist.

Film may be more promising. Numerous films, played before captive audiences in dark rooms, display the ubiquitous role of bodily affect in perception and judgment. The film theorist Steven Shaviro, for instance, explores how "our bodies" are "decisively altered" in the films of Bresson, Fassbinder, and Warhol as we are "agitated and affected in new ways" by choreographed interplay among color, music, rhythms, pace, words, and images.[2] To take a recent example not reviewed by Shaviro, in Stanley Kubrick's *Eyes Wide Shut* we are subjected to a dream story set at a slow pace, with several scenes draped in red followed by scenes in purple and black.[3] We float passively through a kaleidoscope of events in which sexual desire is mobilized, translated into jealousy, suspended, and transfigured into a vague sense of danger. The overt sense of boredom infusing these experiences is punctuated by a strange feeling of tension. The boredom, you might say, partly expresses and partly covers the lower layer of affect, for a feeling of boredom often signifies other energies at work below the threshold of direct inspection. The torsion within this combination may encourage the audience to blame Kubrick for the boredom they feel and to give themselves credit for the thinking it enables. As that combination proceeds we tend to forget the violence punctuating this unerotic adventure of desire, including what happens to the woman who helps Dr. Harford and the fate of the friend who slips the sleepwalker into that tedious orgy. At least these off-scene events were not readily recalled by friends of mine who criticized the film for its boring and ahistorical character. For, as reviewers could not help repeating, the erotic life set by Kubrick in New York City is way out of sync with that operative in the New York scene today. But that's how dreaming works while your eyes are wide shut. Perhaps the film blocks our vision as much as it does that of Dr. Bill Harford, as he wanders through a dreamy sea of affect from one untimely nonadventure to another. At any rate, his nervous system communicates directly with ours as this dream world unfolds. The film places us in a position, after the fact, as it were, to ponder how our eyes can become wide shut too, even as we chuckle at Dr. Harford for his erotic innocence and criticize Kubrick for the historical inaccuracy of his portrayals of New York City.

TV, film, everyday perception, modest experiments upon ourselves, phenomenologies of perception, and engagement with neurological studies of perception—perhaps attention to each site in relation to the others can engender more thoughtful accounts of perception, make them more widely available, and even provide clues about how to intervene tactically in the perceptual process. As we see how soaps draw upon virtual memories and films mobilize affective energy below the threshold of intellectual attention, we might discern more subtly how unconscious mobilizations of affective memory shape the color, tone, and direction of everyday perception. Henri Bergson can help.

Everyday perception, Bergson contended during the early days of film and before the era of television, is constituted by the conjunction of two dimensions. There is the event you encounter and the memory without recollection that help to translate the encounter into a perception. The conjunctions of "virtual" memory and sensory experience format perception. These are, in fact, the same conjunctions that a soap opera deploys as it pulls several story lines across the same program.

The role of memory is crucial, according to Bergson. It is not, as already intimated, an explicit recollection that helps to define a percept. "Virtual" or "motor" memory does that, for "the past survives under two distinct forms; first, in motor mechanisms; secondly in independent recollections."[4] Motor memory allows an encounter to be organized into a perception *because* it subsists below explicit awareness as a repository of cultural life from the past. Perception is quick, as it must be to inform action. The human capacity of explicit image recall is far too slow to keep up with the operational pace of perception as we walk, ramble, and run through action-oriented contexts. So virtual memories are called up rapidly, but their vital role in perception is lost to the perceiver sunk in the middle of action. Perception thus seems pure and unmediated to us. But it is not. It is a double-entry activity guided by the concerns of possible action, not by a spectatorial quest to represent an object in all its complexity. And the action possibilities mobilized through the rapid conjunctions between event and memory often lead to the summoning of additional virtual memories, adding new layers of complexity to perception.

Again, representation by a disinterested spectator would be too slow and disinterested to organize perception. Indeed, the actual organization of everyday perception already verges on being too slow for the pace of life. Luckily, we have a crude, infraperceptual brain subsystem available to deal with high-speed situations—as you will discover by reviewing, after the fact, your quick reaction to a driving emergency. In an emergency your reaction time must be quicker than that allotted to image formation in regular perception. So in an emergency it is not only that explicit recollection gives way to virtual memory, *explicit image formation gives way to rapid information processing without image.* You respond in a split second to cues processed below the threshold of image production. When the image comes into view a half second later, you can then ascertain, if you are still alive, whether you did the lifesaving thing when you jerked the steering wheel to the left even before forming a visual image of the oncoming car. In this instance the relatively slow, complex process of perception gives way to the lightning-fast, crude processing of the amygdala (a small, fast, intense little brain nodule connected to other brain regions *and* to direct, crude preperceptual experience). Let's call the emergency percept *infraperception*, because of its speed and its processing of information without visual imagery. It happens all the time, as when you turn your car in a flash on the road or freeze suddenly while walking in the woods, even before you have formed an explicit image of a car or a snake. When that happens, it reveals something about the layered character of perception in more relaxed settings. For if the information processed in emergency reaction below the threshold of explicit image were subtracted from the visual dimension of the image, everyday perception would be less rich and affectively imbued than it is. Infraperception thereby teaches us about the layered character of everyday perception, as well as about our impressive capacities to respond to emergencies.

Even ordinary perception moves pretty fast, faster than the conscious mind can think. Because it is oriented to dictates of action in a world marked by speed, risk, surprise, need, and opportunity, perception *subtracts* from the incoming sensory material a surplus irrelevant to a small set of action possibilities. Perception is subtractive, and the virtual memories mobilized during it help to determine what is subtracted. Part of the surplus subtracted persists as side perception, potentially available for recall in a different context.

Perception requires forgetfulness to be, first, forgetfulness of elements in the incoming rush of sensory material not relevant to probable contexts of action; second, forgetfulness of cultural images drawn from the past that enter into the virtual memory but do not assume the form of recollection. The subtractive organization of perception involves double forgetfulness; but what is forgotten may nonetheless have effects upon future perception. Bergson summarizes a couple of these points. In perception, memory

> has retained from the past only the intelligently coordinated movements which represent the accumulated efforts of the past; it recovers those past efforts, not in the memory-images which recall them, but in the definite order and systematic character with which the actual movements take place. In

truth it no longer *represents* our past to us, it *acts* it; and if it still deserves the name of memory, it is not because it conserves bygone images, but because it prolongs their useful effect into the present moment.[5]

It is fascinating sometimes to focus on the sounds, sights, and smells of a scene or to wallow in your imagination. Bergson commends it as an excellent way to fold creativity into thinking and judgment. But wallowing can be dangerous in operational perception. That's why, outside the possibilities opened up by film, TV, meditation, and brain/body experiments, it is not all that easy to learn how perception proceeds. Perception does not call attention to itself as it proceeds. It is oriented to action: "Perception, understood as we understand it, measures our possible action upon things, and thereby, inversely, the possible action of things upon us."[6] The closer it is to action, the less expansive are the memories that constitute it. The more delay built into the link between perception and action, however, the more the memories that form part of it can become recollections open to further reflection and assessment. In these circumstances, the virtual memory image expands into a series of explicit recollections.

Each virtual memory also has a characteristic charge of affect mixed into it.[7] Virtual memories are pervaded by affective charges, ranging from a surge of panic through a radiant feeling of joy to myriad other possibilities. As they are quickly mobilized to mediate an encounter — that is, to help translate a sensory encounter into experience — the affective charges help to move thinking and judgment in some directions rather than others. Thinking and judgment are already well under way before they enter the picture as conscious processes.

It is not, again, that you first represent things and then add subjective feelings. Perception is set in action contexts and organized through complex mixtures of sensory encounter, virtual memory, and bodily affect. Sometimes blinding speed is essential and infraperception takes precedence for a split second. At other times merely a fast pace does the job. As your affect-charged biocultural memory deems particular elements unnecessary or unworthy, they are subtracted from the myriad sensory materials rushing in. Virtual memory is crucial. It is memory because it is real and exerts real effects, and it is virtual because it does not take the form of an explicit image. But because "the lesson once learned bears upon it no mark which betrays its origin . . . in the past; it is part of my present, exactly like my habit of walking or of writing; it is lived and acted, rather than represented: I might believe it innate."[8]

"I might believe it innate." The logic of everyday perception seems innate to actors in the midst of action. The quick pace of action in relation to the relatively slow capacities of conscious processing make this necessary. But it is possible to imagine a species, something like us, with quick capacities of explicit memory retrieval. In us, consciousness is slow and linear; parallel processing is reserved for virtual memory prior to consciousness. Maybe this other species of overmen would sew parallel processing into the fabric of consciousness itself, transcending thereby the crude limits of humans. They would seem like gods to us. They would also feel vividly those affects that move us below the level of feeling, perhaps thereby folding more pain, agony, and joy into their lives than we can endure on a regular basis. But because *our* operational capacities are limited in these ways, it is wise for us from time to time to dissect the elements that make up the organization of perception—when, for instance, we are confronted with the cruel effects our perceptual habits have on those marginalized or demonized by them, or when some ingrained habits of perception foster debilitating anxiety or depression. In those circumstances, and many others besides, it becomes ethically incumbent or prudentially important to examine the structure of perception and, sometimes, to devise strategies to work on the cultural dispositions now installed in it. Film can help.

Consider how the flashback in film can teach us about everyday perception if considered in conjunction with Bergson's account of virtual memory. The value of the flashback is not only in representing the causality of the past on the present, although it is often used that way. It can also make visible to viewers how each encounter insinuates into perception affectively imbued memories below the threshold of explicit feeling and visibility. It can help us to appreciate the role of virtual memory in perception. The close-up adds another lesson, as it calls the viewer's attention to side perceptions not placed at the focus of attention by situated actors, even as some of these subsidiary perceptions will survive as remainders to be called up at a later time. It can also alert us to threshold moments in the past that did not seem important then, but now turn out to have been critical to a shift or turn in the trajectory of events.

Bergson himself thought film was too mechanical to address the complexity of perception; but he made this assessment early in its development. It in fact is an excellent medium through which to address and test his theory. In *Being John Malkovich*, to take another instance, the flashback is superseded by the artifice of other human beings actually crawling into Malkovich's head to turn his perceptions, desires, and actions in new directions. In this way the film literalizes the triangular character of sexual desire, making it available for humorous engagement and closer inspection. Such a literalization of the flashback, as it might be called, accentuates the dim perception you sometimes have of something alien inhabiting your desire. It renders such disturbing or delicious experiences more available for reflection. So when a child emerges as the product of heated sex involving Malkovich, the woman who seduces him, and the woman infatuated with her who crawled into Malkovich's head to participate in the action, subliminal elements circulating in perception and desire become more tangible to us. This includes the uncanny sense by Malkovich that his desire is choreographed by strange forces outside his control. The conjunction between film technique and Bergsonian theory, in turn, might encourage reflection on fugitive features of everyday perception that could otherwise remain in the dark.

At a recent gathering in Baltimore, several graduate students recounted a story about a raucous event they had attended. At first I wished I had been there. There was a lot of drinking, dancing, and loud music at this event, held in a row house on a quiet street. The police appeared to quiet things down. Students smoking outside were ordered back into the house. Once inside, they were summarily ordered to reverse course and go outside. As she walked down stairs she had just walked up, a graduate student said, "I know what you are doing, and I will not be intimidated by your tactics." "Okay, you're the one," an officer announced, and she was placed under arrest. She was handcuffed and led to a police car down the street. The other students milled around, wondering what to do. Then the police car moved to the front of the house, the lights inside the car were turned on so that the handcuffed young woman was visible to everyone, and the car sat there for twenty minutes.

It seemed to the revelers, as I prefer to call them, that the cops were inviting them to protest so that new members could be added to the arrest list. They stopped short of doing so, even as they were plagued by guilt for doing nothing. The woman was taken to the police station and strip-searched; she was then charged with disturbing the peace, resisting arrest, and disobeying an officer. She was kept in jail overnight. At last count, she had racked up about fifteen hundred dollars in legal fees.

We were silent for a moment after this story drew to a close. We allowed ourselves, I guess, to absorb the feelings of anger and anxiety surging up as the event was recounted. Perhaps we also resisted, momentarily, the temptation to place it under one or another cliché. "So, finally a student faces real life." Or "The cops have a difficult time keeping order." Finally, I uttered a third banality: "The other students were smart not to take the bait; those cops showed how they are free to act arbitrarily while protecting their deniability." "Yeah," the storyteller said. "But I don't like the effect the whole thing has had on me."

I don't like it either. The choreography of the event colors fear of the police and anger against them into the texture of perception. It takes a toll on those who were there and on others who hear about it as it spreads, fanned by additions, like wildfire across the campus. Now some students tread more carefully in the presence of the police. Indeed, one's approach to authority in general may be colored more darkly as this event merges into one's implicit urban memory bank.

As I awoke slowly the morning after hearing this story, I found myself rehearsing in no specific order a series of encounters with the police, starting when I was a working-class boy in a medium-sized city. About, for instance, the cops who refused to intervene when factory workers beat a fellow worker who lived next door to me nearly to death the day after the House Un-American Activities Committee came to town to expose him as a former communist. Or the cops who harassed me after I chuckled when one of them slammed on his brakes awkwardly to avoid hitting the car in front of him. Or a few years later when I was pulled over after a peace rally by policemen assigned to monitor it. Or the time I was arrested at a peace demonstration and made vividly aware of the power of the police who arrested us and packed us into a holding area. A thin sheet of time regained. As these affect-imbued recollections floated by in nonchronological order, I sensed how they had formed a sheet of virtual memory that had entered into my response the night before. I also saw how hesitant I was to talk about the effects of such past experiences on the color of my perception because of the intensity of affect attached to them.

My experiences pale by comparison to those of young African American males in the inner city, as an incident that took place a few weeks later shows. Police officers in the same city asserted that it had been necessary for them to shoot an African American addict they had captured after he had stolen a car, although several witnesses claimed the police first handcuffed him, tripped him to make him fall, and then shot him in the back of the head as he pleaded for his life. That case is "under investigation."

According to Kandinsky, if "two circles are drawn and painted respectively yellow and blue, a brief contemplation will reveal in the yellow a spreading movement out from the center, and a noticeable approach to the spectator. The blue, on the other hand, moves into itself, like a snail retreating into its shell, and draws away from the spectator."[9] My perception of the Baltimore police force is colored blue.

This is a minor moment in the micropolitics of perception. Such events accumulate to color perception, even as they are variously absorbed by people in different subject positions. It is easy to see how white, middle-class suburbanites could consolidate such events into a law-and-order mentality. Or how more extreme versions of them in the lives of African American youths could accumulate into a pervasive feeling of urban rage. One day a riot will erupt over a minor incident. Perhaps a tough jury decision, reached by middle-class citizens who have absorbed such stories into their perceptions of crime, police conduct, and urban danger, will pull the trigger. The police bring considerable street knowledge to the micropolitics of perception; you hear bits of it in play when they phone you to solicit contributions to the police fund. The producers of soaps also have such street knowledge. The rest of us may still have things to learn.

In the student arrest case, some witnesses want to testify in court, to expose police arbitrariness and perhaps to fortify themselves against the accumulating effects of silence. But the cops involved understand that desire. The student's lawyer, the judge, the police, and the student's concerns about time and money are likely to converge to settle the matter out of court. An object lesson has already been absorbed, although imperfectly and incompletely. Another thing individuals can do in such instances is to use the venues available to publicize the accumulating effects of such micropolitical events on the color of perception. I will reserve until later chapters the dicey question of how to work on a structure of perception already installed in an individual or constituency.

The Neurophysiology of Perception

The account of perception offered by Bergson, who was closely attuned to the biological research of his day, gains considerable support from contemporary research into its neurophysiology. We have already tacked a bit of that research onto his account by introducing the amygdala, for although this intense, crude brain region coalesces with things Bergson says about the color of perception, it was not an object of research when he wrote.

To see how contemporary research supports Bergson's view of the mixing of cultural experience into neural networks in the organization of perception, consider the Held/Heims (now) classic experiment with cats. Two batches of kittens were first raised in the dark and then exposed to light through carefully varied conditions. Both groups were exposed to the same field of visual possibilities, but those in the first group were allowed to coordinate the visual field with their olfactory and tactile experience as they moved, whereas the kittens in the second group were carried around in baskets as they were exposed to the "same" illuminated environment.

When the animals were released after a few weeks of this treatment, the first group of kittens behaved normally, but those who had been carried around behaved as if they were blind; they bumped into objects and fell over edges. This beautiful study supports the enactive view that objects are not seen by the visual extraction of features but rather by the visual guidance of action.[10]

The cats in the first group synthesized visual, touch, and olfactory experience as they *moved* through their environment, while those in the second group were unable to do so. That is why adults who have sight surgically created after never having been able to see have such a difficult time forming operational images. The accumulation of such experiments, with both animals and humans, has drawn many neuroscientists and some cognitive scientists away from the representational models of mind that informed cognitive science in the 1970s. They are moving closer to the "enactive" model adopted by the authors of *The Embodied Mind* and prefigured in the work of Bergson, James, and Merleau-Ponty.

Antonio Damasio, like the authors just cited, also seconds many of the things Bergson says. He situates them in contemporary research into relations between the brain system and bodily zones. Damasio seems unaware of how closely his account tracks Bergson's theory, but he is alert to a debt to William James. And James and Bergson formed a mutual admiration society in the early part of the twentieth century.[11]

Damasio, for instance, connects the recollection of a past event to the affect attached to it. He also emphasizes how memory in the midst of action is dispositional rather than recollective.

> Dispositions are records which are dormant and implicit rather than active and explicit . . . ; moreover, the memories also contain records of the obligate emotional reaction to the object. As a consequence when we recall an object, when we allow dispositions to make their implicit information explicitly, we retrieve not just sensory data, but also accompanying motor and emotional data.[12]

Affect and the "motor image" are as important to Damasio's rendering of perception as they are to Bergson. Damasio has participated in studies, to be reviewed in chapter 4, that measure the brief half second between the beginning of a percept and its consolidation, during which much of the preliminary work is done. In perception, Damasio says, you become aware of many things in the world, but what you do not ever come to know directly is the mechanism behind the discovery, the steps that need to take place behind the seemingly open stage of your mind in order for core consciousness of an object's image to arise and make the image yours.... The time elapsed is minuscule if measured by a stopwatch, but it is actually quite extensive if you think of it from the perspective of the neurons which make it all possible and whose units are so much smaller than that of your conscious mind.[13]

Damasio's story about a patient with "ventromedial prefrontal damage" illustrates how important affect is to memory and perception. The patient has lost access to what Damasio calls "somatic markers" in everyday situations, although his powers of analysis remain intact. These cultural markers inscribed in visceral process form the basis of virtual or dispositional memory. But the capacity to invoke such markers is damaged in his case. Less robustly imbued with markers through which to narrow decision issues to a manageable set of options, this poor guy finds it necessary to reason through every situation as if he were a rational-choice theorist.

His affect/judgment impairment served him well when he was negotiating an icy patch of road one night. Other drivers had to override a socially ingrained instinct to slam on their brakes as their cars slid on the ice, but, in the absence of a panic-stricken impulse, our hero calmly and deliberately steered his car over the icy patch. Awareness of his goal coalesced with a diminution of affect to work well this time around. Things got tougher, however, when he was asked to select one of two dates to return to the clinic.

For the better part of a half-hour, the patient enumerated reasons for and against each of the two dates: previous engagements, proximity to other engagements, possible meteorological conditions, virtually anything that one could reasonably think about concerning a simple date. Just as calmly as he had driven over the ice ... he was now walking us through a tiresome cost-benefit analysis, and endless outlining and fruitless comparison of options and possible consequences. It took enormous discipline to listen to all of this without pounding on the table and telling him to stop, but we finally did tell him, quietly, that he should come on the second of the alternative dates.... He simply said, "That's fine."[14]

If you have attended many faculty meetings, you might be impressed with the patience Damasio and his colleagues showed in this instance. The patient's behavior, says Damasio, "is a good example of the limits of pure reason."[15]

If he had the ability to consult somatic markers acquired through a previous history of cultural transactions, the question would have been framed for him in its timeliness and living significance *before* he began to deliberate; factors irrelevant to the decision could have been subtracted to reduce the number of considerations invoked in explicit decision. This patient is condemned to the infinite imperative of calculative reasoning because he has lost the affect-imbued markers appropriate to contextual decision making. Some rational-choice theorists may be pushed to similar results because they cannot bear the agony of small decisions.

But what is a somatic marker? It is a culturally mobilized, corporeal disposition through which affect-imbued, preliminary orientations to perception and judgment scale down the material factored into cost-benefit analyses, principled judgments, and reflective experiments. If Damasio is right, somatic markers form the seedbed of dispositional memory. A somatic marker operates below the threshold of reflection; it mixes culture and nature into perception, thinking, and judgment; and it folds gut feelings into these mixtures. "Somatic markers do not deliberate for us. They assist the deliberation by highlighting some options (either dangerous or favorable), and eliminating them rapidly from subsequent consideration." They "assist the process of sifting through such a wealth of detail" and thereby "reduce the need for sifting because they provide an automated detection of the scenario components that are likely to be relevant."[16]

Such markers might be triggered when you are invited to a sexually attractive friend's home at the end of a casual evening. Time is short, and you cannot address all the considerations relevant to the decision. You don't, perhaps, ask yourself in detail whether the event may carry future burdens with it, whether your partner would be disturbed upon learning about it, whether you are discontented in your current relationship, whether your future friendship with the colleague could be damaged, and so on. You respond to a series of implicit, affect-imbued judgments gathered from the past before deliberating briefly.

Somatic markers provide ambiguous help in the midst of decision. They make it possible to perceive and decide in a timely manner. But they also fold into these subtractions and accentuations elements that sometimes turn out to be dangerous, unwise, or cruel. You might, for instance, jerk the wheel to the left into an oncoming car. Or turn away the friend merely because a racial stereotype clicks in at the possibility of intimacy. Somatic markers make decisions easier and faster for human beings whose chamber of consciousness is slow in pace and limited in capacity. They can also spur new trains of thought. But, for these very reasons, the weight of somatic markers also generates a need for tactics and techniques by which to work on them when their compressions of experience become too restrictive or destructive.

It is critical to understand that somatic markers are not equivalent to biologically wired predispositions. They have intersubjective and linguistic elements mixed into them. When European Jews went through the Holocaust, for instance, the trauma left effects on several layers of collective experience. The term *Holocaust* became a way to draw up those memories, both virtually in the course of action and in explicit recollection. The term both calls up complex memories on the higher, linguistic register and taps into the visceral dimension of trauma, an intense set of feelings that gather in the gut, the muscles, and the pallor of the skin. When people with such intense collective memories face new circumstances that trigger them, a set of dispositions to perception, feeling, interpretation, and action are called into play. Media such as TV and film, as they mix music, background sounds, words, and visual images together, are particularly adept at invoking such dispositions, and also at working upon them. Attention to the techniques these media deploy can sharpen our perceptions of how such effects are invoked and teach us how to work on ourselves to refine their shape or intensity.

Once somatic markers are added to your ledger, both rational-choice theory and the reduction of culture to an unlayered set of intersubjective concepts and beliefs are thrown into jeopardy. The model of "deliberative democracy," loved by many political theorists, requires modification too. Culturally preorganized charges shape perception and judgment in ways that exceed the picture of the world supported by the models of calculative reason, intersubjective culture, and deliberative democracy. They show us how linguistically complex brain regions respond not only to events in the world but also, proprioceptively, to cultural habits, skills, memory traces, and affects mixed into our muscles, skin, gut, and cruder brain regions. Since we will shortly engage an intersubjective model that flattens out the layered texture of thinking and culture, let me now intimate the implication that Damasio's theory of somatic markers carries for empiricism and rational-choice theory. Here is what the neuroscientist himself says about how the complex relays and feedback loops connecting brain, body, and culture disrupt predictive models of explanation:

> Moreover, the brain is not likely to predict how all the commands—neural and chemical, but especially the latter—will play out in the body, because the play-out and the resulting states depend on local biochemical contexts and on numerous variables within the body itself which are not fully representable. What is played out in the body is constructed anew, moment by

moment.... The brain probably cannot predict the exact landscapes the body will assume after it unleashes a barrage of neural and chemical signals on the body no more than it can predict all the imponderables of a specific situation as it unfolds in real life and real time.[17]

Memory and Action

When you fold Bergson's understanding of the role that human mobility plays in perception into Damasio's exploration of somatic markers, you emerge with a layered appreciation of how perception functions. When that perspective is joined to the insights of some film directors, the credibility and availability of these ideas themselves can be augmented. Take, for instance, the layered image of perception, thinking, and judgment embodied in Orson Welles's *Citizen Kane*.

The film opens with a newsreel about Kane, who has just died. The reporter tells us in objective voice that Kane was a populist, the left-leaning owner of a major newspaper, a scandalmonger, a candidate for governor, a charismatic man, and so on, whose life fell apart when he was caught by his opponent in an affair with a young woman during the middle of his campaign for governor. The newsreel recapitulates the strategies of scandalmongering through superficial objectivity that Kane himself had popularized in the mainstream press. It is played, as it turns out, to reporters in a pressroom. As the reel ends, the reporters' editor, impatient with the veneer of superficial objectivity governing it, assigns a reporter to find out the truth about Kane. Since Kane uttered the word "Rosebud" just before he died, the editor concludes that this is the enigma to be deciphered.

What is Rosebud? The name of a lover? An enchanting childhood experience? An erogenous body zone? A flower that never blossomed? Through a series of long flashbacks, each mediated by an interested witness to a time in Kane's life, the mystery is probed. No flashback simply presents a slice of Kane's past. Each is filtered through the experience of someone invested one way or another in his life. That would be the case for Kane, too; his own flashbacks would be invested with current feelings and concerns inflecting how the past is called into the present. Each memory of the witnesses, then, is itself also shaped to some degree by the affect-imbued context in which it arises. The film enacts Bergson's view that the past is constituted not simply out of the present that it was but during the time it is called into being.

The investments of the witnesses are crudely represented in a poster advertising the film. It places Kane in the middle, surrounded by several faces: "I love him," says a demure woman; "He's a Saint," says the review editor;

"He's a genius," says the editor he replaced; "He's crazy," says his onetime guardian and banker; "He's a dirty dog," says the politician who destroyed him; "I hate him," says the sultry woman looking down from the top left column.[18]

Yes, *Citizen Kane* presents a model of perspectivalism in which no single perspective rises to a place of simple objectivity. But the subjectively mediated flashbacks may also accumulate to form an intersubjective composite exceeding the perspective of any single witness. Together, they put us into filtered contact with selected aspects of Kane's past as they come into play in his later life. But because this composite fails to penetrate the mystery of Rosebud, the assemblage of flashbacks works against the agenda of deep explanation the editor had in mind (and that often governs the use of the flashback). So we must keep digging.

It is unwise to allow the (now) familiar and pertinent theme of perspectivalism to overwhelm Welles's corollary attempt through flashbacks, shifts in perspective, and depth-of-field shots to portray the complex, layered role that the past plays in the present. For through *Citizen Kane*, we now come to terms more vividly with another level of the virtual. The virtual subsists not only as action-oriented memories below explicit recollection at the moment, but also as intensive traces and fragments that have *effects* on judgment and consciousness in new encounters without themselves being susceptible in principle to explicit recollection. Bergson would agree. We now engage three layers of memory: (a) explicit memories called up by an existing situation, (b) potential recollections that operate implicitly in action contexts because time is too short to pull them up as recollections, and (c) effects of the past on the present that cannot take the form of explicit recollection, even when time is available. These latter affect-imbued traces cannot be recollected not because they are repressed, but because the fragmentary form they assume does not coincide with that of an articulable thought or coherent image. This, perhaps, is one shape taken by somatic markers.

Let's see how Welles addresses this third layer. *Citizen Kane* draws toward a close when a worker, visible to viewers but not to the reporter assigned to the case, picks up a sled and tosses it into the fire along with a mess of other items collected by the deceased millionaire. We are then treated to a penultimate scene in which the name "Rosebud" becomes visible on the sled as it goes up in flames, followed by a scene in which black smoke billows from the chimney of the deserted mansion in which Kane lived his last years. Have we—the viewers—now penetrated the enigma withheld from the reporter and witnesses?

The image of the sled may flash *us* back to an earlier scene, one organized through "depth of field."[19] In this scene—presented as a long flashback by Kane's onetime guardian and banker—intensive lighting at the deep back center draws the eye to a window through which a boy can be seen rollicking in the snow on his sled. The intense lighting in the diminutive background is set off from a middle range of depth in natural lighting, where Kane's father watches belligerently from the left as Kane's mother and future guardian settle arrangements at the front right for Kane's adoption and introduction into a more urbane life. Louis Giannetti summarizes some other elements in this depth-of-field shot:

> In this scene... eight year old Charles plays with his sled outside in the snow while his future is being determined by his mother and Thatcher. The boy's father watches impotently, sputtering a few feeble protests. The mise en scene is compartmentalized into twos, with the wall serving as the vertical dividing line. Kane senior and young Charles are grouped to the left; Thatcher and the severe Mrs. Kane dominate the right lower half, their pens poised to sign the contract that will soon separate Charles from his parents.[20]

The shot makes use of tripartite depth division and two-part vertical division, with the viewer's eye drawn to a diminutive, intensely lighted scene of the young boy at the deepest point outside the window while a conversation about him proceeds in less dramatic light in front view in the house. When the scene plays early in the film, we learn that the boy is about to be separated from his parents and his home. When we flash back to it as the sled goes up in flames, we might hope for a moment (unless film critics have already taken that hope away) that it contains the key to the meaning of Rosebud, a key none of the protagonists has been able to turn. We now believe that this fork in Kane's life entered actively into his later decisions. Can we finally decipher Rosebud?

No. The fork does set the table for future perceptions, judgments, and actions by Kane, but it does not by itself determine them. When, for instance, he insists that Susan—the woman he married after their illicit affair was exposed during his electoral campaign—pursue a singing career for which she is ill suited, we might comprehend that response in relation to the early life from which he was pulled away. But a number of other responses might have spoken to the fugitive experience of disconnection as well. Second, when his mother, played by the severe Agnes Moorehead, signed the adoption contract against her husband's wishes, she made it clear to both men (although not to Kane frolicking in the snow) that her primary motive for doing so was to protect her son from future abuse by his volatile father. If Rosebud represented to Kane an idyllic world that might have been—and it is not perfectly clear that it did—it cannot *now* do so for us.

Each time an element in Kane's past is brought into view, it points to a diffuse, affective horizon beyond it. For instance, because we now surmise that other tensions and ambiguities would have been set into motion if Kane had remained with his parents, the snow scene loses its aura as a moment of fullness lost. As each angle of recollection is followed and rendered fuzzy by the next we are eventually pressed to conclude both that the film makes some sense of Kane *and* that it points to efficacious sheets of past working upon Kane's life that exceed anyone's capacity of recollection from any perspective — including Kane's and ours. Each fork is filtered through explicit recollections, but each also points to virtual effects installed below available first-person recollection or authoritative, third-person reconstruction.

Are these latter nonevents, then? In some sense they are, for they can't be represented or articulated. But in another sense they are not. Although no one captures them in a recollection image, they can still have effects in the present when triggered by new encounters. Such affective markers, unsusceptible to explicit recollection, might also be susceptible to some degree to being worked upon by tactical means.

In *Citizen Kane* the eventual placement of the viewer in a superior position to that of the protagonists accentuates the enigma of Rosebud.[21] This tactic, like the use of multiple flashbacks in relation to stories recounted by different witnesses, unsettles the perspectival privilege assumed by the viewer. Rather than completing an explanatory account that had been fragmentary, the flashbacks, depth-of-field shots, and surprising shifts in perspectival privilege encourage us to think more actively about the role that effective, enigmatic sheets of past play in thinking and perception. The Wellesian engagement with depth becomes linked to appreciation of the layered effectivity of the past on the present rather than to pursuit of sufficient knowledge, deep explanation, or narrative integrity. Responding to this development, you may ponder just what prompts you to insist that people, things, and events must be susceptible in principle to deep explanation.

The film will infect your dream life, if you give it a chance, partly because its depth explorations do not issue in deep explanation. Kane's past is tracked by virtual remainders that color his perceptions, inflect his thoughts, and enter into his decisions. Rosebud signifies the complex effectivity of the past. Such a conclusion is supported by the presentation, in later scenes, of the reporter from rear view, of Kane with eyes averted and face partly in shadow, of the loss of resonance in Kane's voice, and by the ominous portrayals of buildings and places as mere edifices and cluttered spaces. At the very end, the film may flash your recollection to a sign at the opening scene in front of the castle. It says, "No Trespassing." It does not say,

"Irrelevant." That recollection, too, is inflected by the new circumstances in which it is pulled up.

Welles is Bergsonian, and Bergson delineates a layered conception of memory and perception anticipating Wellesian cinema. Of course, Freud could be invoked to interpret Rosebud. Indeed, it is difficult not to do so today. But it may therefore be wise to set Freudian theory to the side at first, just so it does not automatically monopolize the possibilities of interpretation. We will explore Freud's theory of primal guilt and memory traces in chapter 4. Bergson's focus on the rapid pace of perception allows us to see how memory, perception, thinking, and culture can be layered without having immediate recourse to heavy explanatory theory. Bergson suggests how "memory traces," as Freud calls them, *might* operate even without expressing primordial guilt (Freud's archaic traces) or, often enough, without being processed through a repression machine. As we shall see, the Bergsonian interpretation opens the door to a wide range of tactics by which to *work* on affective memories that help to structure perception and judgment. Freud's theory — less attentive to the rapid tempo of human perception and unalert to productive potentialities in "religious experience" — limits too-stringently positive possibilities of technical intervention into the habitus of the self and the habits of larger collectives. Put another way, Freud encloses memory traces within a deep interpretation in which he knows the source and shape of the most archaic traces, even though those beset by them do not. The perspective developed here refuses for ethical reasons to join the appreciation of layering and depth to the hubris of deep, authoritative interpretation. We may foster positive experimentation in ethics and politics by joining a layered conception of memory, perception, thinking, and culture to modest schemata of interpretation and explanation. In forging an intertext that includes Welles, Bergson, and Damasio, we address the complexity of perception, and we anticipate how creative thought might be spurred by contingent encounters between virtual memory and new events.

The Texture of Culture

Let's test this layered account of memory, perception, and judgment against a conception of culture that calls it into question. In *Our America: Nativism, Modernism, and Pluralism*, Walter Benn Michaels argues that not only nationalists and nativists adopt racial images of culture; cultural pluralists, against their highest intentions, do so too. How can this be? The problem is that cultural pluralists, trying to match nativists in their appreciation of the texture of culture and the corollary depth of identity, inevitably insert a biological concept of race into the base of culture. The nativists prize racial purity while the pluralists seek diversity. But the way the latter constitute deep pluralism plunges them into the cauldron of pluralist racism.

Culture, for Michaels, consists of "concepts, beliefs and practices." You can get a good sense of how layered his understanding of these media is by attending to his critique of cultural pluralists. Michaels says that cultural pluralists who play up an *obligation* of each constituency to come to terms with its own identity, or to *express* that identity in relations with other groups, or to be *loyal* to it, pour into the injunctions "obligation," "express," and "loyal" a racial conception of culture. They pluralize race under the pretense of eliminating it. The pluralists are driven to this result, he says, through their desire to avoid a "universalism" that they fear fosters an intolerance of "difference."

It is their anxiety about universalism that gets the pluralists into trouble, for to avoid its apparent defects they postulate deep cultural differences "disconnected...from one's actual beliefs and practices." That is, to give depth to culture they incorporate a biological element into its composition that exceeds the concepts and beliefs of participants. "Pluralism makes this disconnection possible by *deriving* one's beliefs and practices *from* one's cultural identity instead of *equating* one's beliefs and practices *with* one's cultural identity."[22] Here is the dilemma in a nutshell:

> The commitment to difference itself represents a theoretical intensification rather than diminution of racism, an intensification that has nothing to do with feelings of tolerance or intolerance toward other races and everything to do with the conceptual apparatus of pluralist racism.[23]

The critique of "the politics of difference" has several implications. One is the restoration of a universalism that Michaels himself neither develops nor defends in positive terms. It is established, rather, by elimination of the other options he recognizes as possible candidates. They don't work because they presuppose a racial conception of identity that is both unwanted by pluralists and at odds with the best biological knowledge available today. To accept this pluralist conception of culture, if you are a pluralist, is thus to get entangled in a performative contradiction: you implicitly presuppose a conception of race that you explicitly reject.

Michaels first reduces every nonracial conception of culture to a set of concepts and beliefs and then shows, through a series of performative contradictions, that each deep conception of pluralism engenders a conception the pluralists themselves can't endorse explicitly. The charge of committing a performative contradiction becomes the most potent weapon of cultural critique in Michaels's armory. If culture were actually constituted as Michaels defines it, the weapon would work effectively. Artfully and relentlessly pursued, it would reduce the contenders to the explicit nativists and implicit racists he opposes and the universalism he endorses. The pluralists would be compelled to adopt his view to avoid implicit racism. And Michaels is very artful . . . within the range of alternatives he acknowledges.

Indeed, a visceral desire to translate the performative contradiction into a master weapon of cultural critique may be one of the things that presses Michaels to give such unlayered readings of "concepts and beliefs," "culture," and "difference." For if that weapon is to win clear-cut victories, it helps to start with a sketch of culture in which the concepts and beliefs that constitute it are clean and flat enough to be fitted into tightly structured arguments. It also helps to act as if everybody must either accept this rendering of culture in the name of clarity or deepen culture through the addition of a biological conception of race.

But a funny thing now happens. It now appears that you can avoid pluralist racism only by enacting a culture as flat as the celluloid world of *Pleasantville* before color, texture, ambiguity, paradox, affect, and passion are folded into it by refugees from the real, embodied, noncelluloid world. Perhaps a reconsideration of the alternatives admitted into discussion by Michaels will help to restore a little color to culture.

Take "difference." On my reading, difference is layered. It operates on several registers, assuming a different level of complexity on each. On one register it is a defined minority that deviates from the majority practice. On a second, it is a minority that varies from other constituencies in a setting where there is no definitive majority. On a third, it is that in an identity (subjective or intersubjective) that is obscured, suppressed, or remaindered by its own dominant tendencies — as in the way devout Christians may be inhabited by fugitive forgetfulness and doubts not brought up for review in daily conversations or in church, or in the way militant atheists may tacitly project life forward after death when not concentrating on the *belief* that consciousness stops with the death of the body. The third register of difference fades into a fourth, in which surpluses, traces, noises, and charges in and around the concepts and beliefs of embodied agents express proto-thoughts and judgments too crude to be conceptualized in a refined way but still intensive and effective enough to make a difference to the selective way judgments are formed, porous arguments are received, and alternatives are weighted. And in a layered, textured culture, cultural argument is always porous. Some of the elements in such a fugitive fund might be indicated, but not of course represented, by those noises, stutters, gestures, looks, accents, exclamations, gurgles, bursts of laughter, gestures, and rhythmic or irrhythmic movements that inhabit, punctuate, inflect, and help to move the world of concepts and beliefs recognized by Michaels.

Michaels, however, will be wary of the third register of difference, and he must avoid the fourth like the plague.[24] Not by disproving it—for it is not clear that he can do so without drawing in advance upon the very model of culture he supports, along with the master mode of argument it makes available to him—but by ignoring, dismissing, or laughing off its expressions and projections by those who are more impressed than he with the animal in us, the spirituality in us, or both. He will say, perhaps, "If it is unknowable, it can't be articulated," supposing in that very formulation an equivalence between *articulation* and *efficacy* that is up for discussion. Or, if he follows the path of dismissal, he may well draw upon cultural resources that exceed his official model of how cultural critique proceeds. Would that be a performative contradiction?

Suppose that Michaels were to project difference, in one of its modalities, as a virtual reality, that is, in Bergson's terms, a real force that has effects on actual feelings, conduct, judgments, and identity but does not itself take the form of a feeling or a recollection image. Or suppose, more modestly, he were to grant this rendering of difference as a contestable reading of a register of cultural life, even though he finds it too messy and unreachable by knowledge to endorse himself. Now the tight connection he has crafted between a culture reduced to concepts and beliefs and the power of the performative contradiction loosens up considerably. The loss of the former reduces the power of the latter in eliminating competitors to his view. For you can now have a deep, layered image of culture without invoking the idea of race to do so. Michaels can disagree with this possibility, but he has now forfeited the sort of arguments needed to eliminate it decisively.

He might now engage with more appreciation a cluster of theists such as Augustine, James, Bergson, Levinas, Merleau-Ponty, and Taylor, as well as nontheists such as Epicurus, Deleuze, Derrida, Butler, Foucault, Nietzsche, and (perhaps) Damasio, who joyfully proclaim that *sometimes* the encounter with paradox, contradiction, aporia, and ambiguity points to a register subsisting beneath close conceptual discernment that nonetheless has effects on the color of perception, the texture of action, and the priority invested in some porous arguments over others. From these perspectives, a performative contradiction is not always a defeat—although it does call for further elaboration of the issue in question. It might point to layers subsisting below disembodied conceptions of cultural life. Augustine treats the paradox of time as a sign of our dependence on God, and Nietzsche treats the paradox of truth ("Suppose truth is a woman") as a sign of our implication in fugitive layers of intersubjectivity that exceeds our best powers of representation. Now culture involves practices in which the porosity of argument is inhabited by more noise, unstated habit, and differential intensities of affect than adamant rationalists acknowledge. The point, at least for me and several of the figures listed above, is not simply to articulate that which exceeds articulation, for each attempt to do that is by definition to move and modify that which is articulated. It is sometimes to draw creative sustenance from this fugitive register of being, as Augustine does in one way and Nietzsche in another. At other times it is to work by *artful means* to magnify, enrich, or modify elements in an affective register not reachable by argument or conscious regulation alone. Now you enter a domain in which technique, faith, cultivation, and conversion infiltrate practices of argument, critique, and deliberation. But this may sound a lot like noise to Michaels, as indeed it is.

In these latter renderings of culture, concepts and beliefs play a significant role, but they are layered into corporeal/spiritual contexts that render it impossible to reduce them entirely to disembodied tokens of argumentation. Culture has multiple layers, with each layer marked by distinctive speeds, capacities, and levels of linguistic complexity. And the relations between the layers are mediated by noise—just as a bit of static can help a single note to stand out more sharply, if the static is not too loud or too soft.

Let me identify a few points at which I concur with Michaels. I agree that an enclave model of pluralism, in which each constituency is obligated only to the group from which it springs, misreads the multiple sources from which operative identities spring and overstates the obligations one has to one's past. I also add that it depreciates the politics of pluralization by which new identities are periodically propelled onto the regime of cultural life from a place below the register of defined identities, although I am uncertain whether Michaels can concur with me in *this* critique of enclave pluralism.[25]

Michaels also helps us to see how a flat conception of concepts and beliefs joined to a quest for deep identity readily degenerates into a racial picture of culture. I agree, too, that some models of pluralism do slide toward a conception of race, even though it is possible to defend a deep, layered pluralism that does not do so. Finally, I concur that concepts, beliefs, and practices play pivotal roles in the consolidation of culture, although I understand these media to be both layered in their degrees of complexity and mixed with other elements that enable and exceed them.

Michaels's tendency to reduce culture to disembodied concepts and beliefs may also flow from a drive to identify the biological with the genetic and the corporeal with the fixed. Hence the reduction of deep pluralism to racism. But, as we have already begun to see, different levels of biological complexity are mixed into culture to varying degrees, and, as we shall see in chapter 3, you can include genetics in cultural theory without succumbing to genetic determinism. Even some birds that are genetically predisposed to sing the songs appropriate to their species vary the forms of their songs depending upon the melodic influences in the environments they are subjected to when young. So, the same problematic assumptions about biology that move Michaels to reduce deep pluralism to a racial view of culture may encourage him to adopt a disembodied, undertextured model of culture.

Take, for instance, his dismissal of "passing," the serious game some members of cultural minority groups play when they pretend to be members of the majority. Michaels asserts:

> The very idea of passing—whether it takes the form of looking like you belong to a different race or of acting like you belong to a different race—requires an understanding of race as something separate from the way you look and the way you act. If race were really nothing but culture, that is, if race really were nothing but a distinctive array of beliefs and practices, then, of course there could be no passing, since to believe and practice what the members of any race believed and practiced would, by definition make you a member of that race.[26]

"By definition," racial passing is impossible unless you presuppose race. Well, it depends on how many elements are folded into the term *race* and, particularly, how textured and layered your understanding of an "array of beliefs and practices" is. So let's transport passing to a venue away from the domain of race. Suppose you are a working-class boy who grew up in Hampden, Baltimore, a neighborhood adjacent to Johns Hopkins University and the one that provided the inspiration for the John Waters film *Pecker* (as well as Waters's *Hairspray* and a couple of others). You have graduated from a commuter college with high grades in English and a couple of stimulating essays to your credit. You are admitted to the English Department at Hopkins and given a free ride. Let the passing begin.

First, there are characteristic modes of pronunciation memorialized in the fine muscles of your jaw, mouth, lips, and tongue. This accent, you fear, will mark you from the start to faculty and graduate students you have observed eating lunch in Hampden. You have seen how they sometimes raise their eyebrows and smirk discreetly while listening attentively to waiters with your accent. So, by paying close attention to the accents of the talking heads on TV, you make a concerted effort to mimic pronunciations that fit seamlessly into the world of the graduate seminar. Of course, you slip up sometimes. That is why you remain as quiet as feasible during the first year. Maybe that initial reserve will stand you in good stead later.

Second, characteristic neighborhood expressions have become part of your second nature, even though it would be an exaggeration to reduce them to a unique set of concepts and beliefs. Nonetheless, they draw your attention to particular features of the world and turn it away from other possibilities. You now work to put some of these expressions on hold, even as you also hold them in reserve for possible use at a later date.

Third, there are distinctive memory traces from your childhood, some of which filtered into your mode of being before you developed sophisticated language skills, for the materiality of culture exceeds the concepts and beliefs that enter into it. They include, for starters, actual hitting, caressing, cuddling, hugging, cooing, bumping, odors, and confinement mixed into conceptually mediated practices of love, anger, discipline, education, and rivalry. Indeed, sometimes a verbal expression of care can be confounded persistently by blows, gestures, and looks that are at odds with it. The effect of such mixtures on your visceral habits of perception, desire, trust, faith, judgment, and inflection of arguments in adult life is likely to be about as strong as the influence of your childhood gait on your adult style of walking. That is, the effect is real without being wholly determinative. This complex mixing of touch, image, smell, sound, posture, concept, affect, and belief in actual conduct is easily forgotten by those whose habits correspond fairly closely to the seminar norm. But its efficacy may become vivid to a bright kid from Hampden working hard to pass as the graduate student he is now defined to be.

Fourth, there are the experiences of dissonance between the academic presentations of culture and class-geographic experiences now embodied in the somatic markers through which your perceptions are marshaled and your identity is crystallized. Such corporeal markers, on my reading, embody a linguistic dimension without conforming to the sophisticated network of contrasts available on the most sophisticated layer of human reflection. That is, there is an interplay between the intersubjective world of linguistic distinctions and the corporeal register. These less refined intensities, moreover, are communicated to the higher, more refined regions, helping to nudge the porous processes of argument in some directions rather than others.[27] They might find expression, for instance, in an impulse to laughter surging up after a literary figure you admire has been convicted of five performative contradictions. You might *then* draw on your street wisdom to identify routes by which to slip through the porous net of these arguments or to convert its apparent defeat into a positive experience.

These are a few of the issues to engage when a working-class kid passes as a graduate student in an elite university—a fair amount of passing without the invocation of race. Still, a brash working-class kid might find pure passing to be humiliating. He might, therefore, occasionally *express* some corporeally ingrained ingredients of his cultural heritage with brazen humor while working out creative connections to the new world in which he now participates. Pecker does walk home on weekends, after all. Or he may alternate between passing and expressing pieces of his background, deploying a combination of silences, jokes, mimicking, and pretense to get through the first year. Gradually he may inject more stutters, guffaws, jokes, and objections into the seminars. These may coalesce eventually to form a distinctive sensibility. That sensibility, in turn, may play an important role in the relative weights he gives to particular arguments, his pleasure in paradox, and the appreciation of the layering of culture he brings to his studies. For he is now even more layered than before. If he is lucky, some of the dissonances, remainders, surpluses, and resistances between his present and his past will elevate his teaching, impart creativity to his literary work, and energize his love life.

You could extend and proliferate such examples without presupposing a biological concept of race *if* you develop an embodied, layered conception of perception and culture: gays passing as straight in a small town or a military unit; straights passing as gay; atheists passing as devout Christians as they run for office; professors passing as hip participants in popular culture; homeless women passing as customers when they need to use a restaurant bathroom. In all these instances the affective layering of identity and culture allows various mixtures of expression, loyalty, disloyalty, passing, resistance, and invention.

Michaels pulls off the dismissal of passing and the reduction of culture it implies by converting each example of the layered materialization of culture into an instance of its racialization. He sustains that formula, in turn, by tacitly equating the biological with the genetic and the genetic with the fixed. Sometimes he gets it right. And he does point to risks accompanying any effort to support an ethos of deep, layered pluralism. But he does not show the negotiation of such a political culture to be impossible. For there is a hell of a lot more to the biological element of thinking, culture, and identity than the dubious genetics of race. The color of perception, the layered texture of culture, and the fugitive energies of becoming are flattened out by such an austere picture of life. Once you restore mobility, color, texture, energy, and ambivalence to culture, life in Pleasantville starts to sing again. But you now lose the ability to say the following and make it stick: "Cultural pluralism is an oxymoron; its commitment to culture is contradicted by its commitment to pluralism."[28]

THREE

Nature, Affect, Thinking...

Nature/Culture Imbrications

EVERY CONCEPTION OF CULTURE, identity, ethics, or thinking contains an image of nature. And the relation goes the other way too. Even the most adamant realist in, say, engineering presupposes a cultural conception of how scientific cognition proceeds. To adopt the correspondence model of truth, for instance, is to act as if human capacities for cognition can be brought into close correspondence with the way of the world separate from those capacities. Nietzsche would say that such a realism preserves the remains of an old theology.[1] Its operational assumption, first, that the world *has* a deep, complete structure and, second, that such a structure is available to the cognition of human agents might appear improbable to a culture in which faith in a world created by a universal, omniscient God did not have a long run. Creationists and realists may slide closer together in their assumptions and hubris than either group today acknowledges.

Absent centuries-long belief in a world completely known to a God, it might seem likely, as it did to some Greeks, that cognition has evolved in ways that help us to intervene in the world rather than to hook onto it as it is in itself. And many contemporary scientists now accept something close to the more modest view.

In this chapter I explore an idea of thinking and culture set in neither a theo-teleological view of nature nor a classical scientific model. I continue this effort through reference to new work in neurocience in the next chapter. The orientation in question, although popular in other times and places, has not gained much popularity in modern Western life. Nietzsche pursued it, but his thought has often been considered to suffer from a poetic conception of nature put to rest by modern science. Given the recent work by Ilya Prigogine and Isabelle Stengers in chemistry and the philosophy of science, respectively, however, now may be a particularly apt time to reopen this issue.

The enterprise we are pursuing has a paradoxical twist to it. Every cultural interpretation expresses an idea of nature; but because the partisans of each are themselves part of nature and culture, they lack a position above the field from which to reach definitive judgments about it. Unless they adopt a transcendental strategy, like Kant, who contended that we *must act as if* nature can be comprehended only through an authoritative model of lawful regularity. But so far every attempt to establish such a transcendental perspective with ironclad authority has bumped into the paradox just identified. I affirm the paradox of interpretation as a condition of possibility for this work, affirming that the perspective defended here will, even if it marshals considerable resources in its support, fall short of establishing its own necessity. It will be contestable, meaning that it is possible for others to support other readings of the nature/culture relation, as they too work to defend the comparative plausibility of their accounts. I agree with Augustine, Nietzsche, and Kierkegaard that thinking itself becomes blunt and dull if it always tries to resolve paradoxes rather than to open up spaces within them and negotiate considered responses to them.

Nature and Unpredictability

Nietzsche's views of science and nature are familiar enough. He defends modern science against a history of attacks by the Catholic Church. He then criticizes early modern science for its insistence that the world is governed by eternal laws discernible to science properly organized. And he finally endorses another model of materialism as a reflective "supposition" or "conjecture." He thinks that the modern regulative idea of a world governed by invariant laws has been useful to human welfare and self-preservation; he even believes he can identify something in the evolutionary development of the human animal that has encouraged adoption of a lawlike model. But he thinks it is also possible and laudable to attenuate those same tendencies, without eliminating them. Here is a statement about the evolution of the human tendency to treat similarities as if they were equalities:

Innumerable beings who made inferences in a way different from ours perished....Those, for example, who did not know how to find often enough what is "equal" as regards both nourishment and hostile animals—those, in other words, who subsumed things too slowly and cautiously—were favored with a less probability of survival than those who guessed upon encountering something similar that they must be equal. The dominant tendency, however, *to treat as equal what is merely similar*—an illogical tendency, for nothing is really equal—is what first created any basis for logic.[2]

These traditions of equalization enter into habits, organic functions, institutional regimes, and the experimental designs of science. They become corporeally encoded into patterns of perception and cultural vocabulary. But they are never completely stabilized. The similarities-rendered-equal and the differences-rendered-similar periodically manifest themselves as rebel forces within habits, linguistic ambiguity, organic functions, and so on. These differential energies and energetic disturbances both enable creativity in thinking and help to propel interventions for reform of the "laws" of science. We have a limited but real capacity to encounter, but not of course to know, some dimensions of the world that escape, exceed, resist and destabilize the best equalizations of nature we have so far enacted and enforced.

The lawlike model of science, however, resists this double-entry orientation by projecting a regulative ideal of nature as completely ordered. It replaces, in Nietzsche's judgment, one kind of ontological narcissism with another. The theo-telological image of the world promised the possibility of eternal salvation by sowing the seeds of an accusatory culture in this life. It ran that risk as it appraised diverse constituencies according to the objective norms it purported to find in nature. The newer, lawlike model promises that we can see our reason reflected in nature and, to a considerable extent, harness nature for the purposes of happiness, preservation, and longevity. If nature can't be for us in the first sense, it must be for us in the second. That is the message of the second image as Nietzsche receives and resists it.

What is the Nietzschean underworld—the world circulating in and around discernible regularities? It can only be characterized cryptically. But if you adjust each element in nature to the speed appropriate to it—a very short time for a neuron firing in the human brain, a longer one for the movement of human consciousness, longer yet for the life span of a human, much more so for the span of biological evolution, and the longest yet for evolution of the universe—you may engage an unpredictable element of "becoming" in each pattern of duration. "The world with which we are concerned [the world of appearance] is false, i.e., is not a fact but a fable and approximation on the basis of a meager sum of observations; it is 'in flux', as something in a state of becoming."[3] Note that after saying this world is false, meaning that it does not exhaust the way of the world, Nietzsche also says that it is an "approximation on the basis of a meager sum of observations." He thinks, indeed, that such accumulations often both approximate reality and play an indispensable role in cultural life. It is just that they often also deserve to be brought into contact with fugitive forces that exeed them. Here is a formulation by Zarathustra that ventures a claim about the world of becoming while seeming to confess how even Zarathustra is unable to pursue this intimation consistently:

> When the water is spanned by planks, when bridges and railings leap over the river, verily those are believed who say, "everything is in flux...." But when the winter comes..., then verily, not only the blockheads say, "Does not everything stand still?"
>
> "At bottom everything stands still." — that is truly a winter doctrine.... O my brothers is everything not in flux now? Have not all railings and bridges fallen into the water? Who could still cling to "good" and "evil"? ... The thawing wind blows — thus preach in every street, my brothers.[4]

The winter doctrine, "At bottom everything stands still." That would mean that the laws of nature are complete and fixed. There is neither excess over them nor asymmetry in them from which long-term changes might be mobilized. It would mean that the experience of history and the arrow of time are illusory when it comes to nature. Does such a presumption throw the evolution of the universe into doubt? What about biological evolution? It depends on whether it is possible to devise laws that explain how the exact course the evolutionary processes actually have taken is the only course they could have taken. No one has done that yet, to my knowledge. But many think it can be done in principle. If that project were to succeed, it would show how both modes of evolution would follow exactly the same course if they started again tomorrow. Until that happens, the regulative ideal of nature stands as a conjecture. Nietzsche contests that conjecture, with an alternative regulative ideal, even as he also resists and challenges creationism.

"O my brothers is everything not in flux now?" That *doesn't* mean that the world is devoid of proximate and approximate regularities. It does mean that even if we were to bring the most refined laws we are capable of formulating to our observation of the initial conditions from which the universe and biology on earth actually evolved, we would not be able to predict the exact future course of either.

Put that way, the formulation hovers in a zone of indiscernibility between a claim about (1) the course of nature separate from our perception of it and (2) our highest ability to chart the course of nature given the ill fit between our capacities and the way of a world not necessarily designed to correspond to them. Zarathustra's perspective is both paradoxical and contestable. He can provide *pointers* to a fundamental mobility of things that may exceed our talent for fitting them into a scheme of calculation, but he cannot now prove the truth of his conjecture. Neither, he thinks, can his opponents do so with respect to their regulative ideals of nature and scientific explanation.

Why entertain his perspective, then? Because of the ethico-political stakes of doing so: the Nietzschean perspective—in conjunction with efforts to overcome existential resentment of a world with these characteristics—invites us to become more responsive to natural/cultural processes by which brand-new things, beings, identities, and cultural movements surge into being. It encourages us to develop more nuanced balances between the comforts and agonies of being on one side and the forces of becoming on the other.

The Nietzschean portrait of nature is often thought to reflect a faulty image of science. The fact that Nietzsche links the scientific problematic to an asceticism previously attributed only to devotees of religious fideism has not endeared him to philosophers of science either.[5] His scattered reflections on nature, then, would be consigned to a dustbin in the history of science if it were not for recent reflections on the character of science by Ilya Prigogine, a Nobel Prize winner in chemistry and an inventor of complexity theory.

Prigogine and his collaborator, Isabelle Stengers, work with physical systems that are "unstable" or "far from equilibrium." Not all systems are in disequilibrium. A system in equilibrium is such that its dynamics are more or less maintained despite environmental changes. A human population is in equilibrium if it remains stable throughout fluctuations in the rates at which people have sex, gather food, encounter disease-producing microorganisms, and so on. However, at far-from-equilibrium states, which abound in the world,[6] molecules begin to act as "singularities," the exact behavior of which *cannot be predicted.* They start to move in exquisite response to each other and to tiny alterations in their parameters.

Unlike their behavior in equilibrium systems, those in "dissipative structures" are marked by an element of internal unpredictability, by capacities of self-development, by periods of significant openness to outside forces, and by a trajectory of irreversible change that endows them with a historical dimension. The Prigoginian update of Epicurean physics and Nietzschean cosmology engages a nature that is sometimes creative and novelty producing, "where the possible is richer than the real,"[7] and where, therefore, new structures come into being over time.

Even though such systems retain a persistent power to surprise and the evolutionary ability to create what has never before existed, they also display a kind of intelligibility retrospectively. This is where Prigogine expresses appreciation for the "approximations" Nietzsche notes. "What is now emerging," writes Prigogine, "is an 'intermediate' description that lies somewhere between the two alienating images of a deterministic world and an arbitrary world of pure chance. Physical laws lead to a new form of intelligibility as expressed by irreducible probabilistic representations."[8] A far-from-equilibrium system is neither the reversible system of classical dynamics nor a condition of constant flux unrecognizable *as* a system. Some read Nietzsche's "flux" the latter way. My Nietzsche, the philosopher of torsion between being and becoming, is closer to Prigogine's contention that "a new formulation of the laws of nature is now possible . . . , a more acceptable description in which there is room for both the laws of nature and novelty and creativity."[9]

The integrable world of classical physics has two defining characteristics: its trajectories are reversible and they are determinist. The trajectories are *reversible*, or indifferent to time, because any possible evolution within the system is defined as equivalent to any other — each is a particular expression of the universal laws of dynamics. And the sequence of equivalents can be reversed without changing the outcome. Kant translates this picture of nature as it is itself into a necessary, lawlike pattern we must attribute to it. He speaks of Galileo, Copernicus, and Torricelli:

> They learned that reason only perceives that which it produces after its own design; that it must not be content to follow, as it were, in the leading strings of nature, but must proceed in advance with principles of judgment according to unvarying laws and compel nature to reply to its questions. . . . Reason must approach nature with the view of . . . a judge, who compels the witnesses to reply to those questions which he himself thinks fit to propose.[10]

Prigogine seeks to modify the regulative ideal of reversible regularity. Prigogine's is a world neither of Newtonian mechanism nor of teleological finalism. When you consider each system in the time frame appropriate to it (a shorter span for hurricanes and a much longer one for evolution of the universe), you come to terms with the element of "becoming" in the world. Here's how Prigogine makes the point: "Matter near equilibrium behaves in a 'repetitive' way. On the other hand, . . . far from equilibrium we may witness the appearance of . . . a mechanism of 'communication' among molecules."[11] Within this mechanism successive repetitions are not identical to each other because they arise out of highly sensitized responses to "initial conditions" that exceed the reach of our capacities for close delineation.

Bifurcation points, as forks that express the play of unpredictability and set new possibilities into motion, can also morph into a new state of *order*. Unstable systems set conditions of possibility, then, for emergent orders. Take the emergence of a termite mound, initiated in an unpredictable way but organized as an effect of stochastic or dicey behavior. You can think of the spots at which a termite drops lumps of earth as underdetermined or "random." But

> in doing so they impregnate the lumps with a hormone that attracts other termites. . . . the initial "fluctuation" would be the slightly larger concentration of lumps . . . , which inevitably occurs at one time or another at some point in the area. The amplification of this event is produced by the increased density of termites in the region, attracted by the . . . hormone.[12]

Practitioners of classical dynamics often acknowledge the artificiality of the nature they examine in the laboratory. But a world of reversibility remains a regulative ideal for them.[13] When singularities or anomalies are observed, they are interpreted as a technical function of the observation process, or of limitations of human knowledge to date, not as *signs* of a world whose subtle powers of multiple causality may exceed our best approximations of it.

But Prigogine and Stengers question the value of this regulative ideal. Stengers writes:

> The deterministic and reversible trajectory that we can calculate for *simple* systems . . . would require, for unstable systems, a mode of knowledge that would only make sense for [a God] . . . who knew the positions and speeds of the entities in interaction with an infinite precision (an infinite number of decimals). That being the case, is it relevant to extend to unstable dynamic systems the ideal of knowledge represented by a deterministic and reversible trajectory? Should we judge as a simple approximation the probability treatment that we *have* to apply to unstable dynamic systems, that is, judge it in the name of a knowledge that for intrinsic and noncontingent reasons we will never have?[14]

Here Stengers articulates a conception of causality in unstable systems with affinities to Nietzsche. For Nietzsche, too, doubts that efficient "cause and effect," as interpreted by nineteenth-century models of science, predominates in nature:

In truth we are confronted by a continuum out of which we isolate a couple of pieces, just as we perceive motion only at isolated points.... The suddenness with which many effects stand out misleads us; actually it is only sudden for us. In this moment of suddenness there is an infinite number of processes that elude us. An intellect that could see cause and effect as a continuum and a flux and not, as we do, in terms of arbitrary division and dismemberment, would repudiate the concept of cause and effect.[15]

"An infinite number of processes that elude us" — this phrase is wonderfully indeterminate between (1) asserting that such processes themselves exceed any possible computational logic and (2) asserting that the logic they may embody either exceeds the coarse capacities of the human animal for close detection and conceptualization or is essentially affected by human interventions into it. Nietzsche adverts to a hypothetical god to highlight this zone of uncertainty between processes undesigned by a god and limits built into the capacities of human beings who have themselves been jerry-rigged through a long, complex process of evolution.

What do Prigogine and Stengers say at this strategic juncture? In one formulation they assert that the image of a calculable "trajectory is not an adequate physical concept" for systems in disequilibrium.[16] That formula leaves poised in uncertainty whether the element of unpredictability flows from the world itself, from powers of observation and calculation, or from dissonant conjunctions between us and the world. Prigogine sometimes projects beyond this zone of uncertainty by speaking of "objective unpredictability," but Stengers increasingly focuses on the relational issue. She conceives science neither as an outsider's discovery of nature nor as a set of processes to which we must bring eternal categories unsusceptible to modification, but as a shifting and dissonant "dialogue" between human assemblages and nonhuman assemblages.

> At both the macroscopic and microscopic levels, the sciences of nature are thus liberated from a narrow conception of objective reality, which believes it must in principle deny novelty and diversity in the name of an unchanging universal law.... They are from now on open to unpredictability... thus they are open to a dialogue with a nature that cannot be dominated by a theoretical gaze, but must be explored, with an open world to which we belong, in whose construction we participate.[17]

Modifying Stengers slightly, it seems reasonable to focus on the dialogical character of science while projecting the element of unpredictability now accompanying that dialogue into the future as a contestable expectation.

It is fair to say that a majority of scientists and philosophers of science today accept a different projection. They adopt the regulative ideal that Nietzsche, Prigogine, Stengers, and I resist. Some treat this as contestable territory, but many do not. Alan Sokal and Jean Bricmont are two red-blooded physicists who object to the perspective of Prigogine and Stengers in the strongest terms. These speculators, they say, "give the educated public a distorted view of the topics they treat"—although "their abuses do not even come close" to those of literary "postmodernists" who distort science for partisan political purposes.[18] The two physicists thus elevate themselves above political partisanship when it comes to the nature of science, even though Sokal perpetrated a famous hoax to expose the shallowness of critical engagements with it. But in calling the views of the Nobel laureate "abuses," Sokal and Bricmont betray the detachment they project. They do not seem to consider a Kantian version of their position. Rather, they act as if the image of science as a mirror of predictable regularities has been definitively established when in fact it remains a contestable regulative ideal. The territory of legitimate contestability, for them, stops at the point where the image of science as science begins, even though what counts as the definitive image has undergone numerous permutations over the past two thousand years.

But what turns on these debates for cultural theorists? Well, when cultural theorists accept the lawlike model as authoritative for all nonhuman systems, they feel pressed either to adopt a reductive model of social explanation or to project a transcendental field that insulates human thinking, reason, and freedom from those lawful regularities. This is the pressure that drives cultural theorists toward Kant, who sought both to accept Newtonian mechanics and to protect human freedom and morality from it.

Here is a question that helped to propel Kantianism into being in the Newtonian age: Where is the thinking of the scientist to be located in a world of reversible laws? *In* nature? Or *above* it? If *in* nature, the image of thought cuts against the possibility of independent powers of human thought in a Newtonian world. If *above* it, the theory demands Kantian transcendental deductions to secure itself. But Kant's deductions over time have shown themselves to be less necessary and more contestable than he imagined. Moreover, as I shall argue in the last chapter, Kant's regulative ideal of reason itself limits creativity in thinking and judgment more severely than advisable. Today, perhaps, many cultural theorists could profit from a layered image of thinking that is not located above biology, or shaped by a reductionist reading of biocultural relations, or governed by a theo-teleological projection into nature. The orientation that emerges will surely be contestable. It is unlikely to defeat its competitors definitively. But it may project another credible candidate onto the field of debate among Kantian, reductionist, and teleological models of human embodiment.

A Zone of Indiscernibility

There are several domains in which a Nietzsche/Prigogine conception of nature could be elaborated and tested. Prigogine applies it to the evolution of the universe, suggesting that in the "preuniverse" matter was not yet organized as a material composite. Instead, nonmaterialized forces generated "an irreversible process transforming gravitation into matter."[19] Matter for him is itself an effect of "becoming," then, to use Nietzsche's locution. It was consolidated out of an irreversible bifurcation. If this is so, "time precedes existence." That is, time precedes the determinate consolidation of matter in the evolution of the universe. Prigogine, then, reinstates within nature a temporality and historicity that modern science had tried to overturn. In a debate with Henri Bergson, for instance, Albert Einstein insisted that the appearance of time in life was an illusion that physics could correct. Later, after a close friend died, he wrote to the friend's wife, saying, "Michele has left this strange world a little ahead of me. This is of no importance. For us convinced physicists, the distinction between past, present and future is only an illusion, however persistent."[20]

A related forum of exploration is the classical theory of biological evolution. Henri Bergson and Stephen J. Gould have already modified the Darwinian reading in ways that resonate with the Prigogine perspective.[21] The course that biological evolution actually has taken, they say, does not conform to the course it might take if it were to be launched again from the same volatile initial conditions. Bergson focuses on how self-regulating biological systems generate, through a series of interactions between virtual capacities and the external forces to which the system is open, "forks" ushering new forms of life into being. These forks could not have been predicted by human beings—had the relevant scientists and sophisticated research technologies been there—with access to the "initial conditions" from which they sprang. Such emergent forms structure surprise, creation, and the new into the evolutionary process. They do so in ways that make evolution irreducible to a mechanistic, creationist, or teleological model. The theory, however, does give creationism a presence of sorts within, rather than prior to, the quirky process of evolution. Consistent with these leads, Keith Ansell Pearson summarizes an innovative theory of the role of genetics in evolution, a perspective that has attracted a significant minority of biologists. After exploring the "curiously awkward history" symbiosis has had in biology, Pearson says:

The importance of symbiotic bacteria in the "origin of species"—repeated bacterial symbioses result in the emergence of new genes—is now widely appreciated.... The detailed organization of the organelles in eukaryotic cells...show[s] that crucial evolutionary processes were not the result of slow accumulation of random changes (mutations) in the genes of ancestral...cells. Rather, it seems highly probable that they were the result of intracellular symbiosis in which some cells incorporated into their own cell contents partner cells of another kind that had different metabolic abilities.[22]

Again, these views contain considerable extrapolation and speculation. But so do the alternative perspectives each is ranged against. Speculation is unavoidable in these domains today. And each speculative theory, in turn, helps to set a specific agenda for cultural and political thought. While the perspective summarized above pushes against the limit of my knowledge of physics and biology, it also resonates with experiences of perception, thinking, culture, and action that make independent claims upon contemporary attention. Nature is always mixed into culture on the image projected here. And culture can be thought of as part of nature in the largest sense of nature as the encompassing whole in which we are set. So if the accentuated velocity of contemporary life, reflected in the pace of trade, mergers, production processes, cinema, TV, air travel, population migrations, disease transmission, climatic change, and so on, heightens the experience of unpredictability, temporality, and creativity in thinking and politics, reflection into those experiences may offer subsidiary support for the Prigogine/Nietzsche conception of nature too.

It is probably clear already that, within this orientation, classical distinctions *of kind* between culture and nature now become translated into interacting layers of biocultural complexity. For it is not only in human culture that perception, interpretation, unpredictability, and history occur. They occur, to varying degrees of complexity and on different scales of duration, in several nonhuman processes as well. Moreover, fairly sophisticated powers of discrimination and communication cut across the classical nature/culture divide. A chimpanzee has more powers of discrimination and communication than a young child, and some types of birds are better equipped to incorporate the songs of other species into their own repertoires when they are young than many human adults are to modify ingrained habits of drinking and smoking.[23]

Perhaps sociobiology reduces culture to regularity because it remains governed by dull readings of nature and biology. To "mix" culture with nature, in this model, is to overwhelm the former with the reductive determinism of the latter. And perhaps *disembodied* theories of cultural intersubjectivity are pulled to the opposite pole because of the same assumptions. If sociobiologists enclose humanity within a crude concept of nature, many intersubjectivists eschew reference to "first nature" because they too tacitly accept a flat, determinist model of it. That is why they often lift language, thinking, identity, choice, and ethics out of it. They implicitly elevate these capacities above biology to preserve freedom and dignity, as they are allowed to conceive them. But to accomplish that task they depreciate the variable degrees of agency and linguistic capacity in nonhuman animals and, at the same time, underplay the layered, biocultural character of human perception, thinking, culture, identity, and ethics. The implications for ecology are not pretty.

The deprecation of nonhuman animals is sometimes accomplished through the implicit adoption of an accordion model of language. Language is construed in open, expansive terms when considered as a human capacity; it includes within its orbit multiple media of expression and most capacities to draw distinctions, express inner states, make discriminations, and modify discriminations already made. But crocodiles and monkeys might participate in *some* aspects of language on this reading. Even bacteria come close. So the idea of language is squeezed back into a narrow range when it comes to the assessment of whether nonhuman assemblages embody linguistic and cultural capacities. Although human culture is in fact composed of essentially *embodied* beings implicated in complex patterns of action, and although some brain nodules in the human brain network are shared with other animals, cultural theorists haunted by determinist images of nature are pressed to dismiss, ignore, or degrade the corporeal layering of language, perception, and thinking in human life. We encountered one example of such a machine in motion in chapter 2.

A multilayered conception of culture and thinking is needed today, one that comes to terms with how biology is mixed differentially into every layer of human culture, even as it addresses the highest modes of intellectuality, artistry, creativity, freedom, and reflexivity of which the human animal is capable. To pursue this end it may be prudent to put scare quotes around the terms "nature" and "culture" on occasion. That pair, in its classically defined form, now impedes creative thinking into the biolayered composition of human thought, action, and intersubjectivity, for human thought carries creative possibilities partly because that which moves below it and feeds into it also moves across a horizon that is not entirely closed. If you subtract the elements of time and creativity from your picture of nature, all the boasting in the world about the creativity of thought will ring hollow. Many governed by a fixed model of nature are tempted both to contract all creativity into thinking alone and to withdraw to a transcendental model of thinking that is ill suited to the creativity they seek to support.

"Nature" and "culture," on my reading, are not defined by categorical differences between the material and the immaterial, or between that which is highly predictable and that which is unpredictable, or between that which is simple and that which is complex, or between that which lacks a history and that which is carried in history, or between that which is governed by logic and that which is not, or between that which lacks a capacity for discrimination and that which expresses such a capacity. It is not even sufficient to say that culture consists of a "symbolic realm" whereas the forces of nature lack symbolism, although the reconfiguration of such a distinction comes closest to filling the bill.

Symbolic activity, judgment, and reflexive consciousness require complex, biological brain systems in which they are set. But the brain network must both engage the linguistically mediated world and respond to multiple signals from the body that bear the traces of past experiences upon them. Again, the human brain system receives and translates innumerable proprioceptive signals as an individual acts in the world, and it depends upon a variety of external media, supports, and techniques to coordinate thought and action. These latter media themselves also modify the microorganization of the body/brain system, as when the energy output in the brains of children with dyslexia is reduced after they are taught to read with new techniques.[24] Human thinking in general involves complex culture/body/brain networks, and each level in this layered, tripartite assemblage is marked by specific capacities of speed, reception, and enactment.

We still don't know enough about what a variety of animals can and cannot do, let alone what the human body can do. And we may never know everything. At strategic intervals new capacities previously unexpected might emerge, along with pronounced shifts in the cultural environment, as when the invention of art and writing enabled humans to record stories and moral codes susceptible to future reference, invocation, challenge, and modification. Natural beings *become* cultural as they acquire capacities of linguistic sophistication, reflexive violence, ethical reflexivity, and artistic achievement.

As biocultural mixtures move toward a middle range of complexity, the difference between "nature" and "culture," as classically represented, glides into a zone of indiscernibility. For if there is an element of artifice in nature and of perdurance in culture, the classical line between them becomes blurred from two sides. This is the zone that deserves much more attention today in cultural theory, the zone that might provide a more energetic focus as intersubjectivists and sociobiologists back away from the dull notion of natural regularity that encourages the first group to bracket culture from nature and the second to reduce culture to natural regularity. It is a zone of indiscernibility because within this zone we are still unclear exactly how the mixing occurs, how complex each layer of capacity is, and how much room there is for mobility and creativity once a set of initial capacities and dispositions has become organized. Even as these questions become more clearly defined, it may still remain a zone of indiscernibility in one sense, because the mixtures may authorize a new set of conceptions that fit into neither the most complex levels of nature then definable nor the simplest modes of culture. Merleau-Ponty suggests how wide and layered this zone may be when he says,

> It is impossible to superimpose on man a lower layer of behavior which one chooses to call "natural" followed by a manufactured layer...in the sense that there is not a word, not a form of behavior that does not owe something to purely biological being—and which does not at the same time elude the simplicity of animal life, and cause forms of vital behavior to deviate from their pre-ordained direction, through a certain sort of leakage and genius for ambiguity which might serve to define man.[25]

Explorations of this zone of indiscernibility show the most promise of superseding the options between intellectualism and determinism debated by many intersubjectivists, rationalists, behavioralists, and sociobiologists. Let's think, then, more about thinking.

Affect, Thinking, Language

Nietzsche, already leaping over the early-modern constitution of the nature/culture dyad, thought things about the layered and creative character of thinking that pull it past the mechanical determinism of reductionists, the transcendence of a two-world metaphysic, and the theo-teleological model advanced by those who will fold nature into culture only if the former is invested with a divine purpose. Thinking for Nietzsche involves a complex process of discord and coordination among multiple theaters of activity. As he puts it, "The chamber of consciousness is small," too small to perform the complex task of thinking alone. That is why, he thinks, intellectualists so ironically underestimate the creative power and complexity of thinking. "Conscious thinking, especially that of the philosopher, is the least vigorous and therefore also the relatively mildest and calmest form of thinking; and thus precisely philosophers are most apt to be led astray about the nature of knowledge."[26] "Philosophers" tend to give too much self-sufficiency to consciousness and to limit thinking too much to the discovery of knowledge. They therefore tend to confine themselves to that part of thinking in which logic plays its most active role. But consciousness is itself pre-organized and moved to some extent by modes of thinking below its reach. Without those processes consciousness would be flat; with them, it is less self-regulating or self-sufficient than intellectuals imagine. And it also may be better equipped both to receive disciplines and techniques applied to rapid processes below conscious regulation and to bring new ideas, concepts, and aspirations into the world. I do not, of course, deny that there are dangers attached to this feature of the human condition. I suggest, rather, that the least viable strategy for liberals, democrats, pluralists, and cosmopolites to adopt is to allow a real concern for the dangers to keep our eyes wide shut with respect to the positive possibilities, for nationalists and dogmatists of other sorts already actively engage this register of being. Perhaps the most dangerous presumption to adopt is that there could be a vacuum in this domain.

On the "lower" layers of being there is a massive filtering or subtraction of sensory material, even though some of the filtered material enters into side perceptions that might become available later for reflection. Then there are, as I will call them, proto-thoughts that, as quick as greased lightning, process the already reduced perceptions further so that consciousness will be able to work upon them. This part of thinking, while it forms distinctions and resemblances that might be called linguistic in a large sense of that term, is too crude and fast to be available to direct conscious inspection or revision. Nietzsche writes:

> We no longer have a sufficiently high estimate of ourselves when we communicate. Our true experiences are not garrulous. They could not communicate themselves if they wanted to: they lack words.... Speech, it seems, was devised only for the average, medium, communicable.[27]

Nietzsche includes within thinking itself the lightning-quick process of filtering alluded to above. In doing so, he ennobles its significance and reach. Part of the reason he *can* do so is that he has already translated the global distinction between nature and culture into multiple layers of biocultural being. Some presentations of Nietzsche misrepresent his account of thinking as "idealistic" because they leave this prior transfiguration of the nature/culture pair out of the picture.

To thematize the intralayered character of thinking is to discern how thought embodies powerful pressures to assimilate new things to old habits of perception and linguistic "equalization." These capacities and tendencies are crucial to thought. But countervailing pressures and possibilities are also at work in the layered corporeality of cultural beings. Thinking bounces in magical bumps and charges across zones marked by differences of speed, capacity, and intensity. It is above all in the dicey relations between the zones that the seeds of creativity are planted. For thinking, again, is not harnessed entirely by the tasks of representation and knowledge.[28] Through its layered intra- and intercorporeality new ideas, theories, and identities are sometimes propelled into being. These new ideas, concepts, sensibilities, and identities later become objects of knowledge and representation. Thinking is thus creative as well representative, and its creativity is aided by the fact that the process of thinking is not entirely controlled by the agents of thought. If thinking is part of nature, as the largest whole in which we are encompassed, then the experience of creativity in thinking provides a piece of testimony in support of the idea that *other* aspects of nature may have variable capacities for creative production as well. Hence Nietzsche's resistance to the lawlike model of evolution in favor of a conception of evolution as becoming—and Prigogine's too.

If you cling to a classical model of nature, it might seem that the creative element in thinking could be preserved only through the elevation of the most refined element of thought to a transcendental register. Hence Kant. But his attempt to secure a refuge for thought while also supporting a Newtonian picture of nature eventually overwhelms the creative element in thinking from another direction. For the Kantian model issues in a set of transcendental arguments that resolve the most fundamental issues about science, morality, and aesthetics in advance. It is true that in Kant the sublime carries counter possibilities within it. And this is a valuable moment to work upon, even against Kant's highest wishes. For he contains those possibilities by claiming that the sense of dissonance inhabiting the sublime indicates a more profound and inscrutable "reason" rising above it. Nietzsche, however, both appreciates the idea that forces beyond representation might be indicated without being knowable and resists the indications Kant projects. He breaks down transcendental reason to leave open the possibility that thinking helps to bring new things into the world not already allowed or disallowed by an authoritative transcendental field. For he dissents from every version of a two-world metaphysic.

William James captures as well as anyone the layered process of thinking alluded to here. He says, "The highest and most elaborated mental products are filtered from the data chosen by the faculty next beneath, out of the mass offered by the faculty below that, which mass in turn was sifted from a still larger amount of yet simpler material, and so on."[29] But how does thought move across these registers? It is here that Nietzsche's resistance to both classical models of human and natural science and transcendental philosophies of the subject may accomplish its finest work. Consider a formulation summarizing points heretofore developed while adding another element to the mix:

> I maintain the phenomenality of the inner world, too: everything of which we become conscious is arranged, simplified, schematized, interpreted through and through. . . . "Causality" eludes us; to suppose a direct causal link between thoughts, as logic does — that is the consequence of the crudest and clumsiest observation. Between two thoughts all kinds of affects play their game; but their motions are too fast, therefore we fail to recognize them. . . . "Thinking" as the epistemologists conceive it, simply does not occur: it is quite arbitrary fiction, arrived at by selecting one element from the process and eliminating all the rest.[30]

"Between two thoughts all kinds of affects play their game." Affect is part of biology, if anything is, and Nietzsche folds it into the very mobility of thinking. Without affect, thinking would lack creativity; with it, thinking is invested with the volatility of nature. Nietzsche's focus on the rapid play of affect in thinking was perhaps easier for many philosophers to ignore before the advent of film; they could do so by "selecting one element from the process and eliminating all the rest." Nietzsche does his best to make it difficult, though. His texts are organized to work upon our thinking by encouraging the movement of affect. Thus the numerous condensed and sometimes outrageous formulations. Or the use of numbered nodules to encourage the reader to construct a series of mosaic connections for further exploration, rather than simply reading the text as a linear story. You might read the nodules in order the first time, and then select a subset from different parts of the text for reading together a second time. More subtly, Nietzsche's use of ellipses (. . .) at the end of some sentences encourages you to break away from the text for a moment. Doing so opens a new round of intrasubjective communication between your virtual register and a conscious line of reflection. After you have done such fugitive work for a while, you might return to the text to see where it picks up by comparison to where your thinking has gone. It is above all in the *encounter* between where you have gone and where Nietasche is going that creative things break out. Nietzsche's use of ellipses in his written texts is in fact remarkably close to the way some film directors today use "irrational cuts" between scenes to encourage us to engage the nonlinear character of time, a technique to which we turn in chapters 4 and 6.

Today a dense series of loops and counterloops among cinema, TV, philosophy, neurophysiology, and everyday life enable people to explore the relation between thinking and affect more readily. Nietzsche's insights about the connections between them are thus much harder to ignore. As film critic Steven Shaviro suggests, cinema, with its concentrated intersections of image, voice, sound, rhythms, and musical scores, often "affirms the powers of the body, and it sees the very opacity and insubordination of the flesh as a stimulus to thought and as its necessary condition." The film close-up of a face in a romantic scene, for instance, may allow you to linger over subtle shifts in the pupils of the eyes, changes in looseness or tautness of the lips, a variation in the pace at which the eyes are blinking, or a change in expression that lasts just long enough to make a difference. The film close-up, in turn, gives you cues to read in other nonfilmic settings that move at a more rapid pace, allowing you to draw a set of side perceptions into sharper focus. And, of course, these cues can also be translated into lessons on how to simulate moods and emotions, adding another layer of complexity to the endless game of expression, pretense, and interpretation. In challenging "the academic tendency . . . to foreground signification at the expense of affect," Shaviro joins Nietzsche in addressing the ubiquitous role of affect inside perception, thinking, and judgment.[31]

Consider the closing scene of *Five Easy Pieces*, a film I saw for the second time in a theater in Canberra in 2000, thirty years after its American release. The closing scene begins after Karen Black, brilliantly playing Rayette, the warm, loving waitress coping with a chronically discontented boyfriend, has gone into a truck stop minimart to pick up snacks for a long drive south from northern Washington State. Jack Nicholson, the man hopelessly divided between a musical, upper-middle-class heritage (as "Robert") and a bare-bones working-class life (as "Bobby"), has given her his wallet to pay for the snacks. He has just walked out of the gas station toilet. As the scene opens, we see him talking to a truck driver without hearing what he says. Then he climbs into the cab of the truck. As Rayette returns to the car on the front left side of the wide shot, she looks around anxiously for her man. The logging truck crawls north on the deep right side of the frame, out of her line of vision. The scene rolls for a few minutes as the credits are played. The absence of dialogue, the sound of the truck's gears grinding up for a long trek, the image of the large truck rolling slowly north toward working-class, macho territory as the car sits in front of the gas pump pointed south, and the uncertainty of the waitress as she looks every which way but north for Bobby—all coalesce to communicate a series of connections and divisions between the two lovers. The fact that we see things outside both characters' lines of vision suggests that we may be in a better position than they to ponder the contradictions of their relationship—but not finally to explain its terms. For there is nothing in the scenes prior to this one that necessitated Bobby's

departure at that moment. It was a spur-of-the-moment decision. It makes sense retrospectively, but lacks necessity prospectively.

An old film, pulled out of its spatiotemporal context of presentation. In Canberra, the audience tarries until the credits are completed, and then
people file out slowly and quietly. As you walk out, a variety of thoughts might be
triggered, depending in part upon the virtual memories each brings to this encounter.
You might recall a star-crossed relationship whose intensity you have never revealed
to the companion strolling out with you. Or, as if from nowhere, you might wish
with sudden intensity that your dad were alive again, realizing only hours later that
his loss was made vivid by the juxtaposition of the closing scene with the one preceding it in which Robert leaves the home of his paralyzed father for the last time.
Or you might wonder, in a flash, what Bobby is running *toward* in Alaska, preceded —
as he is — by the female lovers he had earlier picked up as hitchhikers on their way
to a new life in the north. Or, again, you might wish that films of this sort did not
play so blatantly on emotions you would rather leave in the vault, allowing, finally,
this thought to become the occasion for your first comment to your partner about
the film. For the others had flown by too fast for you to speak them. Then, immediately after that comment, you might think how the superciliousness that often char-
acterizes members of the upper middle class is also resisted or overcome by many of
that class's members (e.g., Robert's sister and occasionally his brother). That thought,
in turn, might bounce your mind to a specific colleague who believes the world
owes him everything because of his aristocratic pedigree. Or, again, you might recall
more vividly than you had for years the chords of Chopin, as your mother occasionally played them on a whim when you were young (and you may realize only much
later — if ever — that this thought was triggered by a series of similarities between
Rayette and your working-class mother). And, a few seconds after that, you may
think how the film, in giving depth mostly to the Nicholson character, tracks the
male-centered tendency of life during the early 1970s. You may now be moved to
think about the gender/class relations in which the film is set, whereas others started
with that thought as they launched the slow trek up the theater aisle. You may, then,
think any number of things in this affectively charged setting, or *all* of the above in
rapid succession before you reach the theater door...

The closing scene of *Five Easy Pieces* could rapidly mobilize a
series of affectively imbued virtual memories and, above them, a set of explicit recollections, even if you do not think it is that good a film. As you stroll slowly up the
aisle, numerous thoughts arrive and depart with lightning speed, faster than they

could be spoken. Their shape and texture are triggered by a series of encounters between scenes in the film and affective memories they trigger in you. Some of these memories work upon you without being translated into explicit recollections. Those are the virtual memories, some of which may surface as recollections later. Others sally forth as explicit recollections, setting off specific trains of thought, even if they too are determined in shape and intensity not by the past alone but by this temporally specific conjunction between the present and regions of the past it calls up. Both tracks recapitulate the way the film presents the past of Bobby/Robert, for it conveys the role of the past in his present through bits and pieces as the story proceeds. A chronology is superseded by selective segments of past ordered nonchronologically in relation to present experiences. The way you and Bobby meticulously review the furnishings of the affluent household of his father when he enters the house after an absence of a few years provides one such occasion. The scene reveals how Bobby's pattern of virtual memory and explicit recollection has already begun to filter into yours, even though you may also retain some critical distance from it. It lends support to Bergson's theory of the layering of memory. As the film unfolds, you piece together the past, not as it is in itself, but as it is filtered through Bobby's experience of the present, giving texture to his character as you do so. By the final scene you are not called upon to *recall* Bobby's past. You ponder conflicts, cruelties, and blind spots in his character, as your appreciation of its formation over time has now *congealed*.

Maybe as you daydream the next afternoon, several of these thoughts will surge up again in rapid succession, and others as well, each bouncing onto stage from the left as its predecessor scampers off to the right. The bumpy course of these lines of thought, with some connected to others by labyrinthine routes too involuted to ponder during the daydream itself and too opaque ever to be captured entirely, forms an assemblage underdetermined by any logical, narrative, or explanatory line of progression. It might go anywhere. Today the pace and number of such thoughts may inspire you to ponder, as if for the first time, those tiny gaps of emptiness that separate each thought from the next. You fall into a reverie as you ponder how, in moments of affective intensity, quick little thoughts often follow one another in rapid succession, with little apparent rhyme or reason. Your thinking now slows down as you ponder how often a few thoughts fly by so fast you can't grab them long enough to explore them, even though you may wish desperately that you could pull this or that one back just after it has disappeared over the edge. These are the escapees: they may or may not return, and if some of them do they are apt to do so in an altered form induced by the changed context of their arrival. As you daydream in this way, the gaps themselves may grow longer. You now make fugitive contact with those recurrent instants of apparent emptiness that set crucial conditions of possibility for new thoughts to arise. You thus slide a little closer to that doorway from which the virtual register opens onto the stage of consciousness. It allows new thoughts to stroll or run onto stage, now and then setting an internal dialogue into motion that brings something new or exciting into being. *Attention to this fugitive doorway discloses how thought is always already under way by the time you place it under the incomplete governance of intentionality and public expression.* You now come to terms more vividly with the indispensability and insufficiency of subjectivity to thought. For between two thoughts all kinds of affects play their game; but their motions are too fast, therefore we fail to recognize them . . .

A multidimensional process of thinking has occurred here. First, there is the dissonant conjunction between the scene and the distinctive thoughts it might rapidly mobilize in people with different, affectively imbued memory banks. Second, the initial encounter may later spur more disciplined thinking about the fugitive relation between the virtual register and consciousness in thought. And third, the conjunction of the first two moments might later yet encourage a disciplined train of thought about the relations among affect, discipline, and technique in both fomenting new thoughts and enabling a disciplined train of thought. For discipline and logic are both essential to a sustained train of thought. We pursue this third track in chapter 4.

Here we focus on a related question: Does attention to the role of affect in the mobility of thought denigrate the role of language? Not at all. First, linguistic distinctions, in the largest sense of that idea, are differentially mixed into affective states at each level of complexity, even if they do not exhaust them and even if many thoughts move too fast to render the linguistic element explicit. Affect would be more brutish than it is without language. It would thus not be able to play the critical role it does in the consolidation of culturally imbued habits and regularities. Indeed, as we shall see more closely in chapter 4, not only is each level of intrasubjectivity invested with an element of intersubjectivity appropriate to its capacity, the *activity of thinking* itself involves a set of layered correspondences between intrasubjective coding and intersubjective props, linguistic supports and nonlinguistic techniques. The body/brain network is indispensable to thinking, but radically insufficient to it.

Second, when you express proto-thoughts and thoughts in conversation, the public context of the expression changes the proto-thoughts brought into being. Expression alters what is expressed in the act of expressing it. Since the pace of thinking moves faster than the pace of public expression, only some things are articulated at any one time. More fundamentally, the public context of articulation has significant effects on what is said, how it is said, and how it is received.

Most critically of all, affect is involved in that tricky process by which the outside of thought is translated into thought. This is the disjunctive connection that expressive theories of language too often either ignore or invest as if by necessity with a predesign of being.[32] Heidegger does not ignore this juncture, however. He suggests that the essence of language is insufficiently disclosed by coming to terms with the way it sets the intersubjective background to thinking and communication. That feature of language must be considered alongside a corollary feature, for language "speaks itself as language" when you find yourself searching for the right word to express a thought and cannot find it. Sometimes you have forgotten, say, the name of a person. That situation is not the one Heidegger has in mind, but before we get to his point, let's first note something in the situation that Heidegger himself bypasses. If you forget a name, there is an absence where you want a presence. But it is not a situation of pure emptiness. Perhaps you remember vaguely the rhythm of the name — da, da, da, rather than da, da — and use that recollection to help you out. Or perhaps you recall a similar name each time you are trying to call up that one, and you see how this is blocking you. These examples show how forgetting does not involve a pure absence, for if it did you could never recognize the correct name when it finally surfaces. They suggest how layered and multidimensional thinking is, for if you forget a name it may be difficult to recall it, but if you forget the rhythm too, it may be lost forever.

Heidegger himself has bigger fish to fry. For "when the issue is to put into language something which has never yet been spoken, then everything depends on whether language gives or withholds the appropriate word. Such is the case of the poet."[33]

"Such is the case of the poet." We have wandered into an even more opaque, yet fecund level of being. To coin a new word or phrase for an inchoate, affectively imbued thought is both to express what has not yet found articulation and to change the dark precursor as it is drawn into an intersubjective network of similarities and contrasts. But to place a new word or phrase into an established network is also to alter the network itself in a small or large way. This is the double process that marks both creativity in thinking and the politics of becoming.

To take a modest example, if, inhabiting a predominantly Christian/secular society, you feel with a vague intensity that the options *theism/atheism* and *believer/nonbeliever* are too confining for the sensibility you strain to express, you might eventually coin the phrase *nontheistic gratitude* to fill the gap. The point of the phrase is to articulate an existential faith that makes contact with dominant alternatives without being entirely reducible to any. The coinage of the new phrase flows from a fugitive encounter between the dominant terms of discourse and a thought bubbling up that touches those terms without finding sufficient space of articulation within them. In this case the experience of absence is filled by an alternative that both recalls an Epicurean philosophy set in a pre-Christian world and speaks to a submerged perspective in contemporary life. The inchoate thought spurring the articulation is changed by the articulation, since the new phrase now becomes situated in a set of contrasts heretofore unavailable to it. But the new articulation, as it becomes sharpened and clarified, also modifies the established web of contrasts by identifying an alternative that can now be brought to bear in characterizing and appraising the dominant orientations. *Nontheistic gratitude* may at first sound like an oxymoron to those who expect the phrase's two terms to retain all the dimensions previously attached to them. This may be particularly true of those who have forgotten how much creative work Augustine and Augustinians once had to do to translate Platonic philosophy into Latin and Christianity. In the phrase *nontheistic gratitude*, for instance, gratitude is now linked to the gift of being as a protean set of energies that enable various identities and exceed the existing pool of identities; it gives priority to a sensibility that affirms this world. In this respect, as we shall see in chapter 5, it makes contact with some mystical traditions within religions of the Book. Similarly, the introduction of *nontheistic* as adjective rather than noun points beyond the idea of *atheism* as the mere denial of belief in God, as that term has traditionally been understood in Christendom.[34]

If you are inordinately lucky, you may eventually find such a phrase accepted as describing a legitimate orientation to being in the world. This hypothetical example brings out several dimensions of language in relation to thinking. There is, first, the *creative effect* that the introduction of a new word or phrase can have upon the web of public contrasts that preceded it, revealing an absence retrospectively where none had been experienced by most before. There is, second, the way public recognition of the new formulation can *express* something in your sensibility as it renders that sensibility more available to others. There is, third, how the sensibility expressed can now become *an object of representation*, and how the represented object, in turn, can now be examined, refined, criticized, and revised in public discourse because of its new status. That is, it can itself become an object of thought, sending thought off in new directions.[35] There is, fourth, the practical opportunity that the coining, expression, and representation of the new phrase creates for you and others to work on yourselves to render your actual sensibilities more congruent with the self-representation you advance. Let us call this fourth element *the self-tactical* or *self-organizational dimension of linguistic expression*. Attention to this dimension shows how thinking crisscrosses between the brains of thinkers and the public worlds in which they participate. Even more, it reveals how public expression faces in two directions: toward the world and toward those individuals and constituencies whose reiterated self-expressions induce effects upon themselves that strengthen or modify their sensibilities. The self-organizational effects of expression are most effective when they work in conjunction with corollary practices of posture, attentiveness, touch, and imagery. Think, for instance, about how while playing tennis you might say to yourself, "Follow through all the way" as you rehearse the requisite motion in the air after having missed your first serve, or "Look the ball all the way in" just after having missed the "sweet spot" when you hit the ball. Augustine illuminated the self-forming or compositional capacities of discursive life when he perfected Christian confessional practices. For him the purpose was both to *express* the faith of Christian believers and to *form* the confessors into more faithful beings.[36] The expressive, representational, creative, and self-organizational dimensions of language often work together: in enabling thought, in regulating it, and in strengthening or modifying the sensibility from which it proceeds.

Let us return to the point in Heidegger's account of language at which the right word could not be found. To attend to this fugitive corporeo-cultural juncture prior to articulation of a new concept is certainly not to come to *know* the unthought before it has been translated into language. Such knowledge is impossible, for this absence, unlike forgetting a name, does not yet conform to the shape of that which is knowable. To attend to such an uncanny moment is to place yourself in a better position to appreciate the role that stuttering, gurgles, smirks, guffaws, tears, timbre of the voice, facial expression, posture, and hand movements play in linguistic expression. Such eye movements, rhythms, gestures, and nonconceptual sounds attached to speech sometimes point to subterranean elements on the edge of thought that do not now find verbal expression. They point to the excess of affect over the context of expression even as they add texture and density to expression. Attention to this uncanny moment also puts you in a better position to work upon those fugitive registers of being that are pertinent to stability or innovation in thought but unamenable to argument or representation. There is much more to thinking than argument.

An expressive philosophy of language, then, points not to the ir- relevance but to the *insufficiency* of both designative and constitutive theories of lan- guage. But it too is insufficient to the affective, layered character of thinking until it acknowledges how affect both becomes mixed into language and is never entirely ex- hausted by those mixtures. As we shall see more closely in the next chapter, some brain nodules in the human brain network have the capacity to register only intense, crude inscriptions, whereas others to which the first are connected are capable of linguistic refinement. *But in the process of thinking, all of them form a complex series of loops and counterloops with each other, the rest of the body, and the larger culture.* The mo- bility of affect not only contributes to the movement of thought, then: it is also a key to that ubiquitous and magical process by which the outside of thought crosses into thinking territory.

You cannot appreciate the creative possibilities in thinking with- out coming to terms with the layered play of affect in it; but you cannot fit thought entirely into a closed schema of logic, narrative, discourse, expression, or explanation if you do attend to the play of affect. It is through the play of affect—partly *within* the orbit of feeling, intention, and consciousness and partly *below* their thresholds— that the creative element of thinking finds its most energetic impetus and possibility. For, again, attention to the role of affect in thought brings out how thinking is al- ready under way as you strain to compose a train of thought. New thoughts bubble, flow, or surge into being from a virtual register hard at work below the threshold of feeling and intellectual attention. Since affect is not entirely under the regulation of consciousness, the flow of thinking exceeds its governance too.

I resist the tendency, sometimes operative in Nietzsche, to en- close thinking entirely within the complex social structure of the individual. Think- ing is not only layered "vertically," so to speak. Several layers within resonate inter- subjectively, endowing culture with interacting levels of complexity. Indeed, the only theory of intersubjectivity worth its salt is one in which intersubjective connections and dissonances move across several registers.

The contagion of affect flows *across* bodies as well as across con- versations, as when anger, revenge, or inspiration is communicated across individuals or constituencies by the timbre of our voices, looks, hits, caresses, gestures, the bunch- ing of muscles in the neck, and flushes of the skin. Such contagion flows through face- to-face meetings, academic classes, family dinners, public assemblies, TV speeches, sitcoms, soaps operas, and films. Affect is infectious across layered assemblages, hu- man and otherwise. Nietzsche knew this, but sometimes depreciated it, as when he treated language as the site of the herd and the average and the unconscious as the site of the singular and unique. This is the juncture, as we shall see in the next chapter, where Gilles Deleuze makes a significant contribution to the Nietzschean image of thought.[37]

The Ubiquity of Affect

So thoughts are invested with affect. That may be one reason corporeal human beings are often so loyal to the thoughts that survive the competition within the subliminal field long enough to enter the field of consciousness for further work. Einstein, for instance, was deeply committed to his idea of the illusion of time, more so than the speculative status of the theory alone required. He is by no means unique in this respect. Part of the affective energy mixed into thought becomes available to consciousness as feelings and concept-imbued emotions; but other thought-imbued energies find symptomatic expression in the timbre of our voices, the calmness or intensity of our gestures, our facial expressions, the flush of our faces, the rate of our heartbeats, the receptivity, tightness, or sweatiness of our skin, and the relaxation or turmoil in our guts. Moreover, the play of affect on some registers is not always entirely consonant with its play on others.

Recent experiments by neuroscientists such as Antonio Damasio and Joseph LeDoux confirm the indispensability of affect to thinking. But if affect retains an element of autonomy that pulls thinking beyond the steady control of intellectual governance, how could this dimension of thinking itself be refined or sharpened? If affect, that is, becomes organized into habits of feeling and judgment that flow into the intellect, by what means can this dimension of being be reeducated? Intellectualists tend to ignore the question, for they assume that it is only at the highest level of intellectuality that thinking and education count. Virtue theorists, on the other hand, attend to it. But they are often prepared to do so only if the question is defined within a theo-teleological matrix. These two parties often concur in thinking that the debate between them exhausts the viable possibilities. One means by which this mutual sense of exhaustion is maintained is through the reduction of Nietzschean nonteleological philosophy to a form of voluntarism that ignores its engagement with the interplay among embodiment, affect, thought, and becoming.

Nietzsche resists this reduction when he poses the question of how to educate affectively imbued dispositions below the level of direct intellectual regulation. Nietzsche—the philosopher who celebrates thinking all the way up and all the way down—explores techniques and arts to work on culturally imbued dimensions of affective thought unsusceptible to direct regulation. As he puts it in a thought pregnant with ethical and political import: "a mere disciplining of [conscious] thoughts and feelings is virtually nothing ... ; one first has to convince the *body*. It is decisive ... that one should inaugurate culture in the *right place*—*not* in the 'soul' ... : the right place is the body, demeanor, diet, physiology, the rest follows."[38]

Nietzsche here looks back to Spinoza, without endorsing the rationalist canopy within which the latter encloses the corporeal adventures of thought. He also anticipates Bergson in his focus on the encounter between inner ("proprioceptive") and outer perception in the organization of perception, thinking, and judgment. While he ratchets down the significance of consciousness by comparison to the transcendental traditions, consciousness nonetheless retains two crucial powers in his presentation. First, it plays an indispensable organizing and regulatory role in thinking, even if it is not self-sufficient or autonomous. Logic and language are thus pertinent to thinking as Nietzsche conceives it—they are just insufficient. Second, consciousness enables humans to devise experimental practices and arts by which to work on affect-imbued thoughts below its direct regulation but pertinent to its conscious deliberations. Nietzsche calls these experimental disciplines modes of self-"artistry." Changing your thinking on something fundamental to your identity often involves work on layers below consciousness, but to assess the effects of those experiments is to bring consciousness back into play.

To ennoble the significance of thinking for life, Nietzsche refuses to put its dangers on ice. He knows, too, that because of the very layered character of thinking others may not be moved to endorse or reject his image by intellectual means alone. Sure, arguments that open up new images of nature and culture are terribly pertinent. And a refined ear for paradox helps. But the suspicion that these modalities are not sufficient to those debates is supported by the fact that today several models of nature, culture, thought, ethics, and science remain locked in competition, with none to date sealed by a transcendental argument or recourse to conclusive evidence that requires all reflective thinkers to adopt it. Put another way, the whisper or screech of affect traverses every argument, helping to nudge the movement of this porous activity (for no discursive argument is airtight) or to foment disturbance inside it. Or both.

What else, then, might nudge the intellect in Nietzsche's direction on the question of thinking? Nietzsche would say that the issue turns in part on the existential orientation to life already installed in you by historical fortuity and institutional design. These previous interventions shape and define, to some uncertain degree, visceral layers that enter into your judgment about how thinking works. In opening the intellect to think anew about the character of thinking, then, *it is useful to run little experiments on ourselves*. Those who from time to time feel little surges

P 18 - Pre-Inscript

What more —

of nontheistic reverence for an abundance of being without intrinsic purpose or final order might work experimentally to install this affirmation of life more actively into multiple zones of the body. You work "to convince the body" to incorporate the image of nature, culture, and thinking that you intellectually entertain as a belief. You might, say, behave experimentally like an immanent naturalist for a month, encouraging yourself to meditate about the abundance of being in an undesigned world as others pray to its designer, to tap into latent feelings of joy that may already accompany such a thought, and to forge "brief habits" that express gratitude for that abundance. Perhaps you will then hold a dance party to music by the Buena Vista Social Club. As you proceed, you read studies about the looping interactions among the eight or nine brain regions of different speed, initiating function and capacity, allowing those studies to sharpen your powers of attentiveness to your own activities of perception, thinking, and judgment. And so on. After a few months you consult your thinking again to see what chords of existential gratitude might have been struck, what ideas are beginning to crystallize, what new possibilities you now seek to enact.

To run such existential experiments is to add a layer of tests to the appraisal of Nietzsche's perspective already in motion. No test has been *subtracted*. You may or may not be converted. The outcome is unpredictable. Whether these experiments do or do not turn the trick, however, your considered judgment may now become inhabited by a deeper sense of modesty and reserve. For while your highest capacities of reflection are now mobilized for or against the Nietzschean image of thinking and nature, you also sense that a series of contestable proto-thoughts behind those thoughts has been mobilized on behalf of that very judgment. So you may strive to fold a measure of modesty and hesitancy into the account you endorse, out of respect for the affective, layered complexity of thinking and for others who engage it differently. To respect the complexity of thinking is to hesitate to reach agreement too fast or too completely on the most fundamental matters.

F O U R

Techniques of Thought and Micropolitics

The Transcendental and the Immanent

Herein I would fain that you should learn this too, that when the primordia are being carried downwards straight through the void by their own weight, *at times quite undetermined and at undetermined spots they push a little from their path:* yet only just so much as you could call a change of trend. But if they were not used to swerve, all things would fall downwards through the deep void like drops of rain, nor could collision come to be, nor a blow brought to pass for the primordia: so nature would never have brought anything into existence....

Now I say that mind and anima are held in union with the other, and form of themselves a single nature, but that the head, as it were, and lord in the whole body is the reason which we call mind or understanding, and it is firmly seated in middle region of the breast. For here it is that fear and terror throb, around these parts are soothing joys; there, then is the understanding and the mind. The rest of the anima, spread abroad, throughout the body, obeys and is moved at the will and inclination of the understanding.[1]

THE NATURALISM OF LUCRETIUS has long seemed too crude and perplexing to muster serious support. It construes the smallest constituents of nature to move so fast and chaotically that they cannot become objects of perception or precise explanation; it treats the mind to be made up of material of the same type—although not the same capacity—as the rest of the body, or animus; it links thinking to the instabilities of sense experience; it locates the mind in the middle region of the breast rather than the head; it has difficulty making sense of free will and responsibility, even while acknowledging the need to do so; its naturalism gives no powers to divinity; it can generate no authoritative basis for morality in the last instance beyond the capacity to achieve a life of tranquility or *ataraxy*; and it counsels its followers to work tactically on the subconscious dispositions that project life forward after death in order to make peace with death as oblivion. Its speculations were too disconnected from the project of deep explanation to gain support in early modern natural science and too committed to naturalism to win praise from the Christian philosophies of Augustine, Aquinas, Kant, Hegel, and Kierkegaard. And most of the Epicurean texts to which Lucretius was indebted have been lost through a long history of cultural war against that philosophy.

Things may be changing. Ilya Prigogine's conception of dissipative structures in nature, as we saw in chapter 3, bears a family resemblance to the physics of Epicurus and Lucretius. And today several neuroscientists conclude that the lower region of the breast, while not as complex as the brain system in the head, houses a simple cortical complex that communicates with higher brain regions to issue intense feelings of disgust, anxiety, fear, and terror. Thinking itself is mixed into these intensities, some of which are felt and others of which move below the level of explicit feeling. The fast, imperceptible units Lucretius called "primordia" bear a family resemblance not only to atoms but to the electrical fields that carry thinking. As Tor Nørretranders says in his review of recent brain research, "A stimulus can be so short that we never become conscious of it but react to it nevertheless."[2]

Moreover, some neuroscientists are moving under their own steam to modify the linear and mechanical concepts of causality that were popular in the field earlier. As Rafael Nuñez, a neuroscientist, says in a review of work in his field, in "the last couple of decades...there has been a tendency to move from a rational, abstract, culture-free, de-centralized, non-biological, ahistorical, unemotional, asocial and disembodied view of the mind towards a view which sees the mind as situated, de-centralized, real-time constrained, everyday experience oriented, culture-dependent, contextualized, and closely related to biological principles—in one word, embodied."[3] Finally, tactical work on dispositions installed below consciousness, while minimized by neo-Kantian philosophies in the traditions of Rawls and Habermas, concerns contemporary neuroscience in a way reminiscent of the tactical orientation to being and thinking propagated by Epicurus and Lucretius.

Recent brain research is suggestive, both in its presentation of nonconscious operations that precede consciousness by a half second and in its suggestions about the role technique plays in thinking and judgment. Take the case of the blind man who could not form images of objects within the range of normal vision. Nonetheless, he, like others with this particular malady, was able to carry out numerous activities, such as riding a bike, usually reserved for those with vision. When presented in a test with a series of arrows pointing in different directions, he was able to identify the correct direction in which the arrow pointed almost every time. He thought he was inordinately lucky. He, however, had "blindsight": the part of the brain that forms images is damaged, while "the other links between the eye and the brain" function well.[4] Here is a dramatic illustration of how large chunks of perception are organized below perceptual awareness. Or consider the sixteen-year-old girl who a team of neurophysiologists at the University of California, Los Angeles, studied to identify the causes of her epileptic seizures. Applying an electric probe to eighty-five separate spots on her left frontal lobe, they eventually hit by chance upon a patch of brain where application of the probe made her laugh. They found that the "duration and intensity of the laughter increased with the level of stimulation current....At low currents only a smile was present, while at higher currents a robust, contagious laughter was induced."[5] The young girl, following the time-honored principle of retrospective interpretation, decided that these researchers were extremely funny guys. These two cases suggest that a lot of thinking and interpretation go on during the "half-second delay" between the reception of sensory material and conscious interpretation of it.[6] They further point to the gaps that often open up between phenomenological interpretations of experience and third-person accounts of it.

A half-second delay? It can be illustrated phenomenologically. When you place your hand over a hot stove, your hand recoils before you experience a feeling of pain, even though you tend to interpret the recoil as if it were caused by the feeling that followed it. The reflex action precedes the feeling commonly thought to cause it; in this case, at least, close attention to the order of action can verify the discrepancy between normal retrospective interpretation of temporal order and the actual order. It seems that "incomprehensible quantities of unconscious calculation"[7] take place during the half-second delay between the reception of sensory material and the consolidation of perceptions, feelings, and judgments. A lot of material is subtracted, and the remainder is crunched into a set of perceptions and thought-imbued intensities that consciousness can now do further work upon. Immanuel Kant, let us say, projects an inscrutable transcendental field into this temporal gap.[8] We

[handwritten notes in top margin: "just neuro w/ mimetico-compulsive & en / memories" — "Perceptual X"]

presuppose this transcendental, supersensible field, he claims, when we explain things according to laws of the understanding; but we cannot inquire further into the concepts of time, space, and causality it sanctions.

> This schematism of our understanding in regard to appearances and their mere form, is an art, hidden in the depths of the human soul, whose true modes of action we shall only with difficulty discover and unveil. . . . The *image* is a product of the empirical faculty of the productive imagination—while the *schema* of the sensible concepts (of figures in space, for example), is a product of the pure imagination *a priori*. . . . It is a transcendental product of the imagination . . . , insofar as these representations must be connected *a priori* in one concept, conformable to the unity of apperception.[9]

The transcendental field provides the understanding with categories necessary to explanation. That same field operates more directly, but with the same necessity and inscrutability, in Kantian moral judgment. The "objective reality of the moral law" is recognized "as an apodictically certain fact, as it were, of pure reason, a fact of which we are a priori conscious." It "can be proved through no deduction. . . . Nevertheless it is firmly established of itself."[10] The closure and rigidity that some discern in Kantian morality—in, for example, his confident commitment to capital punishment and his refusal to allow someone to lie even to save the life of another—may be bound to his insistence that the experience of morality as law takes the form of incontestable apodictic recognition. Finally, aesthetic judgment also falls under the jurisdiction of the supersensible realm. To judge something to be beautiful is to attain a spontaneous accord of the faculties that expresses the dictates of the supersensible realm without being able to conceptualize them.

Apperception in explanation, recognition in morality, expression in aesthetic judgment—the Kantian models of explanation, morality, and aesthetics invoke in different ways an inscrutable supersensible field prior to consciousness that regulates its operations.[11] The introduction of the transcendental field enabled Kant to devise a creative strategy to protect Christian freedom and morality from the corrosive effects of the Newtonian science of mechanics he also endorsed. The crucial move is "to ascribe the existence of a thing so far as it is determinable in time, and accordingly its causality under the law of natural necessity, merely to *appearance*, and to attribute freedom to the same being as a *thing in itself*."[12] The Kantian supersensible field thus subsists below the level of consciousness and above the reach of modification through scientific knowledge, moral decision, or technical intervention. Such a philosophy enabled Kant to disparage naturalists such as Epicurus and Lucretius for deprimees -

sinking into a metaphysical dogmatism that pretends to know the "thing in itself" and for anchoring ethics in something as crude as the sensible realm.

But what happens if we set the half-second delay not in a super-sensible domain but in the corporealization of culture and cultural inscriptions of corporeal processes? What if many messages flowing between multiple brain regions of differential capacities in the same person are too small and fast to be identified by consciousness but are, nonetheless, amenable to some degree to cultural inscription, experimental research, and technical intervention? Does this open a door not to disproof of the Kantian transcendental and proof of the alternative but to a contend-ing interpretation of the transcendental field that moves closer to Lucretius? It may be that Kant's identification of an inscrutable transcendental field is profound, while his insistence that it must be eternal, supersensible, and authoritative in the last in-stance is open to modification. To contest the Kantian reading of the transcendental field, while appreciating that some such field is inscrutable to those implicated in it, is eventually to call into question *both* the Kantian images of thought and morality and the images of those neo-Kantians who often proceed as if they can avoid such a field altogether. Neo-Kantians tend to reduce arts of the self to "therapies" to deal with neuroses or blockages in the powers of normal rationality, recognition, deliber-ation, and decision, rather than ubiquitous exercises, tools, and techniques helping to shape thinking and sensibility in profound ways.

The key move is to translate the Kantian transcendental field into a layered, immanent field. If the unconscious dimension of thought is at once *immanent* in subsisting below the direct reach of consciousness, *effective* in influenc-ing conduct on its own and also affecting conscious judgment, *material* in being em-bodied in neurological processes, and *cultural* in being given part of its shape by pre-vious inscriptions of experience and new experimental interventions, then several theories of morality, ranging from the Kantian model of command through the Haber-masian model of deliberative ethics and the Rawlsian model of justice, to the Tay-lorite model of attunement to a higher purpose in being, may deserve active contes-tation. From the vantage point pursued here, some of the above theories systematically underplay the role of technique and artistry in thinking and ethics while others overestimate the degree to which the cultivation of an ethical sensibility is linked to an intrinsic purpose susceptible to general attunement or recognition.

Immanence and Thinking

By *naturalism*, I mean the idea that all human activities function without the aid of a divine or supernatural force. The specific form of naturalism I embrace questions the sufficiency of the lawlike model of nature endorsed by classical natural science. And it emphasizes how culture gets differentially mixed into natural processes, depending upon the capacity for complexity of the mode of being in question. Let us construe *eliminative naturalism* to be a philosophy that reduces the experience of consciousness to nonconscious processes. Let us construe *mechanical naturalism* to be one that denies any role to a supersensible field while finding both the world of nonhuman nature and the structure of the human brain to be amenable "in principle" to precise representation and complete explanation. I am not sure how many eliminative or mechanical naturalists there are today, although many philosophers and cognitive scientists are represented as such by those critics who endorse transcendentalism. An *immanent naturalist*, by comparison, does not repudiate the transcendental. Rather, it is translated into an immanent field that mixes nature and culture. To immanent naturalism, consciousness emerges as a layer of thinking, feeling, and judgment bound to complex crunching operations that enable and exceed it. The immanent field is efficacious and inscrutable (to an uncertain degree), but not immaterial. It is, you might say, infrasensible rather than supersensible. Moreover, the immanent field, while currently unsusceptible to full explanation and unsusceptible in principle to precise representation, may retain some amenability to both cultural inscription and experimental tactics of intervention. That is, as the practices of Buddhists, Epicureans, and several monotheistic religions have presumed for centuries, human powers of cultural inscription and experimental intervention into the inscrutable domain, while limited, nonetheless *exceed* those of direct conscious control and scientific explanation.

Finally, immanent naturalists resist both a command model of morality set in a juridical rendering of the transcendental field and a teleological image of ethics set in a divine order of things. We do not deny that pressures and directives flooding into consciousness from the infrasensible field often feel *as if* they express "the apodictically certain fact of pure reason"; we simply contest the conclusion that such a recognition actually does express "the objective reality of the moral law itself." To us nature is more diverse and interesting than any god, and the body is more layered, rich, and creative than the soul. Most immanent naturalists support an ethic in which visceral attachment to life and the world provides the preliminary soil from which commitment to more generous identifications, responsibilities, and connections might be cultivated. Such a preliminary disposition is fundamental in that without it further cultivation of generosity and responsibility could not proceed. But it is also fragile in that, while such a gratitude for being is very often mixed into the milk of life, there is no cosmic guarantee that it must be so, or if so, that it will necessarily prevail against experiences of profound injury, loss, violence, or brutality. The admirability of a generous ethos of cultural life is stalked by its fragility.

According to these rough-and-ready standards, thinkers as diverse as Epicurus, Lucretius, Spinoza, Nietzsche, Michel Foucault, Stuart Hampshire, Gilles Deleuze, Jane Bennett, Moira Gatens, Brian Massumi, Paul Patton, and Bernard Williams participate in immanent naturalism. Other (possible) naturalists such as, say, John Rawls, Bertrand Russell, Hans Blumenberg, and Nancy Fraser, while often appreciating the need for cultural diversity and ethical generosity, may still not do so. This is the case partly because they adopt conceptions of nature that are closer to the classical conception of modern science; partly because they do not project an immanent field of perception, thinking, interpretation, identity, and judgment; and partly because they do not actively explore the political issues and ethical possibilities that arise when thinkers engage reflexively the exercises, disciplines, techniques, and impositions that help give shape to thought.

If naturalism in all its forms presents a minority report within contemporary moral and political philosophy, immanent naturalism constitutes a dissenting opinion within the minority report. Its minority status becomes more notable when you think about citizens at large in most western states. Most citizens, particularly in the United States, opt for one or another conception of morality derived from a supersensible realm. Some high articulations of such a perspective, presented by figures as diverse as Charles Taylor, Immanuel Levinas, Paul Ricoeur, Alasdair MacIntyre, and Michael Sandel, ascribe considerable importance in thinking and ethics to the "tacit dimension" and the "embodied self." But they forsake immanent naturalism in the last instance for a divine rendering of the transcendental field. Some of these same figures claim a monopoly over the shape of morality, while others acknowledge the comparative contestability of their own faith and the credibility of immanent naturalism as a competitor.[13] The question is what happens to the monopoly rights over morality claimed by the rest when a set of immanent naturalists rewrite the transcendental rather than erasing it. Even more enchanting are the positive possibilities of selective alliance between theists and immanent naturalists opened up by this intervention, for immanent naturalists join transcendental theists in bestowing considerable significance upon the inscrutable, and several parties on both sides of this divide also acknowledge the profound contestability of their interpretations of the immanent/transcendental field.

To think, according to the *OED*, is "to cause (something) to appear (to oneself)," "to form connected ideas of any kind," and "to form a definite conception by a conscious mental act, to picture in one's mind." These definitions, taken together, have the advantage of including both conscious and unconscious processes under the rubric of thinking. Let us treat thinking, provisionally and roughly, as those activities through which conclusions and judgments are reached and new connections among ideas are generated. That leaves open how layered thinking is, the role of intensity, mood, and sensibility in it, and the relation of technique to it. A technique of thought might be an exercise or other intervention that alters the direction of thinking or the mood in which it is set. An electrical probe becomes a technique of thought when applied purposively to a patch of the brain; clearing your mind of everyday concerns while going on a long, slow run in the woods can be another. Kant, who places thought under the juridical control of inscrutable reason, would distinguish sharply between thinking that conforms to the dictates of reason and thinking altered in its direction by external tactics. Therapies and disciplines can refine or coarsen inclinations outside the medium of thought, but in a Kantian world correct thinking itself is organized under the legislative guidance of reason. A transcendental illusion, for instance, occurs when thinking wanders beyond the limits in which it is properly set. Lucretius, on the other hand, finds that jumps and starts within thinking provide it with some of its creative moments. He commends tactical work on the texture of one's own thought for ethical reasons. You might, for instance, strive to imagine the serenity of death as oblivion every time your heated imagination projects rewards and punishments into an afterlife; you do so to ease your resentment against mortality and, therefore, to render yourself less likely to act cruelly toward others. Stuart Hampshire, indebted to both Lucretius and Spinoza, also finds the Kantian distinction between correct thinking and distortion to be forced. The evanescent activity of thinking occurs as cultural elements are folded into complex neurophysiological circuits. Thinking is irreducible to any of the preliminary ingredients that enable it, but it is affected profoundly by the material medium of its occurrence. Writing in 1970, before the recent surge in brain research, Hampshire says:

> In all probability physical structures of a kind that we cannot now even begin to envisage are involved in the acquisition of language and mathematical skills, in the exercise of memory and of the imagination, and in the formation of complex sentiments and mental attitudes.... Indeed the word "mechanism," which I have introduced, may be thought misleading in so far as it is associated only with types of physical processes, which are not yet recognized, or even envisaged, in contemporary physics.[14]

Hampshire treats the mechanisms "at work at different levels, or in different types of thinking" as themselves potential objects of knowledge and intervention. He agrees with his hero Spinoza in regretting that most philosophers in the past

> could not bring themselves consistently to view human beings solely as one kind of natural object among others. Under the influence of inherited moral and religious ideas, and of their natural pieties, his predecessors had always kept some powers of mind in reserve, treating these superior powers of thought as if they transcended the natural order....They seemed to have assumed that those powers of mind, which are the conditions of any organized knowledge of natural processes, cannot themselves be made the objects of such knowledge.[15]

Immanuel Kant, as Hampshire says, continues the tradition of protecting "those powers of mind" from being "made the objects of such knowledge." He gave the pious tradition new energy and confidence in the eighteenth century by rewriting it to protect it from the challenges posed by Spinoza and Newton, respectively. Hampshire, resisting Kant under the influence of Spinoza, pursues a more reflexive naturalism than that offered by Lucretius. He emphasizes the importance of "shifting attention back and forth from the consideration of persons as active observers of the physical world to the consideration of them as also observed objects, with their bodies in a dual role, as both purposely used instruments of exploration and also as observed objects."[16] Here Hampshire translates the ontological parallelism of Spinoza into what might be called perspectival parallelism. According to Spinoza, thought and extension parallel each other perfectly, so that a change in one of these "attributes" of substance is met by a corresponding change in the other, even though the two do not interact causally.[17] Perspectival parallelism drops the reference to a singular substance with two parallel attributes. It asserts that human beings are unable to translate first-person experiences of perception, thinking, and judgment neatly into third-person observations of the physicochemical processes operative while those activities proceed. That is because the thinking in question draws upon and flows into a larger context or cultural world than that encompassed by the physicochemical processes under observation. Nonetheless, a significant change in the physicochemical process is met by some change in thought process, and vice versa. Appreciating the dual role you play as both thinker and student of brain processes that support thought enables you to explore actively how technical intervention might alter the ethos of thinking. You can apply techniques to yourself experimentally to ascertain what new possibilities become discernible in your thinking, even though you are unable to translate the third-person or external perspective *on* thought into the experiential terms *of* thinking. I share this view with Hampshire. The thinker, Hampshire says, aware of the neurophysical instrument of thinking, knows that if "the condition of the instrument is grossly changed, as by drugs, the power of thought is grossly changed also."[18]

So the reflexive relation between first- and third-person perspectives suggests possible technical interventions, and such interventions can in turn help thought to become more reflexive. The reflexivity Hampshire commends is not reducible to Hegelian self-consciousness, since, as we have seen, he anticipates that the gap between the process of making connections *in* thought and explanations of the mechanisms *of* thought is unlikely to be closed entirely. Hampshire does not endorse the encompassing metaphysic of *Geist,* in which such closure is promised for the future, because *Geist* itself takes the form of an implicit Idea striving to realize itself in the world. Techniques of the self, for Hampshire, can be applied at numerous points where the mind finds its capacity to exercise conscious control over itself limited or constrained. Such techniques aim at unconscious processes below the reliable reach of conscious regulation. Drugs, for instance, are to be neither honored nor depreciated in general, but appraised in terms of the effects and side effects they have on health, thinking, and sensibility. The same goes for ritual, diet, reading, posture, meditation, physical exercise, and films. Of course, many of these activities are typically done for the comfort, sustenance, pleasure, or relaxation they offer; but sometimes these same activities also involve experimental action by the self on its thinking or relational sensibility.

Recent research into body/brain processes and the half-second delay suggests to me that as we come to understand more about the geology of body/brain processes we also see more clearly why lawlike explanations of these processes will remain partial and incomplete. This is partly due to the reflexive arc that forms between new accounts of body/brain processes and the changes in self-interpretation and self-interventions they enable, and partly due to the complexity and variable speeds of the body/brain/culture network. Thus the amygdala, an intense little brain nodule we have encountered before, participates in a system that generates rapid, coarse judgments in dangerous situations operating below the capacity of conscious assessment and feeling. Its relays to other, more sophisticated brain regions may not be susceptible to complete tracking and close prediction, because the amygdala both influences conduct on its own and bumps *intensities* into conscious thinking and judgment that the complex brain regions then process according to their own capacities of reception, speed, and organization. The amygdala is a brain nodule involved in those unconscious crunching operations during the half-second delay, working

"sub-symbolically, in codes that are not decipherable consciously." And "consciousness seems to do things serially, more or less one at a time, whereas the unconscious mind, being composed of many different systems, seems to work more or less in parallel."[19]
The conceptual connections formed in conscious thinking are notoriously irreducible to causal explanation, and the rapid, parallel systems that both affect judgment directly and project thought-imbued intensities into consciousness may be too fast and variable in intensity to submit to close, situational computation as well. Affect is a wild card in the layered game of thinking. Since the effects of one system are bounced or bumped into other systems with different speeds and capacities of reception, you would have to form a god's-eye view of the entire complex as it unfolds in action to "explain" its operations at any specific time. The geology of thought is thus susceptible to third-person understanding, but the interlayering of unconscious and conscious thinking in motion may transcend the reach of the most confident models of scientific explanation. This projection discloses another connection between transcendental and immanent philosophies. The transcendental—which for Kant lies beyond human knowledge even as it regulates thinking—is translated by immanent naturalists into an infrasensible field that transcends consciousness and exceeds mechanistic models of scientific explanation. As such it retains some susceptibility to cultural inscription and technical intervention.
Hampshire tends to bypass affective variations in intensity initiated below feeling and conscious judgment that play such a significant role in the adventure of thought. You may not appreciate the jolts, charges, and flashes through which conscious thinking is sometimes depressed and at other times inspired to new heights of creativity sufficiently until you come to terms with the complex relays and numerous feedback loops in the body/brain system, even leaving to the side for the moment how those relays are linked to larger cultural processes. The following quotation from the neuroscientist Joseph LeDoux indicates some of this complexity:

> When the amygdala detects danger, it sends messages to the hypothalamus, which in turn sends messages to the pituitary gland, and the result is the release of a hormone called ACTH. ACTH flows through the blood to the adrenal gland to cause the release of steroid hormone. In addition to reaching target sites in the body, the steroid hormone flows through the blood into the brain, where it binds to the receptors in the hippocampus, amygdala, prefrontal cortex, and other regions.[20]

Consider a recent development in cognitive science that resonates with Hampshire's recommendation to move back and forth between experimental/

theoretical exploration of body/brain mechanisms and phenomenological attention to the experience of thinking and judging. Researchers have begun to fill out the complex physical processes Hampshire could only gesture toward in the early 1970s. In doing so, they also call attention to the crucial role the world plays in these activities. According to Francisco Varela, Evan Thompson, and Eleanor Rosch, several practitioners of cognitive science are now moving away from the calculative, information-processing, and representational models of mind that governed cognitive science in its early stages.[21] In a way reminiscent of Bergson, Merleau-Ponty, and Hampshire, they now emphasize how the practical activities of embodied human beings give priority to "know-how" over propositional knowledge. They put emphasis on the compositional dimension of thinking while playing down its representational function. People, of course, do form representations. But these are not neutral representations of a world of objects waiting to be copied. They are operational representations by corporeal agents *engaged* in culturally mediated, practical activities of perceiving, working, playing, deciding, evaluating, and judging in a world that simultaneously responds to those operational representations and exceeds them. The "world" for these theorists now shifts from a stable repository of things to be represented to a complex array of operational distinctions "enacted codependently" by human actors and the materials encountered. Such a theme of codependence calls into question the model of pure representation with which modern cognitive science began. This is one of the reasons, Varela and his colleagues think, that the "continued search for parallel processing algorithms has met with little success."[22]

> In fact an important and pervasive shift is beginning to take place in cognitive science under the very influence of its own research. This shift requires that we move away from the idea of the world as independent and extrinsic to the idea of a world as inseparable from the structure of these processes of self-modification. . . . The key point is that such systems do not operate by representation. Instead of *representing* an independent world, they *enact* a world as a domain of distinctions that is inseparable from the structure embodied by the cognitive system.[23]

From my point of view, these authors do not play up enough the fugitive resistances, encounters, slippages, anomalies, paradoxes, and ambiguities that recur to suggest that there is always an outside to any historical system of codependencies engendered. But, still, this shift in cognitive science does call the sufficiency of calculative and representational models of thought into question. It does so by keeping in the forefront of attention how the composition of thinking and judgment is indissolubly bound to complex relays between an intersubjective world and body/brain processes. Calculative models of mind, the authors suggest, are unable to account for how a baby acquires a specific language "from dispersed daily utterances and can constitute meaningful objects from what seems to be a sea of lights."[24]

This movement within cognitive science, then, speaks to Hampshire's point about the tension and interdependence between experimental theories of body/brain activity and the phenomenological experience of perception, thinking, feeling, and judgment.

There are other connections as well. According to Varela et al., there is a turn in experimental research that emphasizes how the dispositions and judgments of the self emerge from complex relays between several systems in the self and the world rather than from "a central coordinator" in the self acting upon the world. And, they suggest, this new insight can be brought into productive engagement with Buddhist practices that help people to overcome the demand to "grasp" a central coordinator not available for grabbing. Refined practices of meditation, that is, can be informed by research into brain activities, and brain/body research can encourage people to explore practices that relax this "grasping" tendency. If you link the findings of recent cognitive theory to practices of meditation derived from Buddhism, the authors suggest, you move into a better position, first, to accept the self without a central coordinator and, second, to respond generously to multiple experiences of being in a diverse world. Such an ethic of cultivation, as I will call it, constitutes their response to the danger of "nihilism" accompanying the critique of "a central coordinator" and "foundationalist epistemologies" previously extant in cognitive theory.

This minority movement in cognitive theory both addresses the aspiration of Hampshire within analytic philosophy and touches Foucauldian and Deleuzian explorations of "tactics of the self" and "micropolitics." I will now probe pertinent resources in the latter tradition.

Thinking, Memory, Cinema

Lucretius concludes that the infinitesimal size, rapid speed, and unpredictable swerves of "primordia" render them ill suited to close or complete explanation. Prigogine and Varela et al. adopt similar views. And the philosophy of Gilles Deleuze resonates with all three of these perspectives. Deleuze projects a virtual register of proto-thought too fast for either conscious self-inspection or close third-person retrieval. This reading meshes with his exploration of how differential degrees of *affective intensity* in thought propel it in some directions rather than others, how such intensities render thinking too layered and wayward to be captured either by a calculative model or a juridical model in the Kantian tradition, and how these intensities sometimes open up lines of flight through which new concepts are ushered into being.

Deleuze translates Kant's story of the governance of thought by transcendental reason in the last instance into one in which thinking is periodically nudged, frightened, inspired, or terrorized into action by strange *encounters*. He treats Kantian recognition as a secondary formation often taken by the innocence of consciousness to be apodictic. New encounters can sometimes disturb this experience of apodicticity. The connection between Kant and Deleuze, amid these differences, is that *both* call attention to the fugitive flash point at which argument ends and either recognition or encounter commences. Both point, then, to the limits of argument in moral and epistemological thought, although too few contemporary Kantians and neo-Kantians acknowledge this critical point of convergence. But, again, whereas Kant thinks the idea that morality takes the form of law is apodictic and authoritative, Deleuze contends that the conscious experience of apodicticity can be subjected to critical interrogation and refiguration. For that which is taken to be apodictic shifts historically and situationally. It can do so because the "syntheses" through which perceptions and judgments are formed are not merely active. Prior to active syntheses, and setting the basis for them, are passive syntheses "which weave their repetitions in the depths of the heart, where laws do not yet exist."[25] Deleuze's interpretation of passive syntheses resonates with interpretations in contemporary neuroscience of body/brain syntheses operating below the level of conscious regulation. Important ethical consequences flow from the historical shape given to passive syntheses.

At its most creative, thinking for Deleuze is the invention of new concepts and possibilities out of the experience of friction, first, between entrenched syntheses and unexpected events that disrupt them and, second, between judgments at one level of being and proto-judgments at a more virtual level. Deleuze agrees with Hampshire in highlighting the importance of the reflexive arc in thinking. But he takes a further step. In concurrence with Bergson, Nietzsche, Prigogine, and Stengers, he also contends that nature itself is unfinished and replete with microdifferentials that periodically accumulate to generate new things. Responding to the "dogmatic image of thought" in which Kant participated, Deleuze says, "Do not count upon thought to ensure the relative necessity of what it thinks. Rather, count upon the contingency of an encounter with that which forces thought to raise up and educate the absolute necessity of an act of thought *or a passion to think*."[26] Thinking is often inspired by surprising encounters, either between new events and established thought-imbued conventions or between those conventions and something mute in the world that has not yet been translated (that is, lifted and altered) onto the register of thought.

> This something is an object not of recognition, but of a fundamental *encounter*. What is encountered may be Socrates, a temple or a demon. It may be grasped in a range of affective tones: wonder, love, hatred, suffering. In whichever tone, its primary characteristic is that it can only be sensed.[27]

"A range of affective tones." Deleuze attends to the dissonant relation between affectively imbued virtual memories and the movement of thought. He suggests that affectively imbued thinking is always already under way by the time consciousness intervenes to pull it in this or that direction. Attentiveness to the multilayered character of thinking encourages him, as well, to think about how institutional disciplines, micropolitical movements, and tactics of the self are deployed to move the affective organization of thought and judgment. It may be that the impressive power of culture to set scripts of thought falls short of governing the oblique encounters, intensities, and connections operative in thinking itself. There is a wild element in the intralayered, intersubjective organization of thinking that sometimes drives it into a black hole and occasionally enables thinkers to usher new concepts and ideas into being. Applying experimental techniques to oneself sometimes fosters a rethinking of cultural conventions. Techniques of thought, then, can function both as disciplines of regularization and as periodic challenges to established scripts of normalization.

Let us examine more closely what Deleuze means by the "contingency of an encounter" and its place in thinking. The idea is introduced in his early work, but developed in the later work on cinema. There Deleuze pursues a line initiated by Walter Benjamin in 1936, when Benjamin explored, against objections from fellow critical theorists, how new techniques of film then emerging had "enriched our field of perception." Just as prior to Freud a slip of the tongue was likely to go unnoticed, and after him it became an object of intense popular interest, "the film has brought about a similar deepening of apperception."[28] Deleuze too claims that by exploring the techniques of "modern cinema"—very roughly, the cinema of a coterie of creative directors between 1940 and 1980—we can map more closely the geology of thought in everyday life. In fact, he claims that a subterranean intertext has been formed between theories in neuroscience and creative film techniques, with each set of practitioners tacitly informed by the possibilities opened up by the other.

Consider a few familiar film techniques. In the imaginary film I have in mind, synchronicity is maintained between sound and image, lighting is designed to promote a sense of realism, most shots are pitched at eye level to augment the spirit of realism, frames are kept open to give the viewer a sense of participating in a scene that has not been closely choreographed, and the cuts between scenes are smooth, suggesting clean transitions between events susceptible to full causal explanation or narrative integrity. Few films actually confine themselves to the above techniques, but the gathering together of such techniques does foster a sense of documentary realism, narrative integration, and linear time. Such a film deflects the viewer's attention from its intensive organization of image, lighting, dialogue, music, background noise, and cuts. It solicits an innocent model of perception.

Deleuze is fascinated by films that break with such techniques or that use them distinctively. In doing so, they sometimes teach us about how memory is assembled, perception is organized, and the adventure of thinking proceeds. Deleuze explores techniques such as closed frames, irrational cuts, experimental lighting, dissonance between sound and image, depth-of-field shots, high- and low-angle shots, and recomposition of the conventional rules of distance between characters. He is interested in how these techniques work upon the visceral registers of viewers. These compositional strategies sometimes call attention to themselves. The viewer is first dragged through a set of choreographed thought-imbued feelings and then encouraged to ponder how they were formatted.

Occasionally such techniques, in conjunction with the story lines they portray, overwhelm the experience of linear time. As Bergson showed, in everyday perception the image is set in linear time; the virtual memories it folds into perception are assembled too fast to surface as explicit recollections. Sometimes however, even a classical technique such as the flashback brings out forkings in time that challenge our linear presuppositions. But why is a flashback needed to disclose a fork in the past? "The answer is simple: the forking points are often so imperceptible that they cannot be revealed until after their occurrence, to an attentive memory. It is a story that can be told only in the past."[29]

Deleuze also presses beyond this point. He seeks to make contact with nonchronological "sheets of past" or "regions of time" from which forks in time emerge. These sheets precede and enable the movement image, but they are left in the shadows by the activity of perception. Bergson himself brings us to the point where this region is touched, for he contends that before a virtual memory is selected to help compose a particular percept, a larger sheet of past must be assembled from which that selection can be drawn.

What is a sheet of past? One shape it assumes is that of a rapidly mobilized set of virtual memories, assembled in nonchronological order from different periods in your life as, say, you encounter a disturbing situation. For example, you hear a man walking at a fast pace behind you on a dark city street. Virtual memories from different events in your adulthood, childhood, and adolescence might be mobilized quickly to help organize your perception and operational response. Since it takes the form of a virtual sheet, the memory does not become a series of explicit recollections. A virtual memory, again, has effects upon the present without taking the shape of recollection. For, as we saw in chapter 2, conscious processing does not move fast enough to meet the action dictates of everyday perception. Rather a sheet of time—of an indivisible pulse of duration—is formed as these layers of memory enter into communication below the threshold of conscious recollection. The assembled sheet is virtual and nonchronological. A response is forged from this affectively imbued encounter between a virtual sheet of time, the present event, and a possible future stretching before you. It may be innovative. Perhaps you walk into the middle of the street with studied casualness. Or yell a friendly greeting to someone up the street, even though you do not know that person.

Inventive thinking draws sustenance from such sheets of time, but it typically does so in settings less constrained by the requirements of action than the one sketched above. During thinking, as the imperious demands of action-oriented perception are relaxed, elements in a nonchronological region of time drift, slide, and bounce into communication with each other. The *creative* dimension of thinking flows from this encounter between a nonchronological region of time, the fugitive present, and an uncertain future. Its *compositional* effect, Deleuze suggests in concurrence with Ramachandran, is engendered by new pathways mapped into the body and brain as new thinking becomes habituated.

The process of thinking might fruitfully be compared to the experience of déjà vu. Déjà vu dwells between a memory that cannot be consolidated and a perception that cannot be completed. It is not exactly a confused state, for that would imply that there is a solid perception waiting to emerge or a settled memory ready to find expression. But in déjà vu experiences neither possibility is present; that which triggers the beginning of each is insufficient to allow either to be completed. Déjà vu is thus a real state of indiscernibility, irreducible to the states it resides between. It feels uncanny because it subsists between familiar modes of experience. It *is* uncanny, first, because its irreducibility to perception or memory signifies darkly how insufficient these rough-and-ready distinctions are to the actual flow of experience and, second, because it illuminates something about the structure of both memory and perception easily left in the shadows. For a sheet of memory is called up by a new encounter in the present, and an encounter cannot be organized into a perception until a sheet of virtual memory has been mobilized. A déjà vu experience teaches us about both memory and perception because it assembles fragments necessary to each without being reducible to either.

Thinking has a comparable structure. It involves a synthesis in the fugitive present between a past that is constructed and a future yet to be consolidated. During thinking, diverse elements in a nonchronological sheet of past enter into communication with each other and with the present in which they are set. Thinking thus occurs in a delicate zone between dreaming and action-oriented perception. It involves an internal "conversation," with some of the voices involved subsisting below the threshold of conscious awareness. Since its constitutive elements coexist in a relation of constitutive instability, it can easily lapse into boredom, dreaming, or action. You might slide toward boredom as you resist the effort or anxiety involved to think something new. It is because thinking subsists within this fugitive zone that it sometimes generates forks of time through which new ideas, concepts, judgments, actions, and sensibilities are ushered into the future.

Deleuze does not make this comparison between thinking and déjà vu, although I think it fits his image of thought. But he does embrace the image of time noted above. He shares the reading of time advanced by Nietzsche and Prigogine. Neither cyclical nor linear conceptions of time capture the movement of thinking. In thinking time is "out of joint," for thinking draws upon nonchronological sheets of past, and it might be nudged in a new or novel direction from the encounter between a sheet of nonchronological past and an uncertain future. Thinking participates in the forking of time because it is suspended in a delicate zone between reminiscence, dreaming, boredom, and action.[30] It is a fragile and vulnerable activity for the same reasons.

Some films, Deleuze says, address the ubiquitous role that sheets of past play in thinking. By attending to these films we gain new insight into how thinking works. I presented in chapter 2, with Deleuze's prompting, an example on the edge of this territory when I mapped a depth-of-field shot in *Citizen Kane* in which the young Kane frolics in the snow in the small, intense back of a shot with three levels of depth. Deleuze himself points to a more complex instance in the same film. Here we view the past working within Susan's life. Susan is Kane's former lover, whose affair with him ended his gubernatorial campaign, who then became his wife, and who was thereafter pressed by him to pursue a disastrous career as an opera singer. In one scene Susan is grieving Kane and regretting the course of her life, when Kane "bursts in through the door at the back..., tiny, while Susan is dying in the shadow in mid-shot and the large mirror is seen in close up." In this suicide scene elements from Susan's past and present communicate back and forth. The scene "directly forms a region of time, a region of past which is defined by optical aspects of elements borrowed from interacting planes."[31] It is perhaps now time to let Deleuze speak in his own voice about how Orson Welles and Alain Resnais link depth-of-field shots to dissonance between sound and visual image to foment an experience of time that agitates thought. The films referred to are *Kafka* and *Last Year at Marienbad.*

> Welles' success in relation to Kafka is that he was able to show how spatially distant and chronologically separate regions were in touch with each other, at the bottom of a limitless time which made them contiguous: this is what depth of field is used for, the areas which are the furthest apart are in direct contact in the background....
>
> This membrane which makes the inside and the outside present to each other is called memory. If memory is the explicit theme of Resnais's work, there is no reason to look for a latent content which would be more subtle; it is better to evaluate the transformation that the notion of memory is made to undergo.... For memory is clearly no longer the faculty of having recollections: it is the membrane which, in the most varied ways (continuity, but also discontinuity, envelopment, etc.) makes sheets of past and layers of reality freely correspond, the first emanating from an inside which is always already there, the second arriving from an outside always to come, the two gnawing at the present which is now only their encounter.[32]

Let us distinguish between *thinking* as an active process that essentially involves language but is not exhausted by it and *thought* as past thinking stored in vocabularies, dispositions, and beliefs. The former cannot be without the latter, but it is not entirely reducible to the latter. Does thinking involve free correspondences between nonchronological sheets of time, mobilized in the fugitive present, pointing toward an unsettled future? Does its *creative* potential expand as you cultivate techniques to extend the fragile zone of indiscernibility in which it moves? Does thinking also carry *compositional* power, participating in modifying old dispositions and forging new habits even as it *expresses* established habits and dispositions? Reflection upon the reflexive, expressive, inventive, and compositional powers of thought enables us to resist the reduction of thinking to cognition alone.

Thinking and Technique

Attention to relays among technique, memory, perception, and thinking in film draws us toward corollary relays outside the celluloid world. How ubiquitous are techniques and rituals in broad daylight? Do they work upon affectively imbued, virtual memories? Consider, for starters, Chuck Knoblauch, the journeyman second baseman for the New York Yankees. According to a piece in the sports pages of the *New York Times*, he repeats nine precise steps prior to every pitch. He sweeps his right foot across the batter's box, taps the right and then the left foot with the bat, places the bat between his legs, bends over and touches his leg, ankle, and knees, stands up again and undoes the Velcro strap of his right batting glove, does the same thing with his left glove, raises the bat with his right hand, holds the bat vertically to get a close grip, and draws the bat down again as he steps into the batting box. This is his unconscious batting ritual, repeated at least fifteen to twenty-two times every game over 188 games. Hitting a baseball thrown by a highly skilled pitcher is a most demanding athletic task. Knoblauch is never sure whether he will encounter a fast ball at ninety-five miles an hour, a sharp curveball breaking away at seventy-eight, a slider at eighty-two, or a change-up that spins like a fastball but travels at sixty-eight miles per hour. Besides all that, he must "decide" in a few nanoseconds whether the pitch is going to be a strike or ball. He thus concocts over time a ritual that helps to clear his mind of extraneous matters while opening it to respond intelligently and subconsciously to a pitch traveling faster than the conscious mind thinks. Knoblauch's techniques of the self, gathered into a ritual performance, enable him to sustain split-second attentiveness to whatever pitch comes his way. "I really don't know exactly what I do because I am thinking about the pitch.... It's all about getting comfortable. It's kind of a fidgeting routine while your mind is at work."[33] Unfortunately, Knoblauch, an excellent athlete, has not succeeded to date in devising techniques to overcome his tendency to convert routine tosses to first base into wild throws.

What are the relations between technique and thinking? And between both and performance? Is technique an occasional aid to thought? Or are thinking and technique bound so closely together that it is sometimes difficult to decide where one leaves off and the other begins? Let's draw up a short list of everyday techniques, both gross and subtle, by which thinking is altered in its direction, speed, intensity, or sensibility. To simplify, our examples for now will be those in which an individual is the object of the technique, and in which the individual either applies the technique to him- or herself or agrees to have it applied by others.

- You listen to Mozart while reading a philosophical text, in order to relax your mind and sharpen its acuity of reception.

- You undergo surgery to increase the flow of blood to the brain, in the hopes of avoiding a stroke and/or improving the quality of your thinking.

- You go for a slow run after having struggled with a paradox or quandary that perplexes you.

- You take Prozac or Valium to relax your nerves and improve the mood in which your thinking occurs.

- You submit to a severe whipping in the hopes of resolving a feeling of guilt that will not subside.

- You expose yourself to an image that, against your considered intention, has disturbed you in the past, while listening to the music of the Talking Heads as you soak in the bathtub and imagine how mellow it would be to dive into crystal-blue water off a Caribbean beach.

- You underline passages in a text while reading it, and then outline the text you have just underlined, remembering as you do how close the relation is between hand gesture and brain processes.

- You give in to a feeling of intense regret that you had previously resisted.

- You concentrate your mind on a practical issue after having gone through several of the activities listed above.

- You introduce full-spectrum lighting into your house during the winter to help lift yourself out of morose thoughts and passive moods.

- You cultivate more expansive powers of reflection and persuasion by giving talks in public settings. On some such occasions you express in public one or two views you have previously stated only in the shower.

- You watch TV ads and films in a new way, analyzing the techniques through which they organize affect and mobilize virtual memory, doing so both to give you more leverage in responding to them and to teach you about how to apply similar techniques to yourself when an old habit or tired pattern of thought needs to be jolted.

- You reach a conclusion after reconsidering familiar arguments and evidence in a mood that has shifted significantly from the last time you engaged the issue.

- You read a book by Spinoza to sharpen your powers of argument and subject entrenched presumptions about mind/body dualism to shock therapy, and then you read Proust to sharpen your powers of perception and memory.

- You introduce the phrase *nontheistic gratitude* into discussions with secularists and believers, knowing that it will sound like an oxymoron to many. You hope, nonetheless, that its introduction will, first, call attention to the forgotten history of its uses; second, open up cultural space in which to articulate an ethical perspective reducible to neither secularism nor monotheism; and third, inspire new strategies by which to work on the lower layers of your intrasubjectivity to bring it closer to the faith you profess.[34]

- You drink three glasses of wine at a social occasion to stop yourself from thinking obsessively about the same topic, or about anything in particular.

- You focus on some new adventure of thought just before going to sleep, in the hope that the dream work done that night will open up new possibilities of thinking in the morning.

- You meditate at the same time every day, striving to loosen the hold the grasping mind has on the self and to open the self to side perceptions that slip away when the first temper prevails.

- You misrepresent a religious or metaphysical perspective that troubles you, to relieve the feeling of disturbance it generates.

- You go dancing to music that inspires and energizes you after hearing very disappointing news.

- You minimize encounters for a time with associates whose dispositions are saturated with existential rage or resentment.

Such examples could be modified along several dimensions and proliferated indefinitely, for technique, in film, institutional life, and everyday life, is ubiquitous. The relays that connect word, gesture, dream, memory, sound, rhythm, mobility, image, and thinking in the application of techniques are particularly close. You could include examples in which others apply tactics to you with or without your awareness, and in which some of these tactics, and more punitive ones besides, are folded into institutional practices. Or you could form a community of, say, immanent naturalists connected by print, phone, Internet, conferences, readings, and travel, the members of which fold several such tactics into their associational activities. Such a formation, indeed, would adapt to the conditions of late-modern life the garden community through which Epicureans responded in their day to the hegemony of polytheism.

But the list assembled above may already be suggestive about entanglements among thinking, virtual memory, technique, habit, mood, and sensibility. It is hard to locate an instance in which several elements are not touched, although the differentials vary. Should we, then, defer the temptation to reduce these diverse interventions entirely to familiar categories, calling, say, one set internal to thought and another external to it? Or to reduce one set of activities entirely to linguistic *expressions* and another to technical *interventions*? What about the difference between invoking the idea of nontheistic gratitude to *express* an orientation to life and doing so to help *compose* that orientation? How radical is the difference between concentrating your mind and taking Prozac to clear it of depressive thoughts? Does the presumption that the difference is one of kind rather than degree tacitly invoke a conception of the supersensible itself open to contestation? What is the difference between smoking a cigarette while reading and underlining passages in a text while doing so? What about tapping into a sheet of virtual memory while dreaming or while running, doing so each time in a way that unlocks a puzzle with which you had been struggling? Or, again, at what point does listening to Mozart while you write shift from hovering in the background of your work to becoming an element in its rhythm and color?

Why press the connection between thinking and technique? Because it discloses something about thinking that might otherwise remain obscure.

Thinking is not merely involved in knowing, explaining, representing, evaluating, and judging. Subsisting within these activities are the inventive and compositional dimensions of thinking. To think is to move something. And to modify a pattern of body/brain connections helps to draw a habit, a disposition to judgment, or a capacity of action into being. Thinking not only expresses our identities; it participates in composing, strengthening, and modifying them. The cognitive — that is, the representational and explanatory — dimension of thinking coexists with its expressive, creative, and compositional functions. If, as Hampshire says, "it is precisely the point of materialism to assert a much closer relation between processes of thought and physical processes than is implied in most of the idioms of ordinary speech,"[35] it may be a creative tactic of reflexive thought to delay placing this miscellany immediately or entirely under the authority of those idioms. For the idioms of ordinary speech may remain too fettered to the logic of recognition, knowledge, and representation while philosophical reflection, brain research, cinema practice, and the accelerated speed of everyday life coalesce to call the *sufficiency* of that logic into question.

Immanent Naturalism and Ethics

An orientation to ethics growing out of immanent naturalism contains several tendencies, although different practitioners nudge them in specific directions. I will sketch a few of these tendencies, scavenging freely from giants in this tradition and inflecting them in the direction I support.

Immanent naturalists, as already indicated, do not ground ethics in a transcendental command or an intrinsic juridical source. Messages flowing from the immanent field to the higher, slower, conceptually sophisticated brain regions are often received *as if* they were lawlike commands or the products of apodictic recognition. But such first-person experiences can be called into question — although perhaps not definitively disproved in the last instance — by investigations from a third-person perspective. Our foray into the neurophysiology of the human brain, for instance, is compatible with the speculation that the apodictic experience of morality as law recorded by Kant does not flow from the noumenal to the phenomenal realm as he contended. It may flow, rather, from the infrasensible dictates of the amygdala into higher consciousness. If so, it may be wise to cultivate an orientation to ethics that draws its *initial* impetus from elsewhere, for the amygdala is implicated in a larger brain system that triggers fear, anxiety, and resentment. Immanent naturalists pursue an orientation to ethics that resists entangling it from the outset in the simplification and cruelty such a system foments. Such a speculation requires further exploration. It is pertinent to note, however, that this speculation has also been supported in a more intuitive way by other immanent naturalists who resist the morality of law. Spinoza, Nietzsche, Freud, Hampshire, and Deleuze all link the morality of law to simplification, cruelty, and violence; and several of these figures strive to supplant it with more positive sources of ethical inspiration. They may be onto something.

With the translation of the transcendental into the immanent, you revise some questions of ethics given priority in the transcendental and quasi-transcendental traditions. You shift priority from the question "Why should I be moral?" or "What is the transcendental or contractual basis of morality?" or "What is the subjective capacity presupposed by the practice of morality?" to "*How* do you cultivate presumptive responsiveness and generosity in a pluralistic culture?" For the practices of obligation, responsibility, and justice one affirms are closely bound up with the sensibility one brings to them. And one can strengthen or modify a sensibility, to some uncertain degree, by working tactically upon the infrasensible register in which it is set.

One possibility to pursue is the cultivation of nontheistic gratitude for the rich abundance of being amid the suffering that comes with being mortal. Such an orientation certainly cannot provide ethical inspiration for everyone. It is, rather, one among several contestable existential faiths from which a positive ethos of engagement might be negotiated between interdependent partisans in a pluralist culture. It is apt to be compelling to those informed by the following experiences: they find intellectualist readings of life to be insufficient to the texture of existence; they experience in conjunction with others religious energies and attachments; they find it to be unconvincing or unacceptable to attach those energies to the idea of a divine being; and they invest those energies in attachment to the earth or reverence for the protean diversity of being. Such an existential combination pulls you away from teleological, Kantian, and secular models of morality. It opens the gate to another possibility.

It is pertinent to emphasize again that immanent naturalists do not reduce ethical sources to "inclination" or "preference," as neo-Kantians often suggest.[36] That is merely how the attachments appear after they have been translated into the confined categorical space Kantians and neo-Kantians reserve for sensibility. Such a representation tells you more about their assumptions than about ours. But what, more closely, is the highest source to which immanent naturalists might appeal for inspiration? For Spinoza that source seems to be the existential joy that accompanies enhanced knowledge of the deep structure of things. But since other immanent naturalists build more contingency and fluidity into the world, such an inspiration is not available to them, at least not in the form espoused by Spinoza.

For many, a presumptive ethos of generosity is inspired by visceral "gratitude for the abundance of life" or "attachment to the world" or "care for being" or (in the case of Deleuze) "belief in this world" already operative to some degree in the identities and interests of people who have a modest degree of good fortune in life.[37] That is, a generous and responsive sensibility is not commanded into being in the first instance; it subsists, when individuals and groups are lucky, as a fugitive disposition on the visceral register susceptible to further cultivation. The element of tragedy in ethical life, according to Epicurus, Nietzsche, and Deleuze, is that such an elemental reverence for life is not always there in everyone, or actively suffused throughout a culture; when it is weak or absent, there is no transcendental guarantee that it can be kindled. The ethical life does not come equipped with a prior guarantee that the energies available for its mobilization will be sufficient to the needs of the time. Even Kant was compelled to admit this point, when he encountered within his own moral philosophy a "perversity" in the will that often exceeds the power of the "autonomous" individual to rise above it.[38]

Immanent naturalists who pursue an ethic of cultivation develop three interconnected strategies to spiritualize positive possibilities on the immanent field. First, we bring other traditions of ethics into contact with sore spots and points of comparative contestability in their claims to uncover solid foundations and/or transcendental sources, doing so to show that the paradoxes and contestability we acknowledge in our ethico-political perspective find corollary points of contact in their own. These genealogical encounters are thus important: they help to qualify and render more modest the automatic stance of superiority through which many transcendentalists and thick universalists respond to perspectives anchored in sensible and infrasensible sources. We will engage one such perspective in the last chapter. Second, we devise techniques and exercises to diminish existential resentment against the absence of such guarantees in the world, for we suspect that visceral resentment of the absence of final guarantees promotes a punitive orientation to difference in many, blunts the capacity to nourish agonistic respect between interdependent constituencies, and diminishes critical responsiveness to new movements of cultural diversification. Third, we *cultivate* further that preliminary gratitude for the abundance of being already there, in the interests of folding more modesty and receptive generosity into entrenched presumptions, established interests, and operational codes. These are not the only strategies available, but this set does enter into selective correspondence with the Buddhist strategies summarized by Francisco Varela in his reconstitution of cognitive theory and ethical practice.[39] That is, it makes contact with a non-Western tradition that plays up the significance of the immanent register to ethical life and plays down the juridical element prominent in several Christian and secular perspectives in Western philosophy.

The most distinctive contribution immanent naturalism makes to contemporary ethical thought is through the retrieval of "self-artistry" (Nietzsche), "tactics of the self" (Foucault), "techniques" (Hampshire), and "micropolitics" (Deleuze). That retrieval connects an ethic of cultivation set in a philosophy of immanence to the monotheistic traditions along one dimension, even as it diverges from them along another. Thus, as Talal Asad has shown in his exploration of medieval Christianity, several monastic orders perfected exercises to cultivate "aptitudes of performance" appropriate to their faith below the register of belief.[40] The role of arts of the self, however, is demoted in Kant's rewriting of Christian morality, although Kant does allow "gymnastics" a modest role in preparing the inclinations to accept the moral law. Contemporary secular, neo-Kantian theories, with their inordinate confidence in argument and deliberation, pretty much jettison this dimension of ethical life.

The exploration in the two previous sections of connections between thinking and technique also makes technique the hinge that links thought (as corporeally stored thinking) to ethical sensibility. In a world in which institutional discipline has become extensive and intensive, such tactics can function as countermeasures to build more independence and thoughtful responsiveness into ethico-political sensibilities. You might, thus, act tactically and experimentally upon yourself to fold more presumptive receptivity and forbearance into your responses to pluralizing movements in the domains of gender, sensual affiliation, ethnic identification, religion/irreligion, or market rationality that challenge your visceral presumption to embody the universal standard against which that diversity is to be measured.

An ethical sensibility, you might say, is composed through the cultural layering of affect into the materiality of thought. It is a constellation of thought-imbued intensities and feelings. To work on an established sensibility by tactical means, then, is to nudge the composition of some layers in relation to others. You work experimentally on the relays between thought-imbued *intensities* below the level of feeling and linguistic complexity, thought-imbued *feelings* below the level of linguistic sophistication, *images* that trigger responses at both levels, and linguistically sophisticated patterns of *narrative, argument, and judgment.* You do so to encourage the effects of action upon one register to filter into the experience and imagination available on others, thereby working tactically upon a dense sensibility whose layered composition is partly receptive to direct argument and deliberation, partly receptive to tactics that extend beyond the reach of argument, and partly resistant to both.

To foreground arts of the self, then, is to flag the insufficiency of argument to ethical life without denying its pertinence. Michel Foucault suggests the significance of such relays when he says, "It is not enough to say the subject is constituted in a symbolic system. . . . It is [also] constituted in real practices. . . . There is a technology of the constitution of the self which cuts across symbolic systems while using them."[41] The thoughtful application by oneself of techniques to one's entrenched patterns of affective thought can both track the institutional technologies through which the visceral register has been organized and activate presumptive responsiveness to new social movements of pluralization. You allow effects promoted at one level to filter into others, doing so to enable new thoughts to come into being or to refine the sensibility in which your judgments have heretofore been set. For thinking, memory, sensibility, and judgment are interwoven.

Ethics and Micropolitics

You can think of micropolitics, in the Deleuzian sense, as a cultural collectivization and politicization of arts of the self. Micropolitics applies tactics to multiple layers of intersubjective being. Because it is often practiced in competitive settings, it contains an agonistic element. The assemblage to which such micropolitical tactics are applied might be a small group, a large constituency, or an interdependent constellation of people holding divergent positions on issues in need of general resolution. Arts of the self and micropolitics are ubiquitous in cultural life, even though they also stand in a relation of torsion to each other.

In a fast-paced world you might try to step out of the cauldron of micropolitics from time to time to work on the ethical sensibility you bring to it.[42] Such a retreat can never be entirely successful in a modern world of intensive institutional discipline, but the effort still makes a difference. That is when arts of the self become particularly pivotal. But it also becomes advisable to step back into the cauldron periodically to enable the sensibility you have cultivated to exert a larger influence, or, sometimes, to compel it to encounter new challenges and pressures. With this proviso in mind about the torsion between arts of the self and micropolitics, we turn to micropolitics.

Over the past fifteen years in the United States numerous trials and hearings have captivated the country. Think of the Pamela Smart trial, the Bork hearings, the Thomas/Hill hearings, the Menendez brothers trials, the Bobbitt wife abuse and penis-severing case, the O. J. Simpson trial, the Clinton show trial, and add to each countless hours of neighborhood gossip, news programs, films, and TV talk shows devoted to them. Barely three months can pass without one trial or hearing assuming the media spotlight just vacated by another. These are vintage events of micropolitics. Their choreography affects us on several intercoded registers of being. Consider, for instance, the TV choreography of the Robert Bork confirmation hearings in the Senate.

> Whatever the seeming naturalness of Senators Kennedy and Biden, they had been carefully rehearsed backstage, with the Harvard law professor Lawrence Tribe. Rehearsals covered not only the appropriate questions to ask but also matters of demeanor and legal bearing.... The front stage of the hearing was that portion of the Senate caucus room that could be or, better, was allowed to be taken in by the camera. That consisted of the table at which Robert Bork and subsequent witnesses sat; the curved, empaneled, and continuous desk or dais at which fourteen senators sat; and the bay which separated them. The only leakage into the stage were glimpses of the audience, usually Bork's family, seated immediately behind the witness, and, behind the senators, their aides listening to the proceedings, moving about, whispering into the ear of their chief or passing documents to the dais. The rest of the back region...was kept from view. At solemn moments the area behind the senators was cleared to minimize distraction and to heighten the dignity of the proceedings; for example, Senator Biden's opening speech...was kept clear of temporal and spatial intrusions. The stage itself was kept free of any action that might contradict the image of rectitude, control and jurisprudential dignity, that might contradict the impression being fostered.[43]

Stage management, a solemnized setting, images of impartial demeanor, carefully crafted correlations between speech and gesture—all mobilized to organize the affective element of intersubjectivity. In this hearing, and numerous others as well, the audience was sharply divided over the guilt or innocence of the parties involved and the motives of those in charge of the proceedings. But such hearings affect the audience at multiple levels of being. The perpetual repetition of such legal and quasi-legal events reflects and promotes a sea change in the political culture, insinuating general effects below the threshold of explicit partisan opinion. It first activates a vague sense of anxiety already in circulation about the moral shape of politics at the onset of the twenty-first century. It then mobilizes that anxiety to give cultural priority to the juridical dimension of political life. For instance, as the political culture becomes more oriented to the search for guilty and innocent parties and becomes more accusatory in character, the implicit presumption to authority of the Supreme Court is elevated and extended.

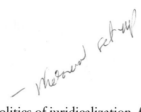

The micropolitics of juridicalization, finding expression in neighborhood gossip, recurrent show trials, national talk shows, and electoral campaigns, slips into the background of macropolitical life. But the micropolitics of cultural juridicalization sets presumptive agendas for macropolitics, ruling a variety of issues and presumptions out of public life. In a setting where unemployment, family life, welfare, drug use, and electoral participation have been moralized, criminalized, or both, it becomes difficult to generate debates about market sources of income inequality or the effects of job insecurity upon crime.

Or take another example, more favorable to the political perspective endorsed here. With the introduction of MIRV (multiple individually targeted reentry vehicle systems) in the 1970s, the old balance of terror between the Soviet Union and the United States was thrown into jeopardy. Between 1979 and 1989 (before the collapse of the Soviet Union) a significant transformation occurred in the operational presumptions about the arms race in both countries. Micropolitics played a significant role in this shift, operating below the veneer of legislative action and military policy. Here, myriad discussions at dinner tables, in churches, and in classrooms activated a gut sense of urgency in many people. Television and the other media eventually picked up on this glacial shift of mood, creating a favorable setting for the Reagan-Gorbachev negotiations and limiting the ability of the Right to mobilize fear against them.

Indeed, each time a new advance is made in the domains of ecology, race relations, income distribution, worker rights, gay rights, religious freedom, and gender diversity it is supported and enabled by micropolitical actions that create resonances across several constituencies at multiple levels of being. Images of a dead fetus flashed to those assessing the legality of abortion; television shows presenting gays as more than cartoon figures in a heterosexual culture; a film about a person dying an agonizing death in a world where doctor-assisted suicide remains illegal; talk-show repetitions of the conviction that you can't be moral or participate responsibly in public culture unless you believe in a God—these examples are merely the steam pouring out of the micropolitical kettle of late-modern life.

Micropolitics is ubiquitous. Immanent naturalism makes a timely contribution to contemporary politics, then, through its appreciation of how micropolitics persistently invades and pervades macropolitics, and through its corollary attentiveness to the connection between techniques of the self and micropolitics.

Several secular conceptions of morality, while some of them too are committed to plurality, underplay the ubiquity and significance of tactics of the self and micropolitics to the texture of public life. They may do so because they invest the deliberative dimension of politics with more autonomy, sufficiency, and purity than it can muster. Instead of thinking about which modes of micropolitics to practice and which to resist, they act as if the micropolitical dimension of life could be expelled altogether. Nothing could be more futile. Immanent naturalists, by comparison, emphasize the complex interactions among sounds, smells, images, rhythms, *and* conceptually refined deliberation in the ethos of public life. Most of us are pluralists who support micropolitical strategies to contest the ugliest dimensions of the culture wars.

It is crucial to emphasize that the sensibility pursued here cannot be generated by the intellectual resources of immanent naturalism alone. The intellectual resources of that philosophy must be linked to other strategies to overcome existential resentment against the limits it acknowledges and to cultivate the sensibility it endorses. That is, it takes a coalescence of a preliminary attachment to the abundance of this world, a philosophy that expresses that attachment, and artful techniques that support these first two movements to entrench this ethical perspective. Some moral theorists, predictably, will criticize this result by saying, "But you have not shown us why we *must* accept the moral philosophy you endorse, merely that you *do* endorse it." But this response already buries the fundamental issue, *for on the view advanced here intellectualism is constitutively insufficient to ethics, and no final moral source to date has ever been vindicated so consummately that all reasonable people find themselves commanded by intellect or revelation to accept it.* This is the point at which immanent naturalists and several religions of the Book converge in breaking with the philosophical imperatives advanced by secular theories: articulation of an ethic requires aid and support from a corresponding sensibility to actualize itself. No ethical perspective, at least to date, sustains itself by argument alone. The sensibility embraced here might be set in a theistic faith or in nontheistic gratitude for being. But there is a strong case to be made that neither it nor its competitors are reducible to argument alone, as even Kant was compelled to acknowledge, and, similarly, that none can generate resources of faith that must command the assent of all. To demand, as many persistently do, that other perspectives establish an authoritative basis commanding universal assent when the carriers of such a demand cannot measure up to that standard themselves is to foster nihilism and cynicism in ethical life per se.

My assumption is that advocates of other theo-ontological perspectives can cultivate similar or complementary sensibilities, proceeding from different existential faiths. Indeed, when devotees of different perspectives reciprocally acknowledge the comparative contestability of the source each honors and also work reciprocally to overcome existential resentment against this persistent condition of being, the prospect of cultivating agonistic respect across difference improves. These are alliances to forge across a pathos of distance. By *emphasizing* the legitimate contestability of the presumptions we honor most in the eyes of others and the insufficiency of argument to ethics, immanent naturalists open lines of communication to theists and secularists prepared to make similar acknowledgments. These lines of connection are strengthened by our efforts to rewrite (rather than simply to reject) the transcendental field endorsed by others, and by our positive orientation to relational arts of the self and micropolitics.

The Fecundity of Thinking

The affective dimension of thought; its multilayered character; contingent encounters in thinking among sheets of past, the fugitive present, and an uncertain future; techniques of thought; the creativity of thought; the compositional power of thought. What about thought, then? A contemporary immanent naturalist, aided and instructed by developments in brain research and film technique, can say a fair amount about *the geology of thinking*. You can show how thinking participates in several layers of being and in every aspect of ethical and political life, including the formation of new identities out of old energies and injuries and the cultivation of critical responsiveness to new events and constituencies. You might eventually outline how each layer contains distinctive speeds, capacities, and intensities that affect the intra- and intersubjective relations of thought; how affective intensities of proto-judgment sometimes surge up from the lower strata, flooding slower and more refined layers of conceptual thought and conscious imagination, overwhelming them for a time or propelling them down new paths of exploration; how these movements sometimes throw thought into a tailspin or open up possibilities of invention for an individual, group, or constituency; and how those lines of flight, in turn, pose questions about what tactics to deploy to educate thought-imbued habits below direct reflective regulation.

To say all that is to speak to the body/brain/culture network in which thought is set, but it still does not dig deeply into the soil from which thinking emerges. There may still be one more zone of passage to address. If thinking encompasses ideas in movement, and if what might be called "the unthought" consists of energetic assemblages that are non- or minimally ideational, then thinking draws part of its material and energy from the unthought as that which does not itself take the form of thought. The fecundity of thinking is bound up with these fugitive passages from unthought to thought, passages that leave signs and remainders but are not themselves susceptible to representation. We here merely allude to such a magical zone, recalling how it was suggested by our exploration of the mixing of nature, affect, and culture in chapter 3.

The factors reviewed in the preceding two paragraphs make it unwise to anticipate a future in which the activity of thinking will be encompassed by lawlike explanations. The "immanence" in the naturalism affirmed here expresses a constitutive element of wildness in thinking. This element, bound to the play of affect within and across registers, is marked by danger, but it also provides a matrix through which something new and wonderful can sometimes surge into being. Arts of the self and micropolitics, when informed by visceral gratitude for the abundance of being, can aid those who must decide which new infusions to support, which to tolerate, and which to resist. For when such context-bending conditions arise, existing rules, constitutions, identities, and principles do not suffice to govern judgment.

Creative thinking may be particularly important to nurture during a time when the tempo of life moves faster than heretofore, when many individuals, constituencies, and states are therefore confronted more often with surprising events that disrupt the sufficiency of established codes of identity, principle, procedure, or judgment. Attention to the layered character of thinking, the inventive potential in it, its compositional character, and the pertinence of technique to it may be particularly appropriate to a fast-paced time in which the established boundaries of normality and morality periodically need to be modified, amended, or reinterpreted. Negotiation of an ethos of presumptive generosity is important during a time when the forking of time and sedimented codes clash. Because creative thinking is so important to contemporary life, freedom of thought and expression—already supported loquaciously by Epicurus, Lucretius, Spinoza, Hampshire, Foucault, and Deleuze—emerge as central principles to embrace in the contemporary period. Most of the above-mentioned figures participate in the contestable faith that as freedom of expression becomes generalized it becomes somewhat easier to thicken a series of fragile connections between thinking, freedom, care of the self, and care for the world. Such connections are often susceptible to disruption. But negotiation of a generous ethos of engagement in a diverse society moving at a faster tempo than heretofore depends upon them.

Thinking is periodically inspired or jolted by unexpected encounters that jar it into motion out of stupor or call into question chunks in the conventional storehouse of thought. Forks in thinking affect, as they become consolidated, the sensibility through which you act. And micropolitical interventions into collective sensibilities installed at several layers of being can make a notable difference to the ethos of public life.

F I V E

Memory Traces, Mystical States, and Deep Pluralism

The Variety of Religious Experience

IT SEEMS SIMPLE. Because life is riddled with mystery and uncertainty, an existential faith may encounter paradoxes that call its claim to universality into question. So a dictum becomes tempting: wherever mystery and freedom meet, a variety of faiths bubble up; wherever, therefore, people prize freedom they will support a significant presumption in favor of honoring that variety. Many give preliminary consent to such a dictum. But it quickly runs into difficulties. Christians have often insisted that because their faith is universal it must be sanctioned by public ethics in the states or civilizations they inhabit. Secularists, while praising religious diversity in private life, typically sanctify this or that rendering of public reason, deliberation, justice, or procedure as the one practice that must be taken to rise above faith. They often fail to acknowledge the element of faith in their doctrine. Freudians, who expose primal elements of dogmatism in the historical religions of Judaism and Christianity, often enough act as if the interpretation that addresses that dogmatism itself rises above fundamental contestability. And numerous defenders of freedom in the United States insist that the very survival of freedom requires general loyalty to the "Judeo-Christian tradition" that enables it. Qualifications and self-exemptions abound, then.

It is difficult to see how such an effect could be avoided entirely by a party enlivened by the faith that animates it. For faith, by its very nature, inclines toward dogmatism. The dictum to support a variety of faiths is thus haunted by a shadow of self-referential exemption that cannot be eliminated entirely. But perhaps it can be worked upon modestly. This very condition of possibility for the dictum not only sets limits to it; commitment to it conveys a responsibility to assess and reassess the specificity of those limits as time flies by. This responsibility is increased by our knowledge of how a tropical undergrowth of limits and exemptions thrives within a habitual practice of pluralism, making it hard for new plants to find a place in the sun. Today the need for reassessment of the limits is accentuated by the acceleration of speed in so many domains of life, by concomitant drives to the pluralization of faith in and across several territorial states, and by fundamentalist reactions to these two developments. There is a growing sense that the historical modus vivendi of secularism carved out of Christendom in a few Western states is no longer adequate to the contemporary demands placed upon it.

Rereading Moses

Sigmund Freud reassessed the animating energies of Judaism and Christianity under distinctive circumstances—in a situation, you might say, of triple urgency. He was dying of cancer, he had been under the fragile protection of a Catholic Church that might turn against him at any moment because of his critical interpretation of monotheism, and he had just fled Vienna in the face of the imminent arrival of troops from Nazi Germany. In these circumstances Freud speaks of the role imagination plays in staging the sweeping historical narratives in which European civilization is set:

> Remote times have a great attraction—sometimes mysteriously so—for the imagination. As often as mankind is dissatisfied with its present—and that happens often enough—it harks back to the past and hopes at last to win belief in the never forgotten dream of a Golden Age. Probably man still stands under the magic spell of his childhood, which a not unbiased memory presents to him as a time of unalloyed bliss. Incomplete and dim memories of the past, which we call tradition, are a great incentive to the artist, for he is free to fill in the gaps in the memories according to the behest of his imagination and to form after his own purpose the image of the time he has undertaken to reproduce. One might almost say that the more shadowy tradition has become the more meet is it for the poet's use.[1]

Freud refers specifically to the role imagination plays in the Jewish story of Exodus and the Pauline story of resurrection and original sin. Moses and Paul are critical to the history he reviews. But it may be reasonable to assume that the statement also speaks to his own role as a countermythologist. For Freud finds it imperative to rethink the archaic origins of Judaism and Christianity during a time when anti-Semitism threatens the very existence of Jews in Europe. He exercises his psychoanalytic imagination upon two discrepant, interlaced stories to see what new possibilities might be squeezed out of them.

The Freudian counterstory is familiar in broad outline. Judaism, a faith grounded in "the law of the father," was founded by Moses, an Egyptian prince with a stammer occasioned by the imperative to speak to the wandering "tribe" in a tongue foreign to him. Moses enforced the alien religion of a universal God, whose image was not to be shown, upon a people who practiced idol worship before his intervention, and who reverted to a volcano god, Jahve, after his death — "an uncanny demon who walks by night and shuns the light of day."[2] Moses used the opportunity the fleeing Israelites provided to inculcate into the Jews the faith his father, Pharaoh Ikhanaton, had tried to install into the Egyptian people in the fourteenth century B.C.E. That faith, as Egyptologist Jan Assmann confirms through evidence unavailable to Freud, insisted that magical rites were superstitions, that other gods were false, and that its God, as stated in the hymn to it, was "the sole God beside whom there is none."[3] The introduction of circumcision, imported from Egypt, both sanctifies conversion to a new faith and carries forward the fragmentary memory of those fathers who enforced celibacy among tribal sons in archaic times. Resenting his implacable rule, however, the tribe eventually killed Moses and covered up its deed. The experience of guilt in that execution is compounded by the "memory traces" it activates of the primal killing by sons of patriarchs in prehistoric times who held a monopoly of sexual rights over women.

Freud's story, as reviewed so far, reflects an interplay between historical evidence and the assumptions of psychoanalytic theory. But why does Freud not just tell a counterstory without attaching those historical hooks? He may think he must do so to counter the power of the official story. In that story, Moses is a Hebrew boy floated down the river in a basket by his mother to save his life; he is then picked up by a pharoah's daughter and then returns to his people as an adult to save them. The traditional story is supported by historical evidence filtered through the texts and assumptions of Judaic faith. It may, then, take a counterstory with historical hooks of its own to disturb and jostle the hold of the official story. And Freud thinks it is essential to disrupt the official story. Moreover, even some nonbelieving Jews (and Christians in turn) may turn out to be more committed to the historicity of the official Moses than they had imagined, once confronted with a Moses said to be Egyptian. Freud may think that he can accomplish the critical effect he seeks only by interpreting available historical evidence through the lens of psychoanalytic theory, rather than merely reconstructing the story from the resources of the latter alone. He *is* working on collective memory supported by a sacred text, rather than trying to develop a historical account separate from that memory; but included in the collective memory he probes is a set of assumptions about correspondences between the memory and facts of history that legitimate it. It is this combination that makes it so shocking to say, "Moses was an Egyptian." For what it's worth—and I don't claim it is worth that much—I suspect that if you could suspend the assumptions and hopes of both believers and Freud, Freud's story would turn out to contain about as much historical doubt and credibility as the one he contests. But again, it is because he purports to hook onto history filtered through the truths of psychoanalysis that the Freudian account is disturbing. This disturbance itself may reveal the extent to which many, at one level or another, invest the traditional story with historical credibility.[4]

But why is it so important for Freud to revise the story in a way that disturbs supporters of the official version? Let us continue with the countermyth. Centuries after its founder's death, the Mosaic faith returns with new vigor to a people whose prophets had never let it die entirely. It is a more intellectual and ethical religion than those preceding it, partly because of its refusal to picture or name the deity and partly because of its resistance to the magical rites of paganism. But the return of the Mosaic monotheistic, universal god is marred. The Jews, expressing darkly the source of their faith in a foreigner and the guilt of their ancestors in killing the foreign founder, define themselves to be the "chosen people" of the universal god. Here is what Freud says at this juncture:

> Still more astonishing is the conception of a god suddenly "choosing" a people, making it "his" people and himself its own god. I believe it is the only case in the history of human religions.... Sometimes, it is true, we hear of a people adopting another god, but never of a god choosing a new people. Perhaps we approach an understanding of this unique happening when we reflect on the connection between Moses and the Jewish people. Moses had stooped to the Jews, had made them his people; they were his "chosen people."

Or again:

> He retained the character of a universal god who reigned over all lands and people; the fact, however, that his worship had passed from the Egyptians to the Jews found its expression in the added doctrine that the Jews were *his* chosen people, whose special obligation would in the end find their special reward.[5]

It now becomes clear why Freud presses the idea that the founder of Judaism was a great stranger, an Egyptian. He not only seeks to underline the syncretic origins of religions that take themselves to be unique and pure, he hopes that his revision in the late 1930s of the story of Exodus will encourage Jews to give up the definition of themselves as the chosen people. To redefine that aspect of the faith would be to subtract from Judaism an element that has historically incited many Christians to anti-Semitism. Freud is willing to risk the ugly label "self-hating Jew" to challenge one characteristic of a faith from which he otherwise draws so much sustenance. "It is honor enough for the Jewish people that it has kept alive such a tradition and produced men who lent it their voice, even if the stimulus had first come from outside, from a great stranger."[6]

It is one thing to risk disfavor from the bearers of a faith with which you identify, another to criticize the Catholic Christianity professed by the majority of people in your host country during the early stages of the Nazi Holocaust. Freud feared that his protection by the Catholic Church in Austria would be relinquished if he published his findings there; the new Moses risked becoming a new voice in the wilderness when he did publish them in 1939 while living in England.

Nonetheless, he proceeds politely and steadily. Pauline Christianity, he argues, is infiltrated by pagan elements, through, for example, the proliferation of divine images, the paradoxical pluralization of divinity in the Trinity, and the veiled reintroduction of a mother goddess in Mary. Pauline Christianity is also anchored in a triple accusation against Jews. First "they" are charged with exposing Jesus to crucifixion. Second, partly because Judaism provided the preliminary materials from which Christian monotheism was crafted, Jews are singled out as a particularly obstinate people, too proud to convert to the universal faith launched in their midst. And third, Jews are implicitly charged with denying the basis of their own faith in the killing of its founder, while Pauline Christians acknowledge the sacrifice of Christ for them and, through Paul's remarkable doctrine of original sin, darkly touch the archaic past, when the sons killed the implacable patriarch governing the clan. The sacrifice of Jesus allows Christianity to become a "Son religion" and opens Christians to the probability of intense resentment against the presence of the "Father religion" on the lands they control.[7] But the basic energy of anti-Semitism can be summarized in the following dictum: Too many northern Europeans, converted as late as the Middle Ages from paganism to Christianity, resent the pious demands and salvational uncertainties of the new faith they explicitly affirm. It is too unnerving to express that resentment against the authorities that be or, even worse, against the Christian God they depend upon for salvation. So it is projected upon the living bearers of that faith from which Christianity is derived, upon those who had been habituated to some aspects of the new faith for centuries but were still too stubborn to bow before the very Christ who grew up in their midst. The Great Refusal of Jews is therefore not only resented actively, it is also envied secretly. Freud writes:

> One might say they [the Christians] are all "badly christened"; under the thin veneer of Christianity they have remained what their ancestors were, barbarically polytheistic. They have not yet overcome their grudge against the new religion which was forced upon them, and they have projected it onto the source from which Christianity came to them. The fact that the Gospels tell a story which is enacted among Jews, and in truth treats only of Jews, has facilitated such a projection. The hatred for Judaism is at bottom hatred for Christianity, and it is not surprising that in the German National Socialist revolution this close connection of the two monotheistic religions finds such clear expression in the hostile treatment of both.[8]

Let us set aside for later discussion Freud's own citation of the "barbarically polytheistic" ancestors of Christianity. This remarkable paragraph condenses the thematic upshot of *Moses and Monotheism*, even though—to my knowledge—that theme has not received nearly as much attention as the Freudian rendering of the origins of Judaism. There is a soft line of repetition between Freud's account of the origins of Judaism, with its theme of the internal mobilization of resentment against the foreign propagator, and his account of the relation between Christianity and the living representatives of the past from which it sprang. The Pauline founding of Christianity, after the death of Jesus, expresses an anti-Semitism that is both doctrinal and visceral—doctrinal in its resentment of the people who provide the inspirational materials from which the new faith is forged because of their very refusal to acknowledge the universal truth it so readily makes available to them, visceral in that resentment by Christians themselves against the stringent demands and salvational insecurities of Christianity sets up this minority inside Europe but outside Christianity to become explicit targets of that animus. What is to be done?

Memory Traces and Practical Exercises

Freud hopes his retelling of the Mosaic story will help to redefine an element in Judaism that foments prejudice against Jews. Perhaps he also hopes that Christian activists will pick up the cudgels from their side in the aftermath of the Holocaust, reassessing elements within Christianity that foster anti-Semitism. Clearly, many have done so in the interim between 1939 and today. Among the philosophically inclined

I would single out Gerald Bruns, Fred Dallmayr, Karl Jaspers, Paul Ricoeur, Elaine Pagels, David Tracy, and Charles Taylor as particularly noble. The problem, though, is that Freud's account of the ugly element within Pauline Christianity identifies a few elements so deeply rooted that it is difficult to see how work on the doctrines and sensibilities of Christians (and Christian secularists) could reach them. To put the point differently, Freud's thesis of the overdetermination of resentment in Christianity pictures a faith in a poor position to become forbearing and generous to those inside and outside the faith who call the universality of its doctrine into question. Since it is unlikely that psychoanalytic faith, which treats "the hypothesis" of monotheism in general as delusional and compensatory, will become the operational faith of most people, it remains pertinent to ask how Christianity could modify itself in the relevant respects. The risk of *Moses and Monotheism* is that its deep story line operates to entrench the phenomenon it seeks to overcome.

To probe that risk, I will focus on Freud's account of "memory traces," paying particular attention to the putative role those alleged "traces" play in Christianity. My sense is that Freud is onto something important in his engagement with traces but that his historical overdetermination of them may be susceptible to revision. A trace, let us say, is enough like a thought to affect linguistically sophisticated thoughts and judgments, and not enough like a thought to be susceptible to direct inspection. A trace is a memory fragment that does not take the form of an explicit recollection. Because it is both fast in its arrival and fragmentary in its shape, it cannot be *recollected* in itself, even after psychoanalysis, although it can be *interpreted* through psychoanalysis. It becomes, however, marked by affective intensity once triggered by an appropriate event. It can thus be powerful in its efficacy in the present, even if not determinant enough to become a clear memory of the past. It is for these very reasons resistant to modification by direct intellectual or interpretive means alone, for it does not assume the shape of a linguistically sophisticated thought demarcated through numerous relations of contrast and similarity to other ideas; nonetheless, it can be fueled by intense energy.

The experience of trauma possesses some characteristics of a memory trace. Years after a distressing battlefield experience, a sudden sound or unexpected smell in some way associated with it can trigger a painful reenactment of that experience. The sound or smell activates a "trace" attached to other painful memories. In a memory trace, the triggering mechanism touches something in the past not susceptible in principle to conscious recollection, although imaginative stories or narratives may touch it in uncanny ways. A triggering event may activate in an adult traces from infancy, even before the individual had access to language. To take an example that Freud alludes to without amplifying, attendance at a bris by a man who was himself circumcised may provoke intense but cognitively vague feelings from the past that infiltrate into the man's contemporary conduct and identifications. Rituals of various sorts, practiced in conjunction with devoutly professed stories, may activate collective traces that would otherwise remain latent.

Freud inserts such traces not only into the early life of the child but also into the early life of the species. He suggests, with a combination of intellectual hesitancy and experimental persistence, that all humans (females too?) carry traces of guilt over the primordial killing of the father by sons who resented his sexual monopoly and identified with his role. This memory is not the repression of a full-scale event that we could picture again if we brought it up for review. It is a trace in that affectively imbued thought *fragments* of the event are deposited in the recesses of the brain. The "archaic heritage of mankind," says Freud, "includes not only dispositions, but also ideational contents, memory traces of the experiences of former generations."[9] These traces became intensively reactivated by the deaths of Moses and Jesus, respectively. They did so because of the similarity the more recent events bear to the primal events. The neuroscientist Joseph LeDoux, for example, would perhaps say that the triggering events tap into the memory of the amygdala, an intense little brain nodule capable of sending, storing, and receiving only crude messages. The amygdala registers traumatic events in a rough-and-ready way. It then both incites immediate action and sends out fast, intense signals to the slower, more refined brain regions for processing in a more complex way.[10]

Memory traces are, as it were, virtual. That is, they are real without being actual: they exert effects (hence are real) without themselves being refined enough to be direct objects of existential inspection (hence lacking actuality). The killing of Jesus, for Freud, awakens the memory trace of the killing of Moses, and the killing of Moses activates a trace of the primal killing. "The awakening . . . of the memory trace through a recent real repetition of the event is certainly of decisive importance. The murder of Moses was such a repetition and, later on, the supposed judicial murder of Christ, so that these events move into the foreground as causative agents."[11] The legacy of guilt and resentment Freud discerns in Christianity, then, is grounded in the prehistory of religion in general as well as in the Pauline founding of Christianity. It is because it is inscribed in that part of the psychic life not amenable to intellectual regulation alone that Freud is so wary of purely intellectual proposals of reform.

Freud, therefore, is confident that his story — his attempt at intellectual reformation — will be implausible at first to most people. Implausible because of the length of time it covers, because of its conflict with the official stories, because of its dependence upon a biological theory of inherited traces, because of the uncertain topography and weird trajectory of those traces carried across innumerable generations, and because of the continued effects of the traces themselves upon those who encounter the revised story. But he nonetheless thinks his story brings out characteristic features of monotheism that otherwise remain inexplicable. He wants the new story to tap into memory traces that could never be uncovered directly as explicit memories, and hence he knows that his story is not in principle susceptible to definitive historical validation. But he seems to hope that his revision could eventually help to modify some of the destructive elements in, or potentialities of, monotheism. Perhaps he thinks that story tokens or story types become deeply inscribed in our brains, so that we keep reiterating the same models even when they are applied to secular materials. And perhaps he wonders whether those tokens themselves could be modified.

I suspect that Freud's idea of memory traces is partly on the right track, while his insistence on grounding them in primordial events is overplayed. It is not that biological theory has definitively disproved the possibility Freud endorses.[12] I doubt that it has done so definitively, despite what people say. And I concede that Freud's interpretation of the staying power of the Pauline doctrine of original sin resonates with his thesis. For he takes that doctrine to be powerful because it refers not only to the fateful actions of Adam and Eve as interpreted by Paul, but also more darkly to the primal killing of patriarchs who were later deified by their killers. Even recent experiments with rats could be taken to reopen slightly a door most of us thought had been closed definitively. These are the rats that react with intense fear upon seeing a cat, even when they have never before seen a cat or been in the company of adult rats who manifest such fear. Nonetheless, I jump nervously off the Freudian bandwagon at this juncture, offering three interwoven rationalizations to vindicate a leap in midair before they were imagined. The first revolves around a doubt concerning whether and how such an intense trauma could be inherited across so many generations. The second revolves around the anthropological (and, as we shall see, Jamesian) idea that the variety of religious experience is less confined and more diverse than Freud suggests. And the third revolves around an unwillingness to lend ammunition to the idea of race that may be implied by this speculative theory of inheritance across innumerable generations. The idea, then, is to *bracket* Freud's presumption of the inheritance of primordial memory traces without closing the door to revisiting it. At the same time, I *retain* the idea of memory traces intersubjectively created and layered into corporeo-cultural life across historical time.

On this view, it takes the reiteration of intensive practices of numerous sorts to transport such traces across generations, and these reiterations, one imagines, acquire significant variation as they are dragged through time. If you bracket the primordial dimension of Freud's theory while retaining a revised idea of memory traces, it still remains clear why intellectual reform — in storytelling, deliberation, argument, interpretation, conscious judgment, and so on — is relevant but inadequate to modification of a faith. Reinterpretation in conjunction with practices and exercises that tap into an affective region of life beyond the reliable reach of interpretation may be needed. This is a disturbing idea, but perhaps also an unavoidable one.

Mystical States and Deep Pluralism

If you attend to the idea of intensive memory traces transmitted imperfectly across generations, you also enter the territory of what William James calls "the religious experience." Such experiences are intensive as well as ineffable.[13] But James explores positive elements in subliminal experience not really registered by Freud. If part of your agenda is to interrogate the supremacy of a father religion and the corollary idea of morality as law inscribed in the Mosaic, Augustinian, and Kantian traditions, then Freud takes you in the right direction, for he treats the experience of guilt and law to be secondary civilizational formations rather than either literally commanded by a nameless divinity or expressive of the apodictic moral subjectivity of humankind. He thus challenges Moses, Paul, and Kant. But in doing so he tends to reduce the religious experience per se to a civilizational neurosis anchored in archaic memories of guilt. He does not find much in the subliminal life itself from which to draw positive sustenance in supporting an ethic of cultivation over a morality of law or a robust tradition of pluralism over frantic insistence upon religious unity. Indeed, he tends to put psychoanalysis in the place just taken away from the one true religious faith.

William James, the hesitant Protestant with Unitarian proclivities, steps into the fray at precisely these points. He emphasizes both the variety of religious experiences and the generic element of the ineffable in them. He does not even demand that faith be anchored in a personal God to count as faith. He thus rules Buddhism in as a mode of religious experience. But, curiously to me, he rules Epicureanism out, even though both Buddhism and Epicureanism take you to the ineffable and neither places a personal god at the end point of its faith. I forgive James this slight against my (quasi-pagan) faith — one that has found minority expression across the long stretch of Western history in the thought of Epicurus, Lucretius, Spinoza, Nietzsche, Deleuze, and Stengers — because his definition of religious experience is otherwise so good at overcoming two risks commonly courted by such attempts. The first is the risk of restricting the appreciation of religious experience so sharply that only your own doctrine could provide a plausible example of it; the second is the risk of locating the religious experience in a form of neurosis that you could overcome only by transcending the impulse to religiosity per se. Paul, for instance, seems to me to succumb to the first risk in his reading of the Jews and pagans of his day; some of Freud's most programmatic statements succumb to the second.[14] Indeed, if a definition escapes the first it already inclines toward the second. And vice versa.

James tries to express the positive element in religious experience by bracketing as far as possible the contending doctrines and institutional practices to which it is attached. This is an impossible objective, in its purity. And he knows it. For example, Jewish experience is underrepresented in this text, perhaps because of James's own emphasis on the significance of the conversion experience. But the attempt nonetheless issues in something productive. The people whose self-reports James quotes at length recall mystical experiences. Interestingly, in terms of his relation to Freud, James finds hypnosis to open a window onto the fugitive taxonomy of religious experience. Hypnosis involves a temporary shift in one's conduct originated below the level of direct intellectual control. The religious experience, like it, wells up from a region below higher intellectual control into the conscious life, but, less like it, is typically a radiant experience that often exercises a profound, long-term effect on one's life.

In seeking, at least initially, an account of religious experience open to interpretation in both theological and atheological terms, James puts himself into conflict with some proponents of Christianity and psychoanalysis alike. Many of the former warrant such experiences as real only if they are given a theistic rendering, and some of the latter contend that they have ample psychoanalytic evidence to enclose such experiences in a naturalistic account. This is how, for instance, James speaks to "orthodox Christians" who might resist his phenomenological readings because they seem to remain agnostic about the role of divinity in them. He is talking about the differences between those who experience a sudden conversion and those who slide into it gradually:

> One word more, though . . . , lest the final purpose of my explanation of suddenness by subliminal activity be misunderstood. I do indeed believe that if the Subject have no liability to such subconscious activity, or if his conscious fields have a hard ring of a margin that resists incursions from beyond it, his conversion must be gradual if it occur, and must resemble any simple growth of new habits. . . . But if you, being orthodox Christians, ask me as a psychologist whether the reference of a phenomenon to a subliminal self does not ex-

clude the notion of the direct presence of the Deity altogether, I have to say frankly that as a psychologist I do not see why it necessarily should.... But just as our primary wide-awake consciousness throws open our senses to the touch of things material, so it is logically conceivable that *if there be* higher spiritual agencies that can directly touch us, the psychological condition of their doing so *might be* our possession of a subconscious region which alone should yield access to them. The hubbub of the waking life might close a door which in the dreamy Subliminal might remain ajar or open.[15]

But perhaps objections to James's reading of mystical experience will also come from another direction, from some materialists and nontheists who doubt that there is such a "subconscious region" of experience, however interpreted. Our engagement with Freud's account of memory traces may have gone some way toward weakening that judgment. Consider as well the work of V. S. Ramachandran, a brain researcher at the Salk Institute for Biological Studies. According to Ramachandran, a small subset of people who have epileptic seizures have a "focal" type of seizure; it generates a process of "kindling" between the lower brain nodules and the limbic system. The result is often something very much like a mystical experience:

> But most remarkable of all are those patients who have deeply moving spiritual experiences, including a feeling of divine presence and the sense that they are in direct communication with God.... I find it ironic that this sense of enlightenment, this absolute conviction that Truth is derived at last, should derive from limbic structures concerned with emotions rather than from the thinking, rational parts of the brain that take so much pride in their ability to discern truth and falsehood.[16]

Let's not worry about the "irony" by which Ramachandran seems to reserve thinking to the higher structures, for he later acknowledges the dependence of the higher brain regions on the limbic structures in thinking and judgment. The point now, perhaps, is to compare the young girl laughing when the probe touches exactly the right spot on her brain (discussed in the previous chapter) to the mystical experience that sometimes accompanies focal seizures. The general capacity the girl has for laughter is triggered by the probe at one moment and by other signs at other moments, when, for instance, funny things are said in her presence. The same thing might be true of mystical experience. The probe and the seizure may both tap into a human capacity that can be triggered in other ways as well—by a seizure in one instance, say, and a religious experience in another. The first question before us is: Do some humans have a capacity for mystical experiences that is more developed than that of most humans? Ramachandran's study lends some support to the idea that they do.

Ramachandran reinforced this point by running an experiment with two clients who reported intense religious experiences. They were exposed to a variety of artifacts, including scenes of violence and sexually explicit pictures and words, all of which stimulate intense feelings in most people. A galvanic skin response (GSR) meter was attached to them:

> What about the patients? The kindling hypothesis would predict a uniform high response to all categories. But to our amazement what we found in the two patients tested was a heightened response mainly to religious words and icons. Their responses to the other categories, including the sexual words and images . . . was normally diminished compared to what is seen in normal individuals.[17]

James, of course, was alert to the biological and psychological research of his day, and his philosophical psychology itself has become an icon of sorts to several neuroscientists engaged in this study. The mystical experiences to which James and Ramachandran allude usually find expression as a radiant feeling of joy and generosity. If Damasio is right, these experiences, flowing into consciousness from a subliminal (or virtual) register, do not pass through the network in which the amygdala is centered, for the amygdala is bound to the generation of fear, anxiety, and depression. As Damasio puts it: "The amygdala, however, has little interest in recognizing or learning about disgust or happiness. Importantly, other structures, just as specifically, are interested in those other emotions."[18] We might say that the Freud of *Moses and Monotheism*, writing under the shadow of Nazism, explored those relays in which the amygdala plays a critical role.

James seeks to explore radiant mystical states, but to do so in such a way that disables any church, faith, or secular authority from dictating to everyone what doctrinal interpretation must be attached to them. His larger point is that absent the mystical or subliminal layer of being, humans would lack the energy, existential trust, and positive affect needed to get on in life. We may differ, however, in the degree to which we have access to mystical states. And we often enough find ourselves plunged into struggles over contending doctrines tied to the very experiences that are, to put it in the mild terms James himself prefers, difficult to articulate, for the sources of such experience subsist below the threshold of pure representation. So

James strives to convert his readers — many of whom have already undergone at least one conversion experience as born-again Christians or born-again atheists — to three themes, each subject to qualification by the others:

(1) Mystical states, when well developed, usually are, and have the right to be, absolutely authoritative over the individuals to whom they come.

(2) No authority emanates from them which should make it a duty for those who stand outside of them to accept their revelations uncritically.

(3) They break down the authority of the non-mystical or rationalistic consciousness, based upon the understanding and the senses alone. They show it to be only one kind of consciousness. They open out the possibility of other orders of truth, in which, so far as anything in us vitally responds to them, we may freely continue to have faith.[19]

It would be easy to deconstruct these injunctions. The first, for instance, contains a qualifier, "usually," that could undercut the robust pluralism it supports if pursued very far; and yet if that qualifier were simply dropped, obvious and immediate counterinstances could be brought against the formula. The phrase "absolutely authoritative" ignores multiple side perceptions within the self that might eventually encourage one to contest the authority invested in that experience, as well as third-person studies that might show how it is induced artificially in some instances.

James also has a tendency to separate the feelings he delineates too sharply from the interpretations that help to fix them. This tendency can be corrected through a highlighting of the paradoxical character of the states themselves: the sources from which the experiences emanate subsist below the threshold of pure representation, yet to become consolidated as experiences, they must be invested with interpretation.

With these qualifications and revisions I receive James's maxims less as fixed formulas and more as an invitation to cultivate a *sensibility* within individuals and an *ethos* in the political culture, a sensibility in which strong presumptions in favor of deep pluralism become embodied in the subliminal field of participants and an ethos of appreciation for pluralism that becomes entrenched in public life itself.

It is inordinate, this call to deep pluralism. It makes the checks and balances of Madisonian and Millian pluralism, situated in the predominantly Christian culture of a time that moved more slowly, look like child's play. We are, so it seems, to honor our existential faith in the first instance, according to whatever work it takes to do so, and then to cultivate self-modesty about its applicability to others in order to promote deep pluralism. We are, that is, not only to be born again, but also to grow up a second time. The latter we do by working on ourselves—within those very religious and secular institutions through which the first faith was consolidated—to activate visceral appreciation of the contestability of that faith and to cultivate a presumption of receptive generosity to other faiths. James thus rejects a bland ecumenism in which the parties connect only through a thin reed of commonality, although he is tempted by that route. He endorses a deep pluralism that places stringent demands on the participants. That idea, as we saw in chapter 2, will seem like an oxymoron to some.

James applies the idea of deep pluralism not only to the bearers of different "religious" faiths, but also to secular, rationalistic, and, well, psychoanalytic faiths that sometimes take themselves to rise above the status of deep contestability. Secularism contains a measure of intolerance to which its proponents are sometimes tone-deaf, if and as it treats its faith in the sufficiency of public reason, deliberation, intellectualism, justice, or procedure to be entirely above faith. And when it ignores or deprecates, as it often does, the significance of the visceral register of being to thinking, judgment, and public culture.

Freud takes a couple of steps in the direction commended by James, through his imagination of Moses as Egyptian and his call to revise selective elements within Judaism and Christianity that render the faith of the other too lowly. Many, however, are likely to find the call to deep pluralism to be sacrilegious, politically unrealistic, or both. But let's continue down the path opened by Freud and James anyway. Negotiation of an ethos of deep pluralism is the most promising way to extend freedom in a state already inhabited by proponents of multiple faiths; it is also the best way to promote generous cross-state and cross-civilizational relations in a diverse world that is smaller than heretofore because it spins faster. It is, of course, "unrealistic." Christianity, Protestantism, secularism, the territorial state, constitutionalism, democracy, feminism, and gay rights were also unrealistic before they surged into being as new formations. And everything not yet consolidated as a new formation always appears implausible or unrealistic to realists. The question is whether it is important to pursue this agenda in the contemporary era—and whether there is some reason to think it may subsist as a possibility to be promoted.

What James does not do is tell us much about *how* such an intercultural sensibility is to be mixed into the experience of faith. Perhaps his decision to ignore the institutional and doctrinal dimensions of religious life contributes to that omission. So Freud identifies traces that exceed the reach of the counterstory he tells, while James celebrates subliminal states that extend below his intellectual call for pluralism. What if deep pluralism requires work upon the same register of life on which radiant religious experience resides?

Deep Pluralism and Relational Arts

Where have we wandered? (1) Faith of some sort is ubiquitous to a species in which ineffable experience and memory traces flow into intellectual life. (2) Partly for that reason, a variety of institutionally organized interpretations of religious experience are likely to flower, unless many flowers are pulled out by the roots. (3) Since the honor of a god, the claim to authority of a state, or the prospect of eternal salvation can hang in the balance, theological disputes are often marked by intense struggle over the type of faith to be sanctioned by the state or the type of state to be sanctioned by faith. One political response to this condition is to have the sovereign define the official religion. Hobbes and Rousseau follow such a line, in different ways. Tocqueville follows it too, by making Christianity a civilizational condition for the success of American democracy. A more valiant response is secularism in which religious diversity is shuffled into the private realm. Rawls and Habermas pursue versions of that approach. But the sovereign response requires violent repression of the diversity already there. And secularism is often blind to the element of dogmatic faith in its conception of reason or deliberation and tone-deaf to the politics of becoming. Its proponents, by remaining deaf to the visceral register in ethical and political life, too often paint an aura of sufficiency around deliberation or public reason that neither can sustain. In response, I explore a third vision—a deep pluralism nourished by a generous ethos of engagement. But such an ethos requires micropolitical work on the subliminal register. And that work itself can sometimes be dangerous to diversity.

Let us, then, explore further the relations among deep pluralism, spiritual exercise, and micropolitics by returning to Freud's attempt to narrow the range of relational arts through which work is done on the visceral register of individuals and groups. Freud moves cautiously toward deep pluralism, but the founder of the talking cure is encumbered by a too-restrictive view of the self-artistry by which receptivity to this end might be cultivated. One reason for this reserve, doubtless, is those memory traces that reach back to primordial times. It would be difficult to modify them if they are as entrenched as Freud takes them to be. You could at most try to overcome them. Which is why Freud (in *Moses and Monotheism*, at least) thinks of ethics mostly on the model of instinctual renunciation. There is also the Freudian idea that ethics at its highest rises above crude instruments such as images, rhythm, ritual, trance, hypnosis, and magic. Moses, "the great stranger," introduced a more spiritual God to the Jewish people, "one as all loving as he was all-powerful, who, averse to all ceremonial and magic, set humanity as its highest aim a life of truth and justice."[20] This means, first, that the intellect is engaged to control the lower instincts and, second, that corporeal gymnastics such as ceremony, image, and magic are to be minimized, because they are historically associated with pagan faiths that pander to "the athletic virtues." So what Freud admires most about the effect of the Mosaic faith upon Jews is how it "formed their character for good through the disdaining of magic and mysticism by encouraging them to progress in spirituality and sublimations."[21] Why? It "signified subordinating sense perception to an abstract idea; it was a triumph of spirituality over the senses; more precisely an instinctual renunciation accompanied by its psychologically necessary consequences."[22] And the athletic virtues, Freud says, are associated historically with cruel, military cultures.

Perhaps it is wise to refuse to represent or picture experiences of divinity that do not assume a form susceptible to representation. Such a refusal could open the self to more creative, experimental relations to mystical, subliminal sources of inspiration. But it is also critical to liberate the "athletic virtues" from monopoly by the martial arts. I agree, of course, that intellectual regulation of socially developed instincts is one critical strategy of ethics. But Freud's syncretic urge hesitates just when it might have drawn more sustenance from pagan practices endorsed by generous, nonmilitary, nontheistic souls such as Epicurus and Lucretius. Freud's depreciation of paganism in general may have encouraged him, first, to invest too much therapeutic efficacy in the talking cure (even though lying on the couch is itself a corporeal tactic); second, to draw the line of distinction between personal therapy and political ethics at the wrong point; and third, to fail to see how crucial relational, multimedia arts are to ethical life.

Mikkel Borch-Jacobsen contends that Freud, after his early period, resisted acknowledgment of the relation between his own practice of therapy and hypnosis. But "transference," the linchpin of the analytic relation, says Jacobsen, is very much like hypnosis. It engenders a magical shift in the organization of affect fostered through identification with the therapist. The clean separation Freud sought between analysis and hypnosis breaks down in the practice of transference.

> Freud made this point in 1912 in an article on "The Dynamics of Transference," and it means among other things that it was becoming more and more difficult, even impossible, to distinguish between the mechanics of analysis and those of hypnosis, even though hypnosis was supposed to have been discarded once and for all. If the transference tends to dominate the whole analytical situation, and if the analyst's silence, rather than keeping the transference at bay, actually provokes it, then one can no longer oppose,

as Freud had done earlier, the pure interpretative listening of the analyst to the direct suggestion of the hypnotist, or the interventionism of the hypnotist to the abstentionism of the analyst.... We might go so far as to say that the whole analytical process moves once again toward the establishment of a hypnotic type of "rapport," in which the subject speaks and thinks like another, and even toward an actual state of trance.[23]

Jacobsen goes on to explore latent connections between analytic therapy and shamanism, treating them as overlapping strategies to reorganize affective dispositions operating below the threshold of representation and intellectual regulation alone. While applauding Jacobsen's attempt to reduce the distance between therapy and shamanism, I want to consider what falls out in the corollary tendency to treat ethical arts of the self as if they were reducible to therapies to relieve neuroses. Freudian and neo-Kantian theory, differing so significantly in other respects, converge in giving low credibility to relational arts of ethical life. Freud does so to ward off the athletic virtues of pagan militarism; neo-Kantians do so to protect the intellectual purity of morality. To call a tactic of the self a "therapy" in the neo-Kantian tradition today is to quarantine it from morality because it falls below action governed by deliberation and the moral will, even though Kant himself maintained a modest role for "gymnastics" in the moral life as he conceived it.

The difference between therapy and ethics, to me, is not that the first adopts a variety of arts for shaping thought-imbued affect while the second operates through the will and intellectual principle alone. Both therapy and ethics in practice draw upon both intellectual capacities and arts of the self. And each is often experimental in the strategies it adopts to reorganize affect. The differences between them are less blatant and elsewhere. You might seek therapy if you suffer conflicts that make it difficult to function in daily life. In the psychoanalytic tradition, at least, therapy occurs under the authority of a trained analyst. Ethical artistry, in its highest forms, is work applied by the self to itself to render its relational proclivities more congruent with principles it professes, or to build up resistance to oppressive institutional disciplines, or to modify a relational pattern of thought or judgment that seems closed, or to put the self in the position of responding more generously to newly emerging identities that call into question the self's implicit sense to embody in its mode of being the dictates of the universal. Ethical work is typically experimental, since it usually occurs in new contexts where established codes show themselves to be too blunt and crude and new patterns of visceral judgments have not yet been consolidated. You do not know exactly what you are doing when you participate in it. But such work is not merely experimental, it is also, as we saw in the last chapter, ubiquitous. We are constantly being bombarded by multimedia tactics applied to several layers of being, and we regularly develop strategies to work on ourselves in modest ways not incorporated into the intellectualist narratives of moral theory.

To appreciate the ubiquitous role of tactics, exercises, and artistry to ethical life, it is necessary either to extend the idea of therapy beyond the treatment of neurosis or to distinguish ethical exercises from therapeutic interventions by attending more closely to a host of corporeal practices already bound to the ethical life. Ethical exercises, moreover, do not merely meld into the sanctified territories of therapeutic and religious practice, they also slide into micropolitics as groups and institutions work on each other through a broad array of tactics. Churches consolidate the faith of their parishioners through multimedia practices such as prayer, ritual, film, liturgy, architectural design, confession, dietary regulations, wedding ceremonies, doctrinal clarification, and music. The professions do it as they organize dinners, award ceremonies, Internet patterns of gossip, informal modes of neglect and punishment, conferences, and editorial boards. Such activities work on intercoded layers of relational being. They help to organize those complex mixtures of word, image, habit, feeling, touch, smell, concept, and judgment that give texture to cultural life. The hope, in these instances, is that the horizontal ties between participants will resonate with the vertical layering within them. And vice versa. The hope for pluralists is that lodged in the interstices between these layers and relays are discrepancies and remainders that generate creative energy for pluralization. Relational sensibilities are sometimes moved or modified by such multimedia means, and, again, this complex interplay between doctrine and tactics works on the affective register of relational life as well as on the conceptual organization mixed into it.

The Apostle

The dense, often intense, relation between mystical/subliminal states and doctrinal representation and interpretation, then, is not only effectuated by gods, genes, traumatic experiences, and neurotransmitters such as dopamine, norepinephrine, serotonin, and acetylcholine, it is also mediated by ritual, tactics, arts, and exercises variously practiced by members of religions of the Book, Buddhists, Freudians, and Nietzscheans, among others.

We can pursue the enigmatic relation between doctrine and exercise within one portion of Christianity by reviewing the experience of an apostle who did not know Jesus directly but nonetheless became a representative of his word. The preacher was at first called Sonny by members of his church, perhaps to mark his special relation to Jesus. He brimmed over with spiritual energy, finding expression in his healing practices, his unrelenting evangelism, his long, Jobian debates with the Lord at night after one disaster or another, and, above all, his exuberant, repetitive appeals to his congregation to chant the name Jee-SUS-uhh in response to his rhythmic questions about faith and doctrine. But it soon becomes clear that Sonny's home life is troubled, the evangelist turns out to be a wife abuser and something of a charlatan. *The Apostle* hovers on the edge of becoming an updated version of *Elmer Gantry*, but it soon turns in new directions.

Life turns sour for Sonny, played brilliantly by Robert Duvall, after he finds his wife snuggling in bed with another Christian. Eventually, overcome by rage, he wields a baseball bat to kill the guy he thinks to be the one, while attending a Little League game in which his kids are playing. After fleeing town he engages in a series of loud, abusive debates with his Lord, late at night. When the two finally negotiate a new peace accord, Sonny christens himself as an apostle in the dirty water of a small lake in southern Louisiana. His self-anointment may invite comparison to Paul, that other apostle who did not know or follow Jesus before his crucifixion. Sonny wanders into a small town, where he eventually founds an interracial, evangelical church among a few down-and-out parishioners. The vibrant mixing of rhythm, music, chanting, and doctrine in this church is inspirational to the struggling parishioners, even as it is bracing to the anonymous, charismatic apostle who ministers to them. It is both disturbing and marvelous to observe the multivalent ways this hard-living man labors upon himself as he works tirelessly on others, transfiguring much of the violence in his soul into evangelical energy. Disturbing because he works so hard to secure an authoritative role above interrogation. Marvelous because his work upon himself to redirect old energies teaches us something about the ubiquity and efficacy of technique. The film closes with the apostle laboring in a work gang after he has been imprisoned for manslaughter.

"Yea, when I walk through the valley of death, who walks with me?" he chants to the gang in rhythm with the swings of their sickles against the thick underbrush. "Jee-SUS-uhh!" they reply in unison with another swing. "Who promises me everlasting salvation?" "Jee-SUS-uhh!" "When I walk down the street who walks with me?" "Jee-SUS-uhh!" "If I go to New York City who walks with me?" "Jee-SUS-uhh," the gang chants again. "Who walks with me in the middle of Times Square?" "Jee-SUS-uhh!" "Who?" "Jee-SUS-uhh!" "Again!" "Jee-SUS-uhh!"

"One more time." "Jee-SUS-uhh!" they chant with louder voices and harder swings. The camera pans out and the scene fades as these thundering questions and answers reverberate in rhythm with the dull thud of sickles against the underbrush.

      The Apostle is marked by a series of "irrational" scene cuts. Jim Jarmusch's *Stranger Than Paradise* is another example of a film punctuated by such cuts. Between the scenes, a black screen stares blankly at you for several seconds, underlining the element of contingency and creativity in the connections forged across scenes. Each cut suggests that you cannot, knowing what you did before, predict the next round of action. That is because *between the scenes* things are happening at the subliminal level, unsusceptible to full self-awareness or third-person representation. After the fact, you can fit the action into a narrative that increases in dissonance and density as it unfolds. This technique resonates with Epicurean-Bergsonian-Prigoginist conceptions of "dissipative structures" in nature that contain elements of unpredictability and self-organization within them, and, even more, with the conduct of passionate, culturally sensitive, linguistically skilled beings endowed with complex body/brain networks.[24] Such cuts, marked in distinctive ways by Nietzsche in written texts (as we saw in chapter 3) and other ways by film directors, signify virtual energies that combine with distinctive events to propel something new into the world. The cuts render the invisibility of these processes visible. Or, better, they represent their unrepresentability. It is precisely these interruptions that are muted by tight narratives, classical natural science, and disembodied theories of culture. We might, then, figure the disjunction between *The Apostle* and its sequel, *The Return of the Apostle*, as an irrational cut.

      The Return of the Apostle has not yet been released, but some who have had a sneak preview are taken with its ability to walk down the forked path of its predecessor. The film, opening at night in the aftermath of a car accident, recalls the opening scene of *The Apostle*. This time, though, the apostle is victim rather than evangelist. He lies alongside an African American companion in a car that has swerved off a deserted road. A middle-aged woman stops to help the semiconscious victims. She hesitates for a moment when she sees the prison shirts they are wearing, but she softens again as she observes the tattered old Bible that has bounced off the dashboard onto the lap of the passenger. Ruth is a woman of working-class background and Jewish heritage. She works for an international computer company and, so it turns out, is clandestinely involved with a group of hackers wanted by the FBI. After giving the two men water from an unfinished bottle of Pellegrino, she takes them to her house, where they hide out for a week.

This woman, it becomes clear through interrogation by the devout escapees, is a Jewish devotee of Jesus.[25] While the apostle is drawn to the Jesus of the Book of John and the letters of Paul, this iconoclastic intellectual is inspired by the earthy Jesus of Luke. She inflects that inspiration in a way that forms syncretic connections to the Reform Judaism she grew up with in Brooklyn. Bookish to a degree, she has been inspired by *The Religion of Jesus the Jew*, as that faith is reviewed by Geza Vermes in a book by that title. She takes seriously the idea that if Moses was an Egyptian by birth or rearing, it makes a comparable difference that Jesus was a Jew. Her eschatalogical Jesus shares something with the Pauline figure, in professing "One God, the Father, maker of heaven and earth, and of things visible and invisible."[26] But her Jesus is not of one substance with the Father; he did not arise from the dead after crucifixion; he does not sit on the right hand of the father, and he shall not return to judge "both the quick and the dead."

Ruth's quirky faith throws the apostle and his companion, Peter, into a quandary. What are they to do with a blasphemous benefactor who is prepared to secure false identification papers for them so they can be born once again? After a series of loud conversations with his Lord, punctuated by a few perusals of Luke, the apostle concludes that Jesus, because his love and beneficence overflow, bestows a variety of religious experiences upon his devotees. This new crisis encourages him to become a bit of a Jamesian.

Peter the hijacker, Ruth the hacker, and the apostle eventually found an interracial congregation outside Memphis called the Syncretic Temple of Jesus. It is Pentecostal in its rhythms, songs, and chants, syncretic in its doctrinal relation to Jesus.[27] Organized as a series of rural temples linked through a sophisticated network of Internet connections, the faith provides a relay point for visceral contact between a large variety of down-and-out people who seek strong medicine, admire the word of Jesus, and inflect that word in theologically diverse ways. Each Saturday-morning meeting, televised from the mother temple, is highlighted by a series of rhetorical questions to the congregation blurted by Peter, the apostle, and Ruth, followed by chants of "Jee-SUS-uhh" from the congregation. In the Syncretic Temple different renderings of the word of Jesus by maverick Catholics, Jews, Protestants, Islamists, and a sprinkling of southern Emersonians are mixed into the rubric of a Pentecostal liturgy. Judeo-Christian Shamanism, you might call it. Or even Judeo-Christian-Jamesian-Shamanism. As one site of doctrinal syncretism and Pentecostal practice, the temple eventually puts pressure on a variety of other faiths to come to terms with elements of syncretism in themselves and the profoundly contestable character of the specific doctrines they confess.

I cannot join the Syncretic Temple at this time. I would, however, be pleased to preach a version of neo-Epicureanism to its members some Saturday morning, if invited to do so.

Pentecostal Pluralization

Freud is wise to respect syncretism, to invoke memory traces, and, therefore, to be wary of pure intellectualism, though his aversion to paganism discourages him from exploring the role of technique and exercise robustly enough. James is astute to invoke mystical experience as a sheet of being that subsists below intellectual sophistication while flowing into the higher intellectual processes, although his study of the varieties of religious experience did not carry him far into the complex relations between institutionalized doctrine and practical tactics. The apostle is provocative in enacting everyday syntheses by which people cultivate trust in life in others even as they work upon their own being, and in suggesting how those practices vary according to the type of medicine needed by people in different subject positions. Ruth is wise too. She knows that in contemporary Western states, with the diverse histories from which each is composed, deep pluralism, among other things, involves multiple readings of the historical meaning and contemporary bearing of Jesus. And some of these readings will extend beyond the cosmology and governance of Christianity. Ruth, in effect, runs a practical test to determine the extent to which a variety of Christians either have always surpassed or now transcend the existential resentment Freud so baldly attributed to them in *Moses and Monotheism*. For Ruth understands that the very practices by which people are inducted into a faith must, in a culture of deep pluralism, be tracked by a micropolitics through which presumptive generosity toward other theistic and nontheistic faiths becomes mixed into the visceral register of being and the public ethos of life. Here the interplay between doctrine and exercise is given a cool twist, as you turn the tactics by which your reflective faith has been secured gently back upon the element of resentment and dogmatism that may be attached to it, doing so out of existential care for different responses to persisting mysteries of existence.

I am not saying that an ethos of deep pluralism is a *probable* achievement today. I am merely suggesting, first, that the actual diversity of theistic and nontheistic faiths today combines with the insufficiency of secular intellectualism to pose the definite need for such an ethos and, second, that the *possibility* of its approximation requires close attention to the relation between practices that impinge on the visceral register of relational life and the doctrinal interpretations we embrace. Political and cultural theory should focus first and foremost on possibilities that speak to pressing needs of the time. Concentration on probabilities alone can be left to bureaucrats and consultants.

A public ethos of deep pluralism does not eliminate politics from life, or sink it into a tub of beautiful souls. It is itself an effect of micro- and macropolitics. It forms the lifeblood of democratic politics by folding creativity and generosity into intracultural negotiations over issues unsusceptible to settlement through preexisting procedure, principle, or interest aggregation alone. On this reading, arts of the self, micropolitics, private and public deliberation, a generous ethos of engagement, and macropolitical action are interconnected, even though valuable dissonances and resistances well up between them.

In the *Ethics* Spinoza says, "Nobody has yet determined the limits of the body's capabilities."[28] That dictum still stands. When you consider the relation of, say, Moses, Jesus, Paul, Freud, and James to the cultural worlds in which they participated and to the world today to which each has added surprising ingredients, it seems pertinent to add a corollary to the first dictum: Nobody has yet determined the limits of cultural capability.

We still do not know, for instance, how deeply entrenched multidimensional pluralism could become. We simply know that it is important today to strive to actualize an ethos of deep, multidimensional pluralism. This is a domain where political speculation, experimentalism, and enactment draw upon the resources of history, knowledge, and experience while stretching beyond them. As the great experiment proceeds, it is wise to pay attention to the registers upon which the cultural dispositions to closure or pluralism are established.[29] Any vision of pluralism that fails to come to terms with the layered texture of being remains imprisoned in a narrow intellectualism insufficient to the world.

S I X

Democracy and Time

A Rift in Time

IN A BRILLIANT LITTLE ESSAY titled "What Time Is It?" Sheldon Wolin contends that the homogeneous, slow time appropriate to a democratic politics of place has been overwhelmed by several "zones of time" moving at different tempos.[1] "Economy" and "culture" now move at a breakneck pace, due to changes in the infrastructure of transportation, communication, and entertainment. The effects on democratic deliberation are pernicious:

> Starkly put, political time is out of synch with the temporalities, rhythms, and pace governing economy and culture. Political time, especially in societies with pretensions to democracy, requires an element of leisure, not in the sense of a leisure class (which is the form in which ancient writers conceived it), but in the sense, say, of a leisurely pace. This is owing to the needs of political action to be preceded by deliberation and deliberation, as its 'deliberate' part suggests, takes time because, typically, it occurs in a setting of competing or conflicting but legitimate considerations. . . . That political time has a preservative function is unsurprising. Since time immemorial political authorities have been charged with preserving bodies, goods, souls, practices and circumscribed ways of life.[2]

Culture and economy are governed by "innovation, change and replacement through obsolescence." The pace they pursue exceeds that appropriate to democratic place and deliberation. Indeed, the contemporary pace of fashion and war threatens to obliterate democratic politics. "Fashion shares with war a certain power: it forces disappearance.... Each is in the business of replacement. Fashion produces new music, dress forms, new language or slogans. Wars produce new economies ('the German miracle'), new cities, new weapons and new wars."[3]

Wolin wants the world to slow down so that democracy can flourish. He wants the politics of place to return. I participate in such a wish to some degree, some of the time. But I also think that it is wise today for democrats to be wary of nostalgia for a world of long, slow time and a circumscribed politics of place. The politics of local place (valorized by Wolin) and the state (valorized by others) are both pertinent to democratic action in the contemporary period. But they are insufficient to it. Those sites of action must be linked to several others. Besides, the very asymmetries of time Wolin delineates can also help diverse constituencies come to terms actively with the historical basis of what they are.

I agree with Wolin that it is possible today to discriminate roughly among several zones of time, in a world where each zone regularly impinges upon the others. The velocity of missile warfare is much greater than that of tanks surging across the border between two desert states, and both of those move much faster than ground troops marching across a border. Rapid eruptions in economic and political life exceed the pace appropriate to democratic deliberation, and the pace of change in religious, moral, sensual, gender, and ethnic identities, while perhaps faster than heretofore, is still slower than the foregoing processes. As we have seen, similar asymmetries of pace operate within the human body/brain network.

It is pertinent to recall how the pace of change in human habit, disposition, sensibility, and cultural ethos does not match the tempo set in the fastest zones Wolin identifies. That's why I am not disposed to assimilate culture to fashion. Thinking, culture, identity, and ethics are stratified processes, involving relays and feedback loops between layers of being operating at different capacities and speeds. So fashion forms a component within culture, rather than serving as the key marker of it. Ethical judgment, for instance, is already well under way before you tend to it consciously.

A world composed of asymmetries of pace is more replete with ambiguity than Wolin acknowledges. On the negative side, the acceleration of speed often supports corporate colonization of new spaces inside and outside highly organized capitalist states. In today's world it is less that the large consume the small, more that fast process overwhelms slow activity. The ensuing politics of capture often foments reactive movements in the name of nationhood and religious purity, expressed as attempts to slow the world down by returning to a unity imagined to have been intact sometime in the past. But to fend off both the takeovers and these reactions to them it is necessary to participate in fast-paced processes. I suspect, then, that coming to terms cautiously but affirmatively with the accelerated pace of life can both foster democratic rule and chasten fundamentalist drives. The irony is that reactive drives to retard the pace of life seldom if ever succeed in promoting that result. They succeed, instead, in locating vulnerable constituencies to hold politically accountable for the fast pace of life.

The acceleration of the fastest zones—and the consequent accentuation of difference in tempo between fast and slow processes—forms a constitutive dimension of the late-modern condition. Only a catastrophic breakdown of the world economy—which is not at all out of the question—could slow down the world enough to conform to the pace of nineteenth-century localism that inspires Wolin's Tocquevillian model of democracy. The acceleration of pace carries danger, then. But it also sets a condition of possibility for achievements that democrats and pluralists prize. The question for me, then, is not how to slow the world down, but how to work with and against a world moving faster than heretofore to promote a positive ethos of pluralism.

There are no guarantees in this domain. But variations of speed do sometimes encourage people to become more modest about what they are in relation to what they are not. The asymmetry between the pace of change in clothing fashion and in school curricula and faith practices, for instance, may have contributed to a positive renegotiation of standards of femininity, piety, chastity, and deference over the past several decades. That new pluralization is still poised in doubt, of course. But, when appropriately addressed, dissonances between zones of time help to nourish a certain modesty about what you are and a spirit of presumptive generosity toward other constituencies. Our engagement with *The Apostle* in the last chapter disclosed one way in which such possibilities can unfold. Evangelical movements often adopt an ambiguous orientation to pace, drawing upon fast-paced media to work upon the visceral register of faith.

A certain asymmetry of pace, then, is critical to democratic pluralism. And yet these same temporal conditions also foster the fragility of democracy. They threaten to turn against the very condition they enable. The judgment that a fast-paced world promotes danger and suffering as well as the possibility of a generous ethos of pluralism encourages me to fold a stutter or break into my vision of democratic politics. A slow, homogeneous world often supports undemocratic hierarchy because it irons out discrepancies of experience through which constituencies can become reflective about self-serving assumptions they habitually use to appraise themselves in relation to others. But in a world marked by asymmetrical zones of speed, it is critical that citizens in a variety of walks of life be provided with structural opportunities for periodic escape and retreat from a fast-paced life. Such retreats enable us to revisit from time to time selective assumptions and dispositions that have gripped us and to refresh our energies to reenter the rat race. In my democratic utopia, for instance, sabbatical leaves would be expanded rather than contracted. Opportunities for midlife education of people in various subject positions would be extended greatly too. Such innovations, of course, are far from sufficient to curtail fixed patterns of hierarchy. But they are pertinent.

Within this preliminary debate between Wolin and me on the relation between democracy and pace there is probably a more elemental difference. To abbreviate, Wolin and I both reject the cyclical image of slow time adopted by many ancients. But I also find myself at odds with progressive, teleological, and linear conceptions of time set against it. Against these four images I embrace the idea of rifts or forks in time that help to constitute it as time. A rift as constitutive of time itself, in which time flows into a future neither fully determined by a discernible past nor fixed by its place in a cycle of eternal return, nor directed by an intrinsic purpose pulling it along. Free time. Or, better, time as becoming, replete with the dangers and possibilities attached to such a world.

A diverse array of thinkers, such as Nietzsche, Kierkegaard, Kafka, Bergson, Arendt, and James, participate in such an image of time. We have already visited versions of it in the thought of Prigogine and Deleuze. Here is the variant enunciated by Nietzsche in *Thus Spoke Zarathustra*. The key statement occurs while Zarathustra is addressing the "vision" and "riddle" of time through reference to the fugitive character of the "moment." He is debating a "dwarf" who embodies the spirit of gravity. They have just halted before a gateway on their walk:

> "Behold this gateway, dwarf!" I continued, "It has two faces. Two paths meet here; no one has yet followed either to its end. This long lane stretches back for an eternity. And the long lane out there, that is another eternity. They contradict each other, these paths; they offend each other face to face; and it

is here at this gateway that they come together. The name of the gateway is inscribed 'Moment.'...do you believe, dwarf, that these paths contradict each other eternally?"

"All that is straight lies" the dwarf murmured contemptuously. "All truth is crooked; time itself is a circle."[4]

It appears at first that Zarathustra supports a linear conception of determinism against the dwarf's cyclical picture of eternal return. That would be ironic for the thinker himself reputed to be a proponent of eternal return. But such a reading soon dissolves into another that folds eternal return into an acyclical philosophy of time. What returns eternally is the dissonant conjunction of the moment. In every moment, the pressures of the past enter into a dissonant conjunction with uncertain possibilities of the future. The fugitive present is both constituted by this dissonant conjunction between past and present and rendered uncertain in its direction by it. Often enough that uncertainty is resolved through continuity; but below the threshold of human attention indiscernible shifts and changes have accumulated, sometimes finding expression in small mutations and sometimes in large events. So occasionally time forks in new and surprising directions. A rift in time, engendered by the dissonant conjunction between complex systems with some capacity for self-organization and unexpected events not smoothly assimilable by them. A rift through which at any moment a surprising fork *may* emerge, ushering microscopic, small, large, or world historical shifts into an open future unsusceptible to full coverage by a smooth narrative, sufficient set of rules, or tight causal explanation. The key to a more generous ethic, according to Zarathustra, is that you work on yourself to affirm rather than resent the rift in time that forms a constitutive condition of existence.

Politics is rendered possible and dangerous by the constitutive rift in the moment. "Becoming"—that uncertain process by which the new flows or surges into being—is rendered possible by the rift. Nietzsche denies that a God stands at the apex or base of being. He also thinks that only a God could have fashioned a world that was both calculable all the way down and fully susceptible to human capacities of cognition and causal explanation. He thinks that nineteenth-century scientific theories that postulate simple linear causality were still feeding off the remains of a theology they purported to transcend. Some modern theists concur with this point. Kierkegaard, Bergson, and James, who place a mysterious divinity at the base of time, nonetheless advance a remarkably similar view. Time forks, either intrinsically or because human capacities of measurement and cognition on one side and world processes on the other do not mesh neatly with one another. It doesn't really matter that much which. Either way, it becomes wise to fold the expectation of surprise and the unexpected into the very fabric of our explanatory theories, interpretive schemes, religious identities, territorial conceptions of politics, and ethical sensibilities. And to work on ourselves subtly to overcome existential resentment of these expectations.

Attention to the rift, however, does sow anxiety in those who seek closure in the above-noted domains, pressing many to reinstate forcefully authoritative understandings most credible in slower and less asymmetrical regimes of time. Anxiety, indeed, can be read as a sign or symptom of the rift, during a time when many are not prepared to come to terms affirmatively with it.

In chapter 3 we encountered in Ilya Prigogine's work an image of science close to Nietzsche's reading of the rift in time. Prigogine explores complex physical systems that engender new crystallizations irreducible to the explanatory resources preceding them. These new crystallizations emerge out of unpredictable "forks" or "bifurcations" in systems that contain both impressive powers of self-organization and exquisite sensitivity to selective changes in the external environment. If you find Prigogine persuasive, you may be encouraged to fold appreciation of the variable speeds of geological processes, biological mutations, and the human body/brain network into cultural theory itself. Such a nonlinear conception of time in nature enables cultural theorists—who too often today read nature out of culture—to fold nature, biology, and human embodiment back into their conceptions of thinking, culture, identity, judgment, and becoming.

While she did not negotiate this last move, Hannah Arendt also embraced the idea of a rift or "gap" in time. She too thought that without such rifts "the new"—exceeding the reach of available stories and explanatory theories that precede it—could not surge into being. With the rift, our established narratives, rules, explanations, and sedimented codes of morality are periodically subjected to surprising jolts and shocks. Drawing upon Kafka and Nietzsche, Arendt says that the present is the gap through which life flows from past into future. It is hence "the most futile and slippery of tenses." It

> is no more than the clash of a past, which is no more, with a future, which is approaching and not yet there. Man lives in this in-between, and what he calls the present is a life long fight against the dead weight of the past, driving him forward with hope, and the fear of a future (whose certainty is only death), driving him backward toward the "quiet of the past," with nostalgia for and remembrance of the only reality he can be sure of.[5]

Arendt fears that the late-modern acceleration of pace accentuates a dangerous nostalgia to return to the "quiet of the past," a quiet placed in
quotes because our contemporary memory of it is unavoidably inflected differently
than it would have been experienced during the fugitive present when the horizon of
the future was open. For the future is never what it used to be, and neither is the past.
This nostalgia for a comforting image of the past expresses anxiety about the security of immortality, existential meaning, moral boundaries, explanatory confidence,
and narrative closure. All these are called into question by the acceleration of pace.
Arendt herself is deeply ambivalent about the condition she diagnoses. I concur in
that ambivalence enough to say that without the pull of the past the horizon of the
future would explode into an abyss. With it, the fundamental issues are, first, how to
engage the rift and, second, how to respond thoughtfully to the acceleration of pace
without falling into either a dangerous insistence upon slowing the world down to a
snail's pace or a crude celebration of high velocity per se. The challenge for those
who embrace the rift is how to reconfigure the balance between past and future in a
world whirling faster than heretofore. And how to respond with agonistic respect to
those who do not embrace the idea of a rift in a context where neither this cosmology
nor those ranged against it is soon likely to receive a definitive demonstration. The
intellectual challenge is how to come to terms productively with the ambiguous relations among time, pace, freedom, plurality, and democracy. None of us may really
be prepared to meet this challenge. But time is short.

You might say that as the asymmetries between different zones
of time widen it becomes easier to discern the rift, which, as Nietzsche, Deleuze,
Prigogine, Arendt, and I contend, is constitutive of time itself. But, again, that very
suspicion may tempt many into a dangerous, reactive response: into a series of familiar political movements to slow time down to conceal the rift. Such reactive
drives are not too likely to grab hold effectively of the processes of capitalist invention, finance, investment, labor migration, geographic expansion, and intraterritorial
colonization, even though these are preeminent forces propelling the acceleration of
pace. For these processes flow through and across states in ways that make it difficult for any territorially organized entity to govern them effectively. The collapse of
the Soviet Union is probably bound up in part with that state's inability either to
avoid these processes or to absorb them into its political economy without transforming it. So now resentment against the acceleration of pace becomes projected
upon religious and nationalist drives to identify a series of vulnerable constituencies
as paradigmatic enemies of territorial culture, traditional morality, unified politics,
and Christian civilization. The atheist, the postmodernist, the gay, the prostitute, the

Jew, the media, the nomadic Indian, and the Gypsy have all been defined as paradigmatic agents of restlessness, nomadism, superficial fashion, immorality, and danger by defenders of close integration among political territory, religious unity, and moral monism. Such definitions displace upon vulnerable constituencies anxiety about the pace of life and the rift in time. The underlying enemy is speed and uncertainty, but it is difficult to grab hold of the capitalist systems in which these processes are set. The hopeful thing is how many contemporary Christians, in the name of Christian love, join others in resisting and transcending these ugly equations.

When Wolin's presentation of the acceleration of pace in several zones of life is juxtaposed to my portrayal of the rift in time, a different picture of the contemporary condition emerges. Uneven pace across zones helps to reveal more poignantly what has always been in operation, a rift between past and future that helps to constitute the essence of time and to enter into the constitution of politics itself. It now becomes possible to come to terms with this condition in a more affirmative way. I do not think, again, that the reading of time I endorse has been proved definitively, nor is either it or the interpretations it contends against apt to be. But this interpretation does pose powerful challenges to those who implicitly treat one of the alternative conceptions of time as if it were undeniable. To embrace the rift is to challenge demands in contemporary social science for consummate explanation, cultural theory for smooth narrative, moral philosophy for thick, stable universals, and popular culture for the sufficiency of common sense.

Even as efforts to slow the world down fail, they do untold harm to many constituencies striving to respond in new ways to injuries imposed upon them and new possibilities opened up before them. Perhaps the best way to proceed is to strive to modulate the fastest and most dangerous military and corporate processes while intervening politically within accelerated processes of communication, travel, population flows, and cultural intersection to support a more generous ethos of pluralism. Such a double orientation does not scrap the advantages of territorial democracy, but it does support democratic movements that extend beyond the parameters of the territorial state as well as operate within it. The challenge is how to support the positive connections among democracy, uneven zones of tempo, and the rift in time without legitimating a pace of life so fast that the promise of democracy becomes translated into fascist becoming machines.

I am not positive how best to negotiate the in-between in a world spinning faster than heretofore. I doubt that anybody is entirely sure how to do so. Nonetheless, to nudge exploration forward a few steps I will first make the case for augmenting Wolin's democratic localism with a practice of cross-border politics that speaks to multiple sites of action and the acceleration of pace. I will then discuss more broadly how the acceleration of pace supports democratic pluralism in some ways while posing risks to it in others. Then in the last chapter I will challenge the sufficiency of two models of politics that reach beyond the parameters of the state while presupposing a concentric image of culture set in long, slow time.

Local Grievances and Cross-Border Movements

Wolin is acute in his understanding of how the initiatives of local constituencies often inspire the most creative and productive drives to democratize life. Here is a formulation that conveys that appreciation:

> The possibility of renewal draws on a simple fact that ordinary individuals are capable of creating new cultural patterns of commonality at any moment. Individuals who concert their powers for low income housing, worker ownership of factories, better schools, better health care, safer water, controls over toxic waste disposals, and a thousand other concerns of ordinary lives are experiencing a democratic moment and contributing to the discovery, care, and tending of a commonality of shared concerns. Without necessarily intending it, they are renewing the political by contesting the forms of unequal power that democratic liberty and equality have made possible and that democracy can eliminate only by betraying its own values.[6]

As he reviews such local movements Wolin inspires anybody inhabited by democratic sentiment. He identifies issues that people in different subject positions can periodically mobilize around together; he plays up the spontaneous character of these creative outbursts; and he contrasts such creative moments to the everyday politics of campaign financing, elections, corporate lobbying, and judicial decision from sites high above ordinary experience. My only concern is that in his laudable effort to highlight a vital *element* in the democratic experience he purifies that experience too much. The desire to purify democracy may contribute to disenchantment with its contemporary complexity, and that could in turn promote disaffection from some of the very sites of democratic action that help to make possible the localism Wolin admires.

One hot issue in Wolin's home state of California concerns the border between Mexico and California. Due in part to economic hard times in Mexico, a large number of Mexicans cross the border to find work in California, Arizona, and Texas. The economic and political trials that propel them to do so are no doubt determined in part by the place allotted to Mexico in the international economy.

The illegal alien, whose life is a constant struggle, becomes a deeply ambiguous figure in the political life of California. As possessors of cheap labor power, undocumented workers are valuable to agribusiness and fast-food restaurants seeking to maintain a competitive edge in the market. But as aliens caught in a miserable situation in a country mobilized around symbols of nationality they are in a poor position to complain about pay levels, organize unions, establish roots in the locality, or participate as citizens in public life. Their labor power renders them valuable while their illegality renders them silent and anonymous. This structural ambiguity intensifies their exploitability. That combination, in turn, further increases their value to agribusiness and fast-food employers.

The structural ambiguity maintains a supply of cheap labor available to corporate elites and small companies. But it also spurs new dimensions of a police state into being as the border between Mexico and the United States becomes a zone of low-intensity war, and as the politics of surveillance spreads to the traditional populace and the interior of the country. Look at customs procedures, conversion of the Social Security number into an ID card, airport surveillance practices, credit card controls, longer prison sentences, compromises of Miranda rights, spread of drug-testing programs, arrest information attached to driver's licenses, interstate sharing of arrest and detention records, highway stop and search policies, and prohibitions against American travel to Cuba, if you wonder what I mean.

"Aliens" are not merely those inside the territory without citizenship rights: they are also coded as strange beings whose presence is threatening to "natives" or, in this case, real citizens. Their ambiguous position intensifies divisions within the citizen class of low-skill workers as a whole, and that too works to the advantage of employers. Traditional low-skill workers, who have formal rights to education, citizenship, and welfare support, feel threatened economically and organizationally by the infusion of aliens. They fear that their jobs, the disciplinary actions they are subjected to at work, or the pay they can hope to earn will be affected adversely. Moreover, they resent the taxes they are called upon to pay to police the border, cover welfare, provide new schools for the children of illegal immigrants, build new prisons, and subsidize emergency health care. The infusion of aliens threatens their sense of security as workers, spouses, parents, and citizens who can raise families and participate in the good life available within the limited resources currently available to them. In this tense situation a racialization of economic and cultural issues readily arises to divide constituencies who would need to collaborate if decent pay, reasonable working conditions, good schools, and secure health care were to be gained. These sharp divisions within the working class also are coded as differences between constituencies thought to be properly located on different sides of the Rio Grande/Bravo.

What emerges from this historical conjunction of contingent elements—including the geographic border between Mexico and the United States created by past wars, the asymmetrical development of the two economies, the structure of the fast-food and agricultural economy in the American Southwest, the organization of illegal entry strategies, the entanglement of the border in the drug trade and an American war on drugs inside and outside the country, the tax and welfare system of the United States, and the racialization and territorialization of ethnic divisions within and around the working class—is a powerful contrivance of economic discipline and political separation. No central power intended it, even though it is bound together by the diverse intentions of agents at multiple sites with differential power. And yet, once it emerges as a contingent constellation, a variety of constituencies caught in it face powerful pressures to adjust their goals, strategies, and interests to its limits and possibilities. The result is a durable pattern of disequilibrium in which the Rio Grande/Bravo border is policed enough to placate American ethnic nationalists but not enough to cut off the supply of cheap labor; in which illegal immigrants are pressed to maintain political anonymity within an arduous system of labor; and in which conservative politicians fan ethnic hostilities to curtail the flow of people and drugs, increase prison construction, expand police surveillance, speed up capital punishment, and cut back state programs for public education, welfare, union support, and affirmative action.

An operational political economy is crafted from numerous such formations. While Marxist theories of capitalist contradiction sometimes tend to schematize the conflicts and trajectory of political economy, and while structuralists formalize them, contemporary cultural theorists of intersubjectivity, in their eagerness to resist these two strategies of schematization, all too often lose touch with how such complex, contingent transstate formations *materialize* specific zones of life.

Such a powerful contrivance of differential economic discipline and political separation is a layered, contingent contraption jerry-rigged from multiple materials. It neither reflects a profound dialectical logic that propels it nor contains a deep structure unknowable to its "role bearers." As a loosely structured modus vivendi crafted out of complex relays connecting the pain of refugees, armed border patrols, the market power of corporate elites, the ideological sanctification of market forces, the demands of consumers, the difficulties traditional blue-collar workers have in making ends meet, the mobilization of layered identity anxieties, the identification of drugs crossing the border with the decline of public morality, widespread frustration with a tax system that does not serve the needs of ordinary people, and interventions by the state, it is likely to contain a variety of leakages, resistances, and potential lines of modification. It may be possible to modify the existing pattern, or even to extract a set of positive possibilities from it. There are no guarantees here, however. Contraptions sometimes fall apart, sometimes keep running for a while, and sometimes become parts of new constructions. The absence of guarantees may be what encourages many intersubjectivists to ignore them, dialecticians to build a historical logic into them, and structuralists to invest them with a deep structure. There are, however, merely contingent lines of possibility to probe and test in a contrivance of discipline and division.

If it is possible to disrupt and reorganize this cross-border contrivance it will surely require political action at multiple sites to do so. The key in this instance may be to devise political strategies to enable immigrants to break out of the anonymity forced upon them by their ambiguous position. Thus, as this historical pattern of immigration has escalated over a few decades, and as recent entrants forge alliances with previous immigrants who are legal citizens and entrenched in several sectors of civil society, it may become possible to mobilize protest movements and electoral strategies to challenge the chauvinism and antiwelfarism that have gained such a strong foothold. It is even possible that labor organizations in the Southwest will track the mobility of the corporations that employ them and explore modes of selective collaboration between workers on both sides of the border. And that an enlarged constituency of workers and consumers will come to appreciate the need to introduce new programs in health care, education, transportation, and so on that reduce per capita costs as they are extended more generally.[7] For the times they are a-changin'. These include changes in the composition of labor and capital on both sides of the Rio Grande/Bravo; the emergence of a healthy cynicism about the sufficiency of market solutions to basic issues of housing, work, job security, education, transportation, and retirement; the critical reaction by large groups of Hispanic voters in key electoral states to campaigns of vilification recently waged against them; and the critical response by other constituencies to their increased knowledge of the ugly character and diffuse effects of these border campaigns. For, again, as even the Republican Party has slowly begun to realize, there is a large Hispanic minority in three of the large states any candidate for president must try to capture to win a national election—California, Texas, and Florida.

If and as such a critical assemblage consolidates, localism will be pertinent but radically insufficient to its effectiveness. Local actions, larger social movements within California and Texas, electoral strategies aimed at these states and the national state, and cross-border, citizen organizations are all relevant to a politics that shakes and moves this contrivance of discipline and division. Moreover, all the public media through which the contrivance has become consolidated must be deployed in political efforts to redesign its balances and possibilities. For sensibilities have to be moved as well as policies. The film *Lone Star* by John Sayles, to take just one example, speaks effectively to these cross-border issues in ways that help to nudge the sensibilities and imagination of possibility of many on both sides of the border. By the time the lead character advises people in a small town in southern Texas struggling with border issues to "forget the Alamo," it has also become clear to a variety of viewers how much futile pain and injustice have been generated by these border hostilities. Radio, television, labor meetings, cross-border citizen actions, films, and Internet connections all play a part in the countermovement. The pace and scale of contemporary patterns of political economy not only help to organize the contrivance in question, they pluralize the media and sites through which to re-fashion it.

That is to say, today you can reduce fugitive democracy to local initiatives or mourn the eclipse of democracy by identifying its crucial dimension with a pace and scale of life that has passed. But to do either is to endanger the complex form of democracy possible in the late-modern time in the interest of pursuing a model of pure democracy that has never existed and is unsuited for contemporary life. In a fast-paced time when speed compresses distance, a plurality of interconnected sites of democratic action must be activated if ordinary people are to have a hand in shaping the working conditions, educational possibilities, forms of identity, income levels, ecological environment, border relations, and citizen entitlements available to them.

Tempo and Experimentalism

We have deferred several pertinent issues. It might be said that if the tempo of economic and cultural life had not accelerated so much, there would be less need for multiple sites of political action and less dissonance between the pace of economic life and the pace appropriate to democratic deliberation. Is there, then, more to be said by democrats themselves in favor of the compression of distance by the acceleration of pace? Can there be a positive relation between the accelerated pace of contemporary life and admirable possibilities of democratic activism and citizenship? To engage these issues I draw selectively upon Friedrich Nietzsche. Despite what a few levelers and simplifiers occasionally say, I do not think that Nietzsche himself was a democrat or that he offers a direct answer to the questions posed here. That is why I seek to rework his ideas rather than merely to represent them. The first time I engaged Nietzsche's thought publicly, I stated that I stood in a relation of "antagonistic indebtedness" to it. Such a relation "would appreciate the reach of Nietzschean thought as well as its sensitivity to the complex relations between resentment and the production of otherness, but it would turn the genealogist of resentment on his head by exploring democratic politics as a medium through which to expose resentment and to encourage the struggle against it."[8] As I have continued to think with and against Nietzsche, and as I have focused on his middle writings, where much of the most pertinent thinking takes place, that stance continues to inform my thinking. What's more, a host of democrats, including Jane Bennett, Judith Butler, Wendy Brown, Daniel Conway, Thomas Dumm, Moira Gatens, Michel Foucault, Gilles Deleuze, Lawrence Hateb, George Kateb, Brian Massumi, Melissa Orlie, Michael Shapiro, Paul Patton, Keith Ansell-Pearson, and Bernard Williams, also draw selective sustenance from Nietzsche in rethinking the question of democracy without identifying him as a democrat. Why would we, in our diverse ways, do so?

　　The general answer is that many of us think that the ideals of democracy bequeathed by Rousseau, Tocqueville, Mill, Dewey, Rawls, Habermas, and Wolin need reconfiguration today. Nietzsche, even as he excoriates actually existing democracy, is distinctive in the late nineteenth century in fomenting some pertinent ideas. We therefore find ourselves criticizing pivotal themes in Nietzsche even as he prompts us to rethink settled ideas about democracy. Our relation to Nietzsche invites comparison to Marx's relation to Hegel, Rawls's relation to Kant, Arendt's relation to Heidegger, and Wolin's relation to Arendt. In none of these cases is the thought of the theorist in question reducible to the thinker from whom the debt is drawn. But there are nonetheless discernible lines of affiliation that help to inspire and shape each perspective.

　　How does this protean thinker contribute distinctive elements to the nobility of democracy while he himself—after a middle period when he flirted with a positive image of a democracy "yet to come"—vigorously disparages it? Several things may be involved. Nietzsche, still dazzled by an aristocratic imaginary he no longer endorses as historically actualizable, could not purge the odor of democratic mediocrity from his aristocratic nose long enough to explore the positive relation of democracy to some possibilities he does admire. His taste was too rarefied to dip into the soup of democratic culture to feel, taste, and smell its nuances and variations. Finally, this protean thinker, prophetic in many ways, was not infinitely so. He overlooked a possibility that many coming after him are better able to see: that some of the most noble elements in his own vision have more chance of finding expression in a democratic culture today than in any other type. The paradox of Nietzsche is that the distinctive sensibility through which he opens a door to the ennoblement of democracy is also one that inhibits him from walking through it. The bind in which he is caught actually mirrors a less familiar one haunting several contemporary advocates of democracy: their enthusiastic endorsement of the generic idea is joined to a failure to rethink its appropriate form during a time when its spatiotemporal conditions of possibility have shifted significantly.

Nietzsche makes significant contributions to the refashioning of democratic thought through the following experiments and explorations:

- In coming to terms with a rift in time and exploring the effects that changes in pace and tempo have on the shape and weight of culture

- In challenging the early-modern idea of nature as a lawlike system through which culture must be defined, either by sharp contrast or dull inclusion

- In bringing out hidden elements in the cultural experience of the "unequal" and "difference" unavailable to those who compress those ideas entirely into a hierarchy governed by a single measure

- In pursuing modes of connection that do not require all the parties to pass through an authoritative center defined either by a nation or by a Christian/Kantian model of the universal

- In exploring those parts of reactive emotion and ethical response that proceed below conscious awareness and the reach of direct self-regulation

- In pursuing an ethic of cultivation or "artistry" that works upon layers of corporeal judgment below the threshold of consciousness

- In pursuing a pathos of distance or noble graciousness irreducible to either agreement or separation

- In affirming a nontheistic, nonjuridical source of ethical inspiration even as he comes to terms with the contestability of such a putative source and the tragic character of being

Of course, each Nietzschean theme must be shaken and reworked to contribute to a democratic problematic. For he was not a democrat. But that is not so difficult. Having addressed Nietzsche on the relations among nature, culture, and thinking in chapter 3, I will here explore how Nietzsche's perspective might inform democratic thought about the connections among a quick tempo of life, arts of the self, and a generous ethos of connection across multiple differences. These are conjunctions that take us to the heart of claims that the tempo of late-modern life is inhospitable to democracy.

What makes it unlikely, to Nietzsche, that a hierarchical, ordered culture of nobility could be rebuilt in the modern age? Several developments are pertinent, but one that he returns to often is the effect the acceleration of pace has on the experience of place and self in modern life. The increase of tempo helps to make aristocratic culture in the old sense no longer possible. The theme is palpable in this statement from a late book, *Twilight of the Idols:*

> Democracy has always been the declining form of the power to organize.... For institutions to exist there must exist the kind of will, instinct, imperative which is anti-liberal to the point of malice: the will to tradition, to authority, to centuries long responsibility, to *solidarity* between succeeding generations backwards and forwards *in infinitum*.... The entire West has lost those instincts out of which institutions grow, out of which the *future* grows; perhaps nothing goes so much against the grain of its "modern spirit." One lives for today, one lives very fast—one lives very irresponsibly: it is precisely this which one calls "freedom."[9]

Lurking within this lamentation is the understanding that a quick pace of life and democracy are interwoven. "One lives for today, one lives very fast." Also lurking there, however, is a theme important to things Nietzsche himself prizes positively. For speed, up to a point, enables more people to come to terms with how unfinished and full of "gaps" nature is; it encourages them to apply a certain experimentalism to themselves periodically; and sometimes it evens supports negotiation of a "spiritualization of enmity" between noble adherents of very different faiths. Indeed, drawing insight from these thoughts in Nietzsche, I will claim that today the accelerated pace of life, inscribed in public media, military weaponry, Internet communications, technological development, cinematic practice, air travel, population mobility, and cultural exchange, is indispensable to pluralization and democratization. So let's pull out the aristocratic lamentation in Nietzsche's characterization. We will not forget the limits, dangers, and risks in doing so; we merely set them aside for a moment.

Nietzsche himself paves the way for this strategy in nodule 356 of *The Gay Science*, a book written before his equation between democracy and a "nursemaid" community hardened into cement. In "How Things Will Become Ever More 'Artistic,'" Nietzsche says that in the "Old Europe" of, say, between 800 and 1000, the ponderous flow of time encouraged people to sink deeply into their roles. They readily forgot how "accidents, moods and caprice disposed of them," and they tended to treat what they were culturally defined to be as what they were divinely and naturally ordained to be. Things change during the opposite ages:

> But there are opposite ages, really democratic, where people give up this faith, and a certain cocky faith and opposite point of view advance more and more into the foreground. The individual becomes convinced that he can do just about everything and *can manage almost any role*, and everybody experiments with himself, improvises, makes new experiments, enjoys his experiments; and all nature ceases and becomes art.[10]

When the pace of life accelerates, nature ceases and becomes art. Inside this exaggeration is an insight. In an up-tempo world people readily become more "cocky," experimental, and improvisational. That is, they become more democratic and less fixed and hierarchical. As these improvisations proceed, people can also become more alert to how "accidents, moods and caprice" have already shaped them. The connection between the shift in the experience of nature and the experience of identity is important, for unless essentially embodied human beings cast off the weight of a teleological experience of nature they are unlikely to come to terms with the element of contingency and fluidity in cultural identity. It is no coincidence that the nineteenth-century critic of both teleological and lawlike models of nature is also an adventurer of the self.

Perhaps Nietzsche constructs a caricature of the premodern world. Perhaps it was not as slow and fixed as he pretends. Even if so, the caricature calls attention to a potential line of affinity flowing through the pace of life, the experience of nature, and the experience of being. As awareness of these connections becomes vivid, people see and feel how some of the habits, prejudgments, and faiths they embody in, say, religion, gender, sexuality, ethnicity, work, and mode of rule could be otherwise. They may even become alert to fugitive currents in themselves flowing in new directions.

This awareness itself opens up the possibility of improvisation and self-experimentation. It encourages artistic work on those geological layers from which our sensibilities are composed and the ethos of public life is assembled. Perhaps you now work to modify one of your relational identities, seeking to squeeze out a background feeling of "ressentiment" that has infiltrated it. Or perhaps a social movement arises that calls into question the transcendental source or civilizational necessity of some aspect of your religious faith, sensual affiliation, or social standing. And if you modify the sense of necessity in what you are in one domain, you may now be prepared to embrace a modest pluralization of identities pursued by others. For you are now no longer so hell-bent on treating culturally entrenched standards of being as if they reflect ironclad dictates of tradition, nature, and God. You are less forgetful of the historicity and temporal fluidity of being.

The acceleration of pace does not, of course, guarantee that such possibilities will be embraced, or that, if embraced, the experimentation they foment will succeed. Nietzsche, as we have seen, resists *both* the lawlike model of nature and disembodied conceptions of cultural intersubjectivity. That means he resists both the project of mastery over nature and the project of complete explanation. He seeks, rather, to *intervene* in the world with some efficacy, not to know it in itself or master it. Readings of the author of the "will to power" that treat him as a philosopher of mastery implicitly project too much of the classical conception of nature into a perspective that resists it. They overlook the extent to which, on Nietzsche's reading, "becoming" is built into nature as well as culture, when each aspect of nature is considered over the appropriate time frame.

Such a shift in the tempo of life generates new possibilities, then. It also poses new *barriers* to the cultural maintenance of innocence about who you are and how you arrived there. When the tempo of life accelerates it now takes *more political work* to protect the assumption that the identities layered into us conform to a universal model commanded by a god or decreed by nature. That is why so many queasy democrats want to slow the world down in the name of democracy. They are worn out by the workload imposed upon them. If you appreciate how nature is differentially mixed into culture—depending upon the layer of culture in question, and if the element of artistry in nature itself also becomes palpable, you are now in a position to transcend theories that reduce culture to natural regularity and also to break the hold of cultural theories that escape stark determinism only by expunging every trace of nature from the idea of culture. Thus spoke Friedrich Nietzsche.

The acceleration of tempo supports the rise of social movements fomented by unforeseen shifts of balance between old identities and new conditions.

And these movements further accentuate the experience of the self as an "actor" who might "manage almost any role." In such circumstances it becomes more credible to balance the politics of recognition against the politics of becoming. The cultural logic of recognition purports to *recall* things that are there intrinsically but have been forgotten, occluded, repressed, or oppressed, while the groan of becoming is that uncertain process by which *new* events and identities reconfigure the established logic of recognition in ways that cannot be captured entirely by tight models of explanation or dialectical advance. For the politics of becoming to acquire greater salience—on the vision pursued here it would be destructive and unjust if it attained full reign—the idea of nature as an inherent set of purposes or laws in which we are set would give some ground to appreciation of an element of contingency, surplus, and mutation in the order of nature. Speed, combined with the expanded scope of communication and connection it fosters, can help to promote that shift too, as people experience more changes, accidents, surprises, and diversities coming into being during their lifetimes. Again, it is not accidental that the nineteenth-century philosopher who raced ahead of his time in thinking about the accelerated tempo of life was the same one who was prescient in challenging *both* the Newtonian and Hegelian conceptions of nature.

Losses and dangers accompany a significant shift in the tempo of life. The biggest loss, to Nietzsche at least, is forfeiture of the ability to build a society of the old sort, the kind of society in which a nobility of the old type could flourish.

> For what is dying out is the fundamental faith that would enable us to calculate, to promise, to anticipate the future…namely, the faith that man has meaning only insofar as he is a *stone in a great* edifice. What will not be built anymore henceforth, and *cannot* be built anymore is…a society in the old sense of that word; to build that everything is lacking. Above all the material. *All of us are no longer material for a society:* this is a truth for which the time has come.

"All of us are no longer material for a society." A pivotal moment in the politics of becoming. The most ominous danger when this becomes the case is that many who resent the uncertain experience of mobility in society and themselves will press militantly to return political culture to a stonelike condition. And do so in the name of democracy. A demand to exercise unquestioned authority by claiming to embody in themselves the commands of God, nature, or transcendental morality may become militant. Or, perhaps more often, the demand to participate in the psychic comforts of obedience to fixed commands may intensify. So speed can foment the drive to experimentalism and to fundamentalism together. It sets two contending cultural dispositions into play, redefining the terms of contemporary politics. For you cannot *be* a stone unless those around you, whose relational identities help to specify how fixed or mobile you are, make up the fixed edifice in which you are set. So, again, the condition of possibility for *democratic experimentalism* also foments the reactive energies of *democratic fundamentalism.*

It is fascinating to see how Nietzsche associates the rise of what might today be called fundamentalism with the emergence of nihilism, and how he associates both with the acceleration of speed. Western nihilism, for him, crystallizes when belief in the traditional Christian picture of the world falls into crisis *and* people nonetheless insist that morality, governance, purpose, and meaning in life are lost unless that world is reinstated. For Nietzsche, who invented the term to apply to exactly this historical configuration, the most promising response to nihilism is to overcome the latter set of demands. It is to accept speed and cultivate new nobilities who can live with its effects. For his opponents, it is to return to what the accelerated tempo of life makes difficult or impossible to reinstate. "Slow the world down, we want to become stones in an edifice again."

The futile drive to reinstate the old picture through force and repression, rather than to forge new values for new circumstances, is the key to modern nihilism as Nietzsche understands it. Such a drive, while unlikely to succeed in its positive agenda, can certainly foment cultural war. When such negativity prevails, one extreme or another will triumph. For "extreme conditions are not succeeded by moderate ones but by extreme conditions of the opposite kind."[11] In that regard it is pertinent to listen to the traits of character Nietzsche thinks are most conducive to negotiation of a world conforming to neither extreme. These traits, represented by him as unusual achievements, are precisely the qualities I find to be most conducive to a democratic culture in a fast-paced world. They foster critical responsiveness to new constituencies seeking to move onto the legitimate register of identity, and they encourage agonistic respect between constituencies already on that register who honor diverse moral sources. Nietzsche writes:

> Who will prove to be the strongest in the course of this? The most moderate; those who do not require any extreme articles of faith; those who not only concede but love a fair amount of accidents and nonsense; those who can think of man with a considerable reduction of his value without becoming small and weak on that account: those richest in health who are equal to most misfortunes and therefore not afraid of misfortunes—human beings

who are sure of their power and represent the attained strength of humanity with conscious pride.[12]

"Those who do not require any extreme articles of faith." In the nodule of *The Gay Science* with which we started, Nietzsche associates the drive to return to society in the old sense with the anarchists and socialists of his day. Others might select new candidates for that honor today, such as the Christian Right or fervent advocates of the nation. Whoever your candidates are, listen to Nietzsche's account of what they yearn to become:

> It is a matter of indifference to me that at present the most myopic, perhaps most honest, but at any rate noisiest human type that we have today, our good socialists, believe, hope, dream, and above all shout and write almost the opposite. Even now one reads their slogan for the future, "free society." Free society? Yes, yes! But surely you know, gentlemen, what is required for building that? Wooden iron! The well-known wooden iron. And it must not even be wooden.

"Wooden iron" is an old German expression for an unbreakable contradiction. Self-proclaimed democrats who relentlessly pursue a world in which life is slow would, through fulfillment of that wish, crush the highest form of freedom to which democracy is connected. They unconsciously project an ideal world in which everyone becomes a peasant. In pursuit of stolid role sedimentation, they would destroy the actor in the self and, above all, expunge the element of artistry from the actor. By freezing actors into stones, they would expunge the very traits of citizenship crucial to a fast-paced world. For *it* is not going to slow down.

Let there be no mistake. While Nietzsche himself admires the effect of pace upon the few he thinks can handle it, he resists it for the large majority, even though this marginal member of the middle class refuses to define the majority (or "the herd") by a socially fixed category of class or income. The "herd" is always an indispensable element in each and all of us, for we need commonalities of language to be. But it becomes overwhelming for those in any sociological category who seek to sink into the roles assigned to them. As Nietzsche puts the difference between the few and the many, "Man's greatest labor so far has been to reach agreement about very many things and to submit *to a law of agreement*—regardless of whether these things are true or false."[13] This comes most readily when they/we participate in a leisurely pace of life, one in which solid conventions become consolidated into the experience of transcendental truths. Here the many are molded into beings of "*virtuous stupidity*, stolid metronomes for the slow spirit; to make sure the faithful of the great shared faith stay together and continue their dance." Only "we others"—Are you one? Am I?—can rise above such a condition. "We others are the exception and the rule."[14] So Nietzsche, for the seventh time, is not a democrat. But he may discern more presciently than many erstwhile democrats the connection between an acceleration of pace and experimentation.

I disagree with Nietzsche about defining a majority as "solid metronomes" while an exceptional few experiment upon themselves. The hope to fold something like this combination into the democratic state may be the agenda governing contemporary Straussians. It is governed by a fear of what might happen if too many people lose touch with the traditional boundaries that give them meaning and security. But it does not plumb carefully enough the dangers of acting upon that fear under contemporary conditions, under conditions when circumstances beyond anyone's control make the boundaries shaky.

I concur with Nietzsche, then, that a fast pace of life democratizes possibilities he would confine to a few. And that there are risks and dangers attached to this development. Unlike him and many contemporary conservatives who would insulate most people from the effects of fast tempo, I endorse the democratic possibilities supported by such a pace even as I support efforts to temper and qualify some of its most destructive effects. A quick tempo of life, to put it bluntly, sets a crucial condition of possibility for the vibrant practice of democratic pluralism.

My wager is that it is more possible to negotiate a democratic ethos congruent with the accelerated tempo of modern life than it is either to slow the world down or to insulate the majority of people from the effects of speed. It is important to reach a judgment on this issue, for the downside of pace without negotiation of a generous ethos is as bleak as its upside is enchanting. And the attempt to slow the world down under contemporary conditions of life is almost certain to devolve into a search for scapegoats held responsible for the effects of a rapid pace of life that cannot itself be derailed. What is needed today is at least a large minority of people located in several "subject positions" (such as class, age, gender, ethnicity, faith, region, sensual affiliation) acting as individuals and as constituencies to translate the positive possibilities of a quick pace of life into a generous ethos of engagement. Of course, a tense balance must be maintained in such an ethos between the claims of regularity, predictability, and commonality and those of experimentalism, artistry, and becoming.

Let us plumb more closely the risks and costs of trying either to slow the world down or to insulate the majority from the effects of rapid pace upon their experience of identity. The contribution a modern capitalist economy makes to pace is typically insulated from such cultural wars. For the prospects of slowing capitalism itself down are dim, and to exempt it from criticism functions to protect the system of inequalities many defenders of a slow world admire. These devotees of community act as if locality, community, family, neighborhood, and church could be blocked off from the mobilities of capital, labor, travel, fashion, and communication. Such a selective hostility to speed pulls its proponents toward an ugly politics of cultural war against those who both lack institutional power and challenge through their mode of being the claim of traditional constituencies to embody final moral authority in themselves. That brings us back to the familiar tendency to treat "Gypsies," "Jews," "women," "homosexuals," "Indians," "prostitutes," "welfare freeloaders," "Blacks," "atheists," and "postmodernists" as paradigmatic agents of nomadism, fashion, promiscuity, style, instability, anchorless amorality, nihilism, or narcissism by those who both insulate capitalism from critique and express nostalgia for the long, slow time of the putative nation. The resentment against speed and the refusal to challenge its most salient institutional sources combine to foster such an accusatory culture.

Some proponents of long, slow time actively resist these ugly temptations, and they are to be congratulated for it. Sheldon Wolin is exemplary here, except perhaps for the slick equation he sometimes promotes between "postmodernism" and "capitalism." Others now more carefully select their targets to avoid countercharges of racism or anti-Semitism.[15] But the temptation persists, and many succumb to it. So that temptation itself must be included in any calculus of the best orientation to adopt toward the contemporary nexus between speed and democracy.

Nobility and Grace

Let's tarry over the positive possibilities of a fast-paced democracy a moment longer. During a time in which people become more like actors, it also becomes more possible to work on ourselves artistically. We can attempt to modify, adjust, or sublimate destructive orientations to diversity entrenched in our identities, instincts, and moral codes. To be an actor is not the highest thing, then. An actor, for instance, might become the pawn of arbitrary authority. The actor merely sets a (dangerous) condition of democratic possibility. Nietzsche is wary of the actor as a self-sufficient type. But he and I both admire immensely the possibility of artistry, where people act upon themselves, thoughtfully, modestly, and experimentally, to "become what they are."

So you might be an actor without becoming an artist, but you cannot cultivate self-artistry without first stepping onto the stage of the actor.[16] The language through which Nietzsche makes these points uncannily anticipates the interplay among film, TV, and the staging of ordinary life so densely developed to-day. The noblest thing is to become more artistic in relation to other constituencies and to fugitive elements in yourself. Nietzsche thought such artistic experiments could promote a "spiritualization of enmity" between nobilities of different types occupying the same politically organized territory, if and when these projects are joined to the task of overcoming existential resentment. I call the *democratization* of such a spirituality between constituencies honoring different moral sources a gener-ous ethos of engagement. Everything most noble about democracy is connected in some way or other to this ability to become a little more artistic in our relations with others and with diverse parts of ourselves. The acceleration of pace helps to gener-alize that possibility even as it foments risks and dangers to the possibility. Pace thereby sets an ambiguous condition of possibility for a generous ethos of engage-ment in a pluralistic, pluralizing democracy.

I have been appropriating Nietzsche's thought selectively, as promised, working on it as we proceed. Let's turn now to his new conception of no-bility to see how it might be picked over. The old nobility is not possible anymore, as we have seen. So Nietzsche promotes a "new nobility." He divides the new ideal of nobility into three interdependent and dissonant parts.

Those who are noble in the Nietzschean sense, first, work on themselves to overcome existential resentment against the lack of intrinsic meaning in life (or the uncertainty attached to the judgment that there is such a meaning). The base treat themselves as if they were born to be what chance and power have made them. The difference between nobility and baseness, again, is not distributed according to the usual categories of class, income, or educational level. Anyone might be noble, but, according to Nietzsche, most won't be. "But we, we others who thirst after reason, are determined to scrutinize our experiences as severely as a scientific experiment — hour after hour, day after day. We ourselves wish to be our own ex-periments and guinea pigs."[17] To be noble, then, is to be your own experiment and guinea pig, even as you realize — if you follow Nietzsche on this point too — that modesty in method and objective is appropriate to the uncertain process of self-ex-perimentation.

But, second, the noble also cultivate a grace and ease of conduct best accomplished through long practice. To be noble is both to be one's own guinea pig and to cultivate grace of self. The first is a condition of the second. But the two don't coalesce smoothly. Final harmony between these two interdependent and dis-sonant components cannot be attained, particularly in a world of rapid pace and more than one nobility.

The third dimension of Nietzsche's new nobility is that for any nobility to be it must enter into affirmative relations with other types of nobility. "For many who are noble are needed, and noble men of many kinds, that there may be a nobility. Or as I once said in a parable: Precisely this is godlike, that there are gods, but no God."[18] This means, when you read it in combination with Nietzsche's call for a "spiritualization of enmity"[19] between noble Christians and non-Christians, that some of the new nobility will accept Nietzsche's reading of existence while others will put a God, a transcendental law, or apodictic recognition at the pinnacle of experience. But each noble party will respect the fact that its projection is apt to be profoundly contestable in the eyes of others. The advocates express their existential faith, but they also affirm the profound contestability of the "conjecture" they honor the most.

To democratize the Nietzschean conception of nobility, then, is to generalize the noble ethos he admires. It is to support a multidimensional pluralism of democratic life irreducible to the national or local pluralisms often associated with democracy; and it is to pursue the possibility of common action in that network through negotiation of an ethos of engagement between constituencies who fold into their relational identities the three qualities Nietzsche associates with the new nobility. The dissonant interdependence among these three elements—self-experimentalism, grace, and plurality—is precisely the condition of being appropriate to democracy in a fast-paced world. So let's think further about how grace is cultivated, according to Nietzsche, and what connection its cultivation has to a noble democratic ethos in which appreciation of plurality reigns.

The cultivation of grace involves not only direct intellectual self-regulation but also tactics or artistry applied by the self to corporeal layers of being not sufficiently susceptible to direct conscious control. "For to say it once more":

> Man, like every living being, thinks continually without knowing it: the thinking that rises to consciousness is only the smallest part of all this—the most superficial and worst—for only this conscious thinking *takes the form of words, which is to say signs of communication.* ... The emergence of our sense impressions into our consciousness, the ability to fix them, and, as it were, exhibit them externally, increased proportionally with the need to communicate them to others by means of signs.[20]

In the nodule from which this statement is drawn Nietzsche tends to equate the difference between conscious and nonconscious thinking with that between general cultural orientations and thought-imbued intensities unique to each individual. At other times, however, he sees how cultural intersubjectivity itself becomes mixed into corporeal habits through affectional ties, general patterns of repetition, and collective techniques of punishment. We now encounter formulations such as "states of consciousness, beliefs of any kind, holding something to be true, for example—every psychologist knows this—are a matter of complete indifference and fifth rank compared to the value of the instincts"; and "our true experiences are not garrulous"; and "our invisible moral qualities follow their own course—probably a whole different course; and they might give pleasure to a god with a divine microscope."[21]

    Both noble arts of the self and negotiation of a democratic ethos of agonistic respect among diverse constituencies depend upon making distinctive implantations in those "concealed plantings and gardens" that precede consciousness, influence conduct independent of it, and exert some influence over conscious reflection. That is why Nietzsche both resists those who would eliminate social rituals in the name of a more rational secularism and opposes those who would give any church monopoly over ritual. For ritual is a generalization of arts of the self. And the cultivation of nobility cannot be attained by intellectual argument and acts of will alone. Argument, deliberation, and stories, while pertinent to self-cultivation, are not sufficient to them. The self, rather, nudges the organization of its own proto-thinking, mood, and prejudgment by artful means. As we have seen in previous chapters, the generalization of such arts, and the negotiation of a generous ethos between constituencies who honor different ethical sources, forms the micropolitical dimension of life in a pluralist culture.

    How do such arts proceed? It depends upon the issue and the context. That's why it is most pertinent to discuss relational techniques of the self case by case.[22] We isolated in chapter 3 a few techniques by which one already tempted by the Nietzschean image of thinking might come to embrace it more actively; we explored techniques to spur creativity in thinking in chapter 4; and I have discussed such tactics with respect to one's orientation to criminal punishment, doctor-assisted suicide, and same-sex marriage in other studies. Here is an example that is particularly relevant to the issues posed in this chapter.

    Suppose you find yourself attached to either a linear or teleological image of time, even while a series of events increasingly presses you to call that image into question. Part of you insists that a viable concept of causality and a reliable concept of morality depend upon this image. Moreover, a sense of anxiety surges up when it is called into question. Perhaps it is connected to your faith in a salvational God or to the sense that life is meaningless unless the possibility of steady progress is projected forward. On the other hand, you've been around for a while, and you recall several instances in which either your projection into the future or your established judgment of conduct was thrown into crisis by unexpected events or new movements in the politics of becoming. You have reached the point where you suspect that it is unethical to accept without complication the linear concept of time bound to your current vision of causality and morality. How to proceed now?

The first thing, perhaps, is to rehearse this autobiographical history of disconcerting events more closely. They may include the rise of a feminist movement, the emergence of a gay rights movement, the unexpected collapse of the Soviet Union, the unexpected upsurge of religious fundamentalism, and the birth of a movement in support of doctor-assisted suicide. The point now is to review the events that surprised and unsettled you initially, trying to bracket the interpretive and/or ethical adjustments you later made in response to them. Each such event, of course, might have been incorporated *later* into your understanding, because you are a smart dialectician. In fact, it is difficult not to do so, since subtraction and forgetting are closely bound up with organization of memory. But now you suspect that this very dialectical skill encourages you to forget the agonizing and intensive work you actually did on your explanatory projections and moral sensibility to adjust to new and initially surprising conditions. Moreover, this very forgetfulness may render you less prepared than otherwise to respond reflectively to the *next* set of surprises. You now suspect that history is intrinsically replete with surprise, and that your implicit image of time operates as a screen to protect you from this disturbing realization. Sure, you will unavoidably continue to project things forward on the basis of established understandings and to judge them according to the best recipes heretofore fashioned. But now you try to build into that very sensibility another dimension dissonant with it, one that affirms the probability that some of the very projections you make will be disturbed, unsettled, or overthrown at unexpected moments. Following Bergson's account of how operational perception promotes a linear image of time, you now strive to build into your sensibility a second-order appreciation to correct the first impression. For the first image, while useful and ethically laudable much of the time, may also conceal something that needs to be drawn into your thinking. Spinoza recommended something akin to this in the seventeenth century, when people were adjusting to the idea that the phenomenological experience of the sun revolving around the earth was at odds with second-order evidence that the earth revolves around the sun. He thought that once you absorbed the second-order understanding, the initial phenomenological experience would both persist and be infused by self-corrective tendencies.

After such a series of rehearsals it might now be possible to consolidate more deeply the idea that time is out of joint. Deleuze, as we saw in chapter 4, reviews in *Cinema 2: The Time-Image* a series of films that convey this second image of time more vividly. Another film that does so is *Stranger Than Paradise*, by Jim Jarmusch. One remarkable thing about that film, as noted briefly in chapter 5, is the irrational cuts between scenes, joined to a bracing musical score that links them in mood and temper. We are first treated to a scene in which a series of connected events unfolds; then to a blank, black screen for a few seconds; and then every now and then to a new scene that neither we nor the actors could have anticipated. We might retrospectively make sense of this break, at least to some degree. It is this retrospective power that provides the crooked line of continuity connecting the scenes together. But we could not predict the turn prior to its occurrence.

Exposure to the repetition of such irrational cuts can work upon your subliminal experience of time, if you have now reached a point where you are receptive to such work. You now sense more vividly that below the threshold of attention things go on too small and fast to know, but cumulatively effective enough to issue in surprising twists and turns in time. It is hubristic to think that you could capture all these elements in the detail and depth needed in the course of living, and it is possible that some of those elements lack the shape or structure amenable to full intellectual capture in principle. As this latter sense sinks into your sensibility, you may gradually find yourself projecting an orientation to meaning and ethics that affirms a rift in time as an intrinsic part of them. You begin to experience meaning less as something to be discovered and more as an *investment* you make in selective activities and events. Now the attainment of meaning and a rift in time become intermeshed. And that part of freedom that is tied to becoming may now appear closely bound up to a rift in time too. Soon, rather than treating the rift in the moment as a crisis in the fabric of causality, meaning, and morality, you have begun to see how each, after appropriate revision, becomes intermeshed with the others. We started to think about the relevant idea of causality in chapter 2, and we will pursue further the connection between ethics and the rift of time in the next chapter.

After a series of such reflections and interventions, you might *now* be moved to consider in a more receptive mood the conceptions of nature developed by Epicurus, Lucretius, Nietzsche, Prigogine, Stengers, and Stephen Gould, for their images of nature are congruent with a rift in time in history.

What is initially treated as a set of intellectual themes to explore can next be translated into a series of experimental interventions into the character of your sensibility. This is the translation process through which the compositional dimension of thinking comes into its own, although it is always at work in the background. Suppose, after all this, you watch *Stranger Than Paradise* again, priming yourself this time to let your dream life enter more actively into the picture. You review the issues before going to sleep, thinking, too, about how you have already begun to translate the intellectual issues into experimental strategies of self-composition. According to some researchers on sleep, it takes both deep, slow wave sleep and rapid eye movement (REM) sleep to consolidate new experience. "During the first two hours of slow-wave sleep . . . certain brain chemicals plummet and information flows out of the memory region called the hippocampus and into the cortex." Then, "during the next four hours," the brain engages in a kind of internal dialogue "that distributes this new information into the appropriate networks and categories." Finally, in the last two hours, "brain chemistry and activity again change drastically as the cortex goes into an active dreaming state." The cortex now "re-enacts the training and solidifies the newly made connections throughout its memory banks."[23] After several such bouts of synthesis or "processing," you may move closer to the double experience of time initially projected intellectually. It finds expression in the occasions and tone of your laughter, and in a readiness to draw upon an ethical reserve of generosity exceeding the dictates of your official doctrine when you encounter new twists and turns in time.

You thus participate, repetitively and experimentally, in a series of intercoded activities that impinge upon the self at several levels, allowing a *mixture* of images, gestures, rhythms, memories, arguments, and ethical concerns to become folded into your sensibility. You do so to recode modestly your experience of time and the ways that experience is now joined to modified ideas of meaning, ethics, and causality. If the double image of time begins to take, the possibility to work further on the relevant images of meaning, ethics, and causality has also become enhanced.

Such strategies might be adapted to work on your preliminary orientation to border politics in the American Southwest, or to engage religious or irreligious faiths that challenge your presumption to monopolize the final source of morality, or to reconfigure modestly any number of dispositions disturbed by the emergence of a new movement sowing uncertainty or panic in this or that aspect of your identity.

If and as the background feeling of anxiety diminishes, new and more generous thoughts, images, feelings, and judgments might become available, emerging as if from nowhere into the conscious register of thought, perception, and judgment. If some of these filter into your dream life, more work yet may be accomplished on the lower layers of subjectivity. In Nietzsche's more grandiose language, those artists of the self who "give style" to their character "survey all the strengths and weaknesses of their nature and then fit them into an artistic plan until every one of them appears as art and reason. . . . Here a large mass of second nature has been added; there a piece of original nature has been removed — both times through long practice and daily work at it."[24]

Nietzsche, again, contests the secular ideal in which the admirable refusal to make a single orientation to God the defining mark of a whole political regime is joined to the less thoughtful relegation of ritual and arts to churches in the private realm. Too many secularists slide over or denigrate those culturally mediated layers of unconscious corporeality that flow into consciousness without being under its complete governance. For to embrace pluralism is to tap into depths beyond the shallow waters of secular intellectualism.

The key, as Nietzsche himself makes clear in the nodule in question, is that those who practice such arts "attain satisfaction" with themselves. His idea of satisfaction is not reducible to that calculus of uncultivated pleasure valorized in some versions of British utilitarianism. For such a feeling could be set in an underlying mood of resentment against the lack of intrinsic purpose in the world. It, rather, involves an enhanced feeling for existence, a "gratitude" for the abundance of life that many people, if and when they are fortunate, are already inhabited by to some degree. Nietzsche's idea of satisfaction is actually closer to the Buddhist sense of "the ultimate nature of awareness," and "fathomless well spring of intuitive wisdom, compassion and power" attained through arts of meditation than to a utilitarian calculus of pleasure, although his emphasis on maintaining dissonance among activism, experimentalism, and grace may not mesh entirely with the corollary balance in Buddhism.[25] The feeling for existence Nietzsche seeks to amplify through self-artistry also touches those "background feelings" that Antonio Damasio addresses in his study of the neurophysiology of affective thought. Such a sense gives tone to a life. "A background feeling is not what we feel when we jump out of our skin for sheer joy, or when we are despondent over lost love. . . . A background feeling corresponds instead to the body state prevailing *between* emotions. [It] is our image of the body landscape when it is not shaken by emotion."[26] It is the affirmation of existence that Nietzschean arts seek to fold into the background of being. The goal is to fold a visceral affirmation of life more robustly into being, even as you understand that disaster or misfortune might overcome it at some point. Nietzsche, the modern Sophocles, thereby tracks several religions in their appreciation of ritual, music, and rhythm in spiritual life, but he does so without himself adopting a theology of transcendence. The close connection between enhancement of the feeling for existence and a generous ethical sensibility surfaces in the following formulation. It is crucial that a "human being should *attain* satisfaction with himself, whether it be by means of this or that poetry or art. . . . Whoever is dissatisfied with himself is continually ready for revenge, and we others will be his victims."[27]

It is pertinent to underline again that this advocate of "nobility of many kinds" and "the spiritualization of enmity" does not demand that every noble practice of artistry endorse the same fundamental interpretation of being he himself embraces. While he *contests* many who endorse, say, Christian love, Buddhist compassion, Judaic responsibility to a nameless divinity, or the Kantian presumption of pure practical reason, Nietzsche at his best—which is often enough—seeks to establish noble relations of agonistic respect between the carriers of such alternative faiths, as participants in each come to terms with the contestability of their fundamental faith in an affirmative rather than resentful way. That's one reason Nietzsche respected Jesus, even while dissenting from him. For Jesus, too, seeks to overcome existential resentment. Arts of the self, as Nietzsche presents them, both move in the region of religious ritual and aim at installing reciprocal appreciation of the contestability of different fundamental interpretations of being. The time of the old nobility, where one tradition secures its authority on the same territory, has passed, if it ever existed. That's why this defender of nobility as "nobility of many kinds" calls his most fundamental orientation a "conjecture."

But you may still contest elements in my reading of Nietzsche. No matter. Let me gather a few together, fold them into a vision of democratic pluralism, and put the result in my own voice, so the issue will be clear. In my rendering, arts of the self and micropolitics can help pluralistic democrats residing on the same territory affirm without existential resentment the profound contestability of the existential faith each honors the most, whether it has at its pinnacle a designing god, a voluntarist god, a loving god, a commanding god, an inscrutable, unnameable divinity, the emptiness of being, a moral god as a subjective postulate, or an abundant, opaque, mobile world without a god. Such an orientation goes beyond the intellectualism of liberal tolerance precisely in the way it links artistry to the layering of presumptive generosity into visceral dimensions of the self and the materialities of cultural life; and it stretches liberal tolerance precisely to the degree it extends "critical responsiveness" (as I call it) not merely to already existing identities but to the politics of becoming by which new constituencies periodically surge into being from an opaque netherworld of difference, injury, and energy.

We have seen how arts of the self work for Nietzsche and to what layers of being they might apply. What, more closely, is the relation between self-artistry and a noble ethic for him in his middle writings? "Most of us," Nietzsche says, "are our whole lives long the fools of the way we acquired in childhood of judging our neighbors (their minds, rank, morality…) and of finding it necessary to pay homage to their evaluations." The absolutization of childhood judgments by priests, parents, politicians, political theorists, and philosophers further insulates these codes from ethical work. Ethics, as Nietzsche understands it, is intimately bound up with the work adults do on themselves to reconfigure crude childhood codes received as laws and to reconsider the intrinsic authority in which those codes are said to be anchored. He contends that we "have to *learn to think differently* — in order at last, perhaps, very late on, to attain even more: *to feel differently*."[28] Arts of the self are thus bonded to the project of folding nobility and grace into cultural relations between different faiths in the same regime. The main difference between Nietzsche and me is that he thinks it best to reserve this effort for a small set of freethinkers, while I think the compression of distance by the acceleration of pace makes it wise to pursue it among a large number of citizens in a variety of subject positions.

Nietzsche thought that morality in Christendom, as the latter was transformed by Paul following the death of Jesus, encourages people to impose rigid restraints on others and their own potential selves. Democracy, for him, compounds the problem. There is evidence to support his judgment, in the long history of Christian orientations to paganism, heresy, schism, science, inquisitions, the New World, Judaism, atheism, homosexuality, and women. But there are also important developments that press against that judgment. Above all, the post-World War II period has seen a significant development toward deepening and extending pluralism. The European Holocaust against Jews fomented a profound rethinking. And general changes in the pace and scope of public culture expose more Christians than Nietzsche ever anticipated to the experience of historical contingency in aspects of their religious identities and to the reasonable contestability in the eyes of others of their most fundamental beliefs. Although the issue is still very much in doubt, a larger number of Christian/secular democrats today cultivate dispositions in favor of multidimensional pluralism than Nietzsche ever allowed himself to imagine. During a time when things move faster than heretofore, the nobility Nietzsche admired at his best finds its most active expression in a democratic culture. For, although there can be no *guarantees* in this domain, democracy, speed, plurality, and a graceful ethos of engagement set preliminary conditions of possibility for each other.

Since Nietzsche did not explore the ennoblement of democracy, he did not appreciate, either, how much its ennoblement involves the reduction of inequalities in income, educational opportunity, and participation in governing. The noble philosopher of becoming, further, overlooked the *democratic politics of becoming* by which new events, identities, faiths, and conditions are ushered into being. That is why the philosopher of speed, the gateway, arts of the self, the cultivation of grace, and nobility as multiple nobilities both advances themes pertinent to a pluralization of grace and requires transfiguration by democrats who stand in a relation of agonistic indebtedness to him.

Over the past fifteen years or so, I have sought to valorize productive tension in democratic life between, on one side, being, recognition, predictability, rights, governance, and tolerance and, on the other, disturbance, becoming, critical responsiveness to the surge of the new, and a generous ethos of engagement between constituencies honoring different final sources. The torsion between these two forces constitutes, for me, the key to democratic pluralism. The ideas of the layering of culture, a rift in time, an ethic of cultivation, nontheistic gratitude, deep contestability, the politics of becoming, agonistic respect, critical responsiveness, studied indifference, multidimensional pluralism, and an ethos of engagement speak to a fast-paced world in which care for the protean diversity of life already has some existential foothold and no transcendental *or* nontranscendental source of morality is susceptible to universal recognition. The drive is to nourish an intracultural ethos capable of democratic governance between interdependent partisans honoring different moral sources. Each of these ideas, in turn, draws part of its inspiration from a distinctive theme in Nietzsche. His aristocratic presentations of the dissonant conjunction of the moment, a pathos of distance, nobility as multiple nobilities, being one's own guinea pig, the unequal as difference exceeding a single authoritative measure, modesty as strength, the immorality of morality, the creativity of nature, ethics as artistry, and the spiritualization of enmity provide fertile ground for plagiarization and transfiguration by those who treat democracy as the crucial cultural formation through which to sustain torsion between being and becoming. It can be left to the academic police to decide whether my transfigurations depart too far from Nietzsche as they understand him. The significant question is whether the complex can stand on its own as a network of dispositions and practices appropriate to democracy in a fast-paced world. That one remains open.

Let's note in closing a moment in Nietzsche's thought when he experimented briefly with some of the positive possibilities in democracy pursued here:

> Democracy wants to create and guarantee as much *independence* as possible: independence of opinion, of mode of life and of employment.... For the

three great enemies of independence...are the indigent, the rich and the parties. I am speaking of democracy as something to come.[29]

Nietzsche, like Wolin after him, speaks here of a connection between equality and independence in democracy, with each needing the other to develop. Like Wolin too, he focuses on democracy not as something that is, but as "something yet to come." The fragility of democracy and the element of becoming in it. To the extent a vision of democracy supports tension between the weight of existing plurality and the politics of pluralization, to that extent it is pertinent to think with and against the nineteenth-century philosopher of becoming, nontheistic gratitude, nobility, grace, and a rift in time.

S   E   V   E   N

Eccentric Flows and Cosmopolitan Culture

The Ambiguity of Speed

SHELDON WOLIN seeks to save local democracy by slowing down time. Paul Virilio lifts the issue of speed into the ether of global politics itself. It would be difficult to overstate the importance of Virilio to exploration of the effects of speed upon the late-modern condition. Everybody who engages the issue is indebted to him, even when they disagree with him profoundly. When speed accelerates, Virilio says, space is compressed. And everything else changes too: the ability to deliberate before going to war; the priority of civilian control over the military; the integrity of the territorial politics of place; the capacity to think with concepts in relation to images; the ability to escape the eye of surveillance; and so on and on. Not only does Virilio chart the multiple effects of speed, he develops an arresting vocabulary to fix these effects in our minds: the war machine, the unspecified enemy, the nonplace of speed, the negation of space, the perpetual state of emergency, the miniaturization of action, the disappearance of the present, and the integral accident. These pithy formulations encapsulate in their brevity the compression of time they represent, giving us a double dose of the phenomenon Virilio warns against.

And the danger is great. Little doubt about that. If you treat the war machine as the paradigm of speed, as Virilio does, it seems that sometime during the 1960s the ability to deliberate democratically about military action was jeopardized by the imperative to automatize split-second responses to preemptive strikes a minute or less away from their targets. My concern, nonetheless, is that Virilio allows the military paradigm to overwhelm all other modalities and experiences of speed. Virilio remains transfixed by a model of politics insufficiently attuned to the *positive* role of speed in intrastate democracy and cross-state cosmopolitanism. He underplays the positive role speed can play in ventilating dogmatic identities in the domains of religion, sensuality, ethnicity, gender, and nationality. And he remains so sunk in the memory of the territorial nation as the place of democratic deliberation that he too quickly dismisses the productive possibilities (I do not say probabilities) of cosmopolitanism in the late-modern time.

Let's listen to some moves in Virilio's presentation of the correspondences between speed, temporality, territory, democratic deliberation, nationhood, and belonging.

> The speed of the political decision depends on the sophistication of the vectors: how to transport the bomb? how fast? The bomb is political . . . not because of an explosion that should never happen, but because it is the ultimate form of political surveillance.

> Social conflicts arise from rivalries between those who occupy and preserve an eco-system as the place that specifies them as a family or group, and that therefore deserves every sacrifice, including sudden death. For "if to be is to inhabit,' not to inhabit is no longer to exist. Sudden death is preferable to the slow death . . . of the man deprived of a specific place *and thus of his identity.*

> Contraction in time, the disappearance of the territorial space, after that of the fortified city and armor, leads to a situation in which the notions of "before" and "after" designate only the future and the past in a form of war that causes the "present" to disappear in the instantaneousness of decision.

> "Unlike cinema," Hitchcock said, "with television there is no time for *suspense,* you can only have *surprise.*" This is . . . the paradoxical logic of the videoframe which privileges the accident, the surprise, over the durable substance of the message.

> In the first instance, it [war] involves the elimination of the *appearance of the facts,* the continuation of what Kipling meant when he said: "Truth is the first casualty of war." Here again it is less a matter of introducing some maneuver . . . than with the obliteration of the very principle of truth. Moral relativism has always been offensive, from time immemorial.

> The more speed increases the faster freedom decreases.[1]

But what if, as I began to argue in the last chapter, the compression of distance through speed has some of the effects Virilio records while it *also* supports the possibility of democratic pluralization within states and the periodic emergence of citizen cosmopolitanism across states speaking affirmatively to issues of ecology, peace, indigenous minorities, the legitimation of new identities and rights, and the better protection of old rights? Then acceleration would carry positive possibilities as well as dangers. And a single-minded attack on its dangers would forfeit access to its positive possibilities. Let me, then, summarize my contentions:

- The contemporary accentuation of tempo in interterritorial communications, entertainment, tourism, trade, and population migration exposes more constituencies more actively to the comparative particularity and contestability of faiths and identities they may heretofore have taken to be universal or incontestable.

- The accentuated pace in the experiences of accident, innovation, and surprise, listed by Virilio only as a destructive effect of speed, can also function over time to disrupt closed models of nature, truth, and morality into which people so readily become encapsulated, doing so in ways that support revisions in the classical paradigms of science and more active appreciation of positive possibilities in the politics of becoming by which new identities and rights are engendered.

- Virilio's identification of the territorial *nation* as repository of democratic unity and of *slow pace* as the temporal condition of national deliberation deprecates pursuit of a more expansive ethos of multidimensional pluralism that speaks to diversities, both submerged and visible, already extant on most politically organized territories.

Speed is dangerous. A military culture organized around missiles accentuates danger and compresses the time in which to respond to it. At a certain point of acceleration speed in other domains also jeopardizes freedom and shortens the time in which to engage ecological issues. But, as already suggested in the last chapter, the crawl of slow time contains significant injuries, dangers, and repressive tendencies too. Speed is therefore profoundly ambiguous. The positive possibilities in this ambiguity are lost to those who experience its effects only through nostalgia for a fictive time when a slow pace, the centered nation, the security of eternal truth, the experience of nature as purposive organism or set of timeless laws, and the solidity of thick moral universals governed experience of the world and enabled democratic deliberation.

Today, ironically, the most virulent attempts to slow things down now take the form of national and religious fundamentalisms that deploy media sound bites and military campaigns of ethnic cleansing to return to a slow, centered world. Indeed, the ambiguity of speed finds its most salient manifestation in the paradoxical contest taking place in our souls, our states, and our interstate actions between the pluralization of public cultures and their fundamentalization. Fundamentalism is the shape the desire for a slow, centered world takes when its temporal conditions of possibility are absent. The drives to pluralize and to fundamentalize culture form, therefore, two contending responses to late-modern acceleration. Each propensity intensifies under the same temporal conditions. And that struggle goes on within us as well as between us. As that contest proceeds it also becomes clear why democratic pluralists must embrace the positive potentialities of speed while working to attenuate its most dangerous effects. We explored these issues in chapter 6 primarily within the compass of the territorial state. We turn now to that dimension of citizen politics that reaches across states.

Kant and Cosmopolitanism

When Kant penned his great essays on universal peace and cosmopolitanism in the 1780s and 1790s, clocks did not have second hands; it took a week to set the print for a newspaper run, weeks to travel across Europe, months to sail across the Atlantic, longer yet to sail around the world. European engagements with people, religions, and languages in Asia and Africa were circumscribed by the slow media of travel and communication in which they were set. Such a pace of life may show itself in Kant's racial hierarchy of civilizations, with Europe at the top and Africa at the bottom; it may also find expression in his judgment that only Christianity is truly a moral religion and that the morality applicable to the entire world finds its deepest spiritual anchor in Christianity.[2]

Kant's genius finds expression in his quest for a cosmopolitanism that rises above the particularity of a single nation; but the limits of that cosmopolitanism are bound to the temporal assumptions in which it is contained. That cosmopolitanism, as we shall see, gains a grip in Kant's moral imagination only because it flows from a transcendental imperative to act *as if* the world were filled with a *providential direction* that stretches beyond the reach of human agency. Kant's moral transcendentalism enables cosmopolitanism to function as a regulative ideal in his time. But the form that transcendentalism is constrained to assume also folds an element of European superiority and dogmatism into cosmopolitanism.

What, exactly, is the relation between Kant's image of universal morality and his injunction to cosmopolitanism? Morality, according to the famous Kantian dictum, takes the form of a categorical imperative that applies universally. He devises simple tests to help people decide when a candidate for moral law passes muster. But prior to those tests, making them possible and necessary, is the insistent idea that *morality itself takes the form of a law binding on everyone.* How does Kant know this to be so? How does he conclude so authoritatively that diverse theorists of ethics in Europe such as Epicurus, Lucretius, Spinoza, Montaigne, and Hume, as well as vast numbers of people outside Europe adopting other sources of ethical inspiration, are mistaken in deviating from this fundamental dictum? He does not, he acknowledges, *know* it. He cannot, he agrees, prove this fundamental dimension of his theory by any argument. Rather, Kant treats this categorical judgment about the very form of morality itself as a fundamental *recognition* always already achieved by every ordinary person who has not been confounded by individual perversity or thrown astray by the dictates of an underdeveloped civilization.

Kant's critique of pure reason in the domains of explanation and understanding does set limits beyond which understanding and "speculative" reason cannot proceed. These are limits to which contemporary realists, neorealists, rational-choice theorists, and empiricists would have to conform if they abided by the Kantian dictates of modesty in explanation. But morality, as practical reason—that is, as non-theoretical reason—*is* pure and unmediated. Here is how Kant distinguishes the two:

> For whatever needs to draw the evidence of its reality from experience must depend for the ground of its possibility on principles of experience; by its very notion, however, *pure practical reason cannot be held to be dependent in this way.* Moreover, the moral law is given, *as an apodictically certain fact, as it were, of pure reason....* Thus the objective reality of the moral law can be proved through no deduction, through no exertion of the theoretical, speculative, or empirically supported reason; and even if one were willing to renounce its apodictic certainty, it could not be confirmed by any experience and thus proved a posteriori. Nevertheless, *it is firmly established of itself.*[3]

The fundamental character of morality is not known by conceptual reasoning; it is recognized apodictically. And all of Kant's characteristic strictures about the moral effect of *publicity*, the proper role of *philosophy* in the university, moral *enlightenment, universal history, perpetual peace*, and *cosmopolitanism* reflect the practical implications of the apodictic recognition that precedes, enables, and requires them. These ideas are not forms of knowledge but (variously) postulates, hopes, and dutiful projections that follow from apodictic recognition of the proper form of morality. As we shall see through Kant's encounter with Spinoza, however, these postulates and *as if* injunctions also function secondarily as props to the very recognition that grounds them. For if the postulate/props were pulled away, the initial, apodictic recognition of morality as law would begin to unravel too. How solid and universal, then, is the linchpin? How solid or fragile is apodictic recognition?

The cultural attainment of Kantian recognition may depend in part on the tempo of life in which it is pursued. I want to suggest, at any rate, that the steadfastness and generality of Kantian recognition is even more difficult to sustain today than it was in Kant's time. And it faced difficulties then. As distance between places becomes abridged and plurality within each becomes enhanced, what appears in Kantian philosophy as an unavoidable moment of universal recognition increasingly becomes a critical site of cultural contestation. Today, the Kantian recognition of the constitutive form of morality is endorsed fervently by some, rejected intensely by others, ignored by many, and strained through a vague sense of uncertainty by yet others. It can be confessed as a contestable act of faith; it might even be imposed through cultural war as the official judgment of an entire country or even civilization. But it cannot be shown without doubt to function, as Kant thought it must, as an apodictic, spontaneous basis of morality achieved prior to moral argument and cultural induction.

Moreover, it never was all that secure. The Kantian model of recognition carried with it the translation of the Christian God heretofore confessed directly and "dogmatically" (as he put it) into a necessary subjective postulate of morality. Both the model of recognition and the demotion of the God were criticized in Kant's time by those who confessed direct obedience and devotion to a loving/commanding God and, although in much smaller numbers, by others who supported a nontheistic ethic of cultivation over the command and teleological models set in the theological tradition. Kant got into trouble with ecclesiastical and state authorities for giving morality priority over ecclesiology. But he joined them in castigating and marginalizing others who adopted an ethic of cultivation that did not place a god either at the highest site of command or as the implication of a necessary morality of command. Kantian cosmopolitanism cannot tolerate plural sources of morality.

If apodictic recognition—as the linchpin of Kantian morality—is even more contestable and contested today, this shift in its status throws into question the model of cosmopolitanism derived from it. It does so, moreover, in a time when the need for a cosmopolitan dimension of politics is greater than ever. Let's look more closely, then, at the connection between his conception of morality and his model of cosmopolitanism. Both "realism" and "idealism," as defined in contemporary international relations theory, find places within the Kantian system. If Kant had accepted "theoretical reason" but scrapped "pure practical reason," for instance, he might be a realist of the most uncompromising sort.[4] He would discern no sign of progress in history; he would counsel states to be governed by narrow self-interest; he would predict an endless series of wars and other catastrophes. History would appear to Kant as "an aimlessly playing nature" in which "hopeless chance" governs.[5]

The undeniable integrity of *practical* reason changes things. It demands, despite what actual history may teach, that we act *as if* nature and history are intelligible. It suggests, further, that we act *as if* there is a guiding thread in history that pulls us, beyond the reach of effective human agency, toward a cosmopolitan world in which peace between nations can prevail. Practical reason tells us to "assume" that an "idea" of progress operates within the ugly empirical history of war and commerce; it tells us to "regard" history and nature as "providential"; it enables us to "hope" that the dictates of the moral will might be aided in the individual by grace and in collective life by a providence that exceeds the possible reach of human agency. Here is a formulation expressing the idea:

> I will thus permit myself to assume that since the human race's natural end is to make steady cultural progress, its moral end is to be conceived as progressing toward the better. And this progress may occasionally be *interrupted*, but it will never be *broken off*. It is not necessary for me to prove this assumption; the burden of proof is on its opponents. For I rest my case on my innate duty...—the duty so to affect posterity that it will become continually better (something that must be assumed to be possible).[6]

The "innate duty" to cosmopolitanism, the practical assumption of its possibility, and the idea of providence in nature and history all flow from the same slender reed of apodictic recognition at the base of Kantian morality. That is why Kant says—to the realist in others and in himself—that "empirical arguments against the success of these resolutions, which are based on hope, fail here."[7] International relations theorists who criticize Kantian cosmopolitanism on empirical grounds miss this point. They address the historical probability of cosmopolitan efficacy, not the moral necessity to act as if it were possible and could become efficacious.

It is clear to Kant that human agency by itself is radically insufficient to realize the cosmopolitan idea in his time. The slow pace of history helps Kant to adopt a subjective postulate of providence to supersede the reach of human agency. So the Kantian trust in providence in the otherwise uncertain flow of commerce, wars, migrations, and natural disasters speaks to "what human nature does in and with us so as to compel us to a path that we ourselves would not readily follow." But the assumption of providence itself flows in part from a disjunction between the historical fact that "while men's ideas *[Ideen]* can extend to the whole as such, *their influence cannot*, not just because it is too vast for them, but primarily because it would be difficult for them to freely unify their conflicting plans into a single purpose."[8]

Kant projected dramatic possibilities into the future as he sought to find signs in history of the progress he was obligated to project into it. He projected an "unbroken" historical progress promoted by the beneficent effects of "pathological" wars, the extension of gentleness in commerce, and the gradual cultivation of a higher moral culture by these and other pathological means. But he did not anticipate—nor could he be expected to have done so—the late-modern compression of global distance, the tightening of global interdependencies and inequalities, the accentuation of diversity on politically organized territories and the multiplication of global dangers through the acceleration of speed in military delivery systems, communication networks, production processes, commercial activity, cross-territorial migrations, refugee movements, tourism, disease transmission, criminal networks, ecological effects, drug trade, interstate social movements, nuclear danger, and climatic change. Had he done so, he might have sensed how the apodictic recognition of morality he took to be implicit in every normal person and every culture could be challenged through an intensification of intraterritorial pluralization and cross-territorial compression. And he might have seen how the gap between the scope of possible agency and the aspiration to cosmopolitanism could close somewhat through speed.

Today the specific terms of that cosmopolitanism have not only become even more contestable, they continue to carry within them elements of a dogmatic Western imperialism still in need of reconstruction. One key, in my judgment, is to relinquish the demand that all reasonable people in all cultures must actually or implicitly recognize the logic of morality in the same way Kant did. Or even as neo-Kantian universalists do.[9] Once this pivot of Kantian morality is transfigured into a contestable act of faith finding its most active expression in states

shaped by the history of Christianity on the European continent and the settler societies it spawned, it becomes more feasible to engage a late-modern world of speed
and dense interdependencies. For today cosmopolitanism involves the difficult task
of coming to terms receptively and reciprocally with multiple and contending final
sources of morality. Some of these sources predominate in this or that area of the
world, but several contenders also find active expression *within* a variety of territorial states. Kantianism can provide one noble moral faith within a plural matrix of
cosmopolitanism. But this cultural particularism can no longer pretend to set the
universal matrix of cosmopolitanism itself.

Concentric and Eccentric Culture

Today, when speed compresses distance and intercultural action transcends state
boundaries, the cosmopolitan dimension of politics becomes both unavoidable and
diverse. There are military, corporate, Christian, Islamic, Jewish, Muslim, ecological, aboriginal, and feminist modes of cosmopolitanism for starters, with each type
containing considerable variety in itself and involved in a series of alliances and
struggles with several of the others. Even fervent nationalists of a decade ago are
hopping onto the bumper of the cosmopolitan bandwagon. Thus Samuel Huntington,
recently a devotee of the nation-state and the provincial citizen, now invokes what
might be called *civilizopolism*. This is Huntington's implicit concession to the compression of territory by the acceleration of speed: The territorial nation, he concludes, is no longer large enough to secure the political unity essential to military security and civilian governance. It must be secured by a more encompassing civilization.[10]

Unlike Kant, Huntington does not project a (Western) universal
that non-Western cultures might someday hope to emulate. Rather, he now defines
"Western civilization" as a *unique, nonuniversalizable territorial formation* that exceeds
the size of any territorial state and must be protected from migration and other as-
saults from other territorial "civilizations." But even as he cuts the Kantian universal
down to civilizational size, he shares with Kant *a concentric model of political culture*.
For Kant culture radiates out from the individual through the family to the nation,
and he projects a future whole in which all nations participate in the same "moral religion." The latter forms the largest circle of concentric culture. Huntington adopts
another variant of the same image of culture. The world is organized for him into
several territorial civilizations. And "Western civilization" forms the largest circle
of identification in which Huntington himself participates. Identity in "the West,"
Huntington thinks, flows from the family to the neighborhood to the community to
the nation to Western civilization and back again, with each arc in this spiral resonat-

ing with identities, mores, customs, values, and interests in the others. So Huntington and Kant split on the debate between "particularism" and "universalism." But they both locate that debate within a concentric image of culture. In fact the familiar debate between particularists and universalists is often set in a concentric model of culture elevated above critical interrogation by the disputants.

In a fast-paced world "the West" cannot be self-sustaining. So Huntington gives primary responsibility to "the core state" within Western civilization, that is, to the United States. Its job is to protect the larger civilizational complex from multiculturalism on the inside as well as economic and military threats from the outside. To sustain this model of civilizational governance, however, Huntington must anticipate citizens whose identifications and allegiances do not stop at the boundaries of the state within which they reside. Some dimensions of membership, such as the sense of belonging and support for cross-state, intracivilizational actions, extend to the edges of Western civilization as such—wherever those edges are. As Huntington puts it in a formulation expressing succinctly the concentric image of political culture, "A civilization is an extended family."[11] Huntington, the former defender of national interest narrowly defined, has remade himself into a civilizopolite.

The need today, however, is to complicate the images of nationalism and civilizopolism by paying attention to numerous eccentric connections that exceed them. The idea is not to delegitimate all concentric identifications as such. For you may well have a sense of belonging to the family that nourishes you or wish to participate in the state that governs you. It is to appreciate how—particularly during a time when speed compresses distance—concentric circles of political culture are complicated and compromised by numerous crosscutting allegiances, connections, and modes of collaboration. It is to lift the experience of eccentric culture above the automatic connotation of isolation, perversity, and marginalization that itself reveals the extent to which the concentric image prevails, doing so to identify eccentric flows of flight, compassion, connection, allegiance, identification, legitimacy, responsiveness, and responsibility that exceed the concentric image of how political culture does and must function. Even more, it is to take advantage of the possibilities created by the compression of distance to *enact* a more vibrant plurality of eccentric connections cutting through and across concentric enclosures. You might cultivate ties to ecologists or feminists in South America more significant than those you share on these two issues with some neighbors, in-laws, or corporate leaders in your state. You might support cross-country citizen networks designed to protect rain forests in several countries (including your own), or to reduce toxic emissions in the world, doing so to support future life anywhere and everywhere on the planet.[12]

You might support movements to honor a plurality of moral sources within and across states, perhaps finding more allies among atheists in Europe, Buddhists in Tibet, Arabs in Israel, and secularists in Australia than in your neighborhood or professional association. And you might cultivate a network of interconnections among these territorially dispersed constituencies. You might forge extrastate lines of connection with aboriginal peoples, targets of state torture, refugees, or boat people, partly because you extrapolate from experiences of minority standing in your own state to these more radical conditions, partly because your state may have helped to produce the injuries involved, and partly because you realize that cross-state citizen pressure is often needed to modify oppressive state, interstate, and international corporate practices.

In these cases, and numerous others, your participation may require creative political tactics, such as the formation of e-mail networks to protect the rain forests, or a cross-border citizen divestment movement to end apartheid, or the organization of cross-country boycotts against corporations using child labor, or the introduction of cross-border labor negotiations with international corporations, or the creation of global tribunals to try symbolically tyrants who remain beyond the reach of effective tribunals in their own states.[13] The key point is that such assemblages involve activists in advanced capitalist states listening and responding to the initiatives of migrant workers from other states, indigenous leaders within your state, women seeking educational opportunity in India, and participants in insurgent movements in Africa. Those who have been diasporized through complex histories of colonization, migration, creolization, asylum, and flight provide key mediating links through which new assemblages of cosmopolitan action are forged: cosmopolitan connections moving across the concentric dimension of culture as well as in its circles; a cosmopolitanism organized through ec-centric connections as well as concentric attachments. Still, the question is inevitably posed, if Kantian universalism does not provide the highest circle of guidance for cosmopolitan movements in a world marked by ec-centric and concentric connections, what else does or could? How do you connect to others elsewhere without a firm universal accepted by all? Are such efforts necessarily devoid of inspiration and guidance? If so, do they collapse into relativism, subjectivism, provincialism, or narcissism? Martha Nussbaum thinks so. She thinks that unless "we" reach a consensus on a thick, vague experience of the universal, there will not be enough to draw upon to inspire and inform citizen actions that stretch beyond the circle of the "country." Nussbaum is a cosmopolite who reaches beyond the moral circle of the nation in the name of the universal. Here is what she says:

We should *recognize humanity wherever it occurs*, and give its fundamental ingredients, *reason and moral capacity*, our first allegiance and respect.

We should give our first allegiance to no mere form of government, no temporal power, but to *the moral community made up by the humanity of all human beings*. The idea of the world citizen is in this way the ancestor and source of Kant's idea of the "kingdom of ends." ... One should always behave so as to treat with equal respect *the dignity of reason and moral choice in every human being*.

They must learn enough about the different to recognize *common aims*, aspirations, and values, and enough about these common ends to see how variously they are instantiated in many cultures and their histories.

If one begins life as a child who loves and trusts his or her parents it is tempting to want ... an idealized image of a nation (as) a surrogate parent.... Cosmopolitanism offers no such refuge; it offers *only reason and the love of humanity*, which may seem at times less colorful than other sources of belonging.[14]

There are things to admire in Nussbaum's position, particularly by comparison to that of Huntington. She refuses to curtail connections and obligations to others once you reach the boundaries of your "nation" or your "civilization." In *For Love of Country* Nussbaum's case for extending such commitments beyond the states we inhabit derives primarily from Kant, as these quotations amply indicate. She does not, however, evince any appreciation of the dicey role that apodictic recognition plays at the very base of Kantian morality. And that presents difficulties if she wants to forge ec-centric connections beyond the historical orbit of Christendom. Nor does she address the intrastate diversity of fundamental moral sources, one that becomes urgent when migrations and internal mutations draw many who are neither Christian nor Kantian into states with a predominantly Christian heritage.

In another essay, however, Kant gives ground to Aristotle. I do not know how Nussbaum squares her Aristotle with her Kant, but I imagine she might proceed by saying that the Kantian element provides the authoritative basis for moral obligation to people in other cultures (but must they accept that basis too?), while her modified Aristotelianism fills out (more than Kant would) the functional universals to which to appeal in cross-cultural engagements.

Nussbaum calls her list of universals "thick and vague." I like that characterization, as a first approximation. These formulations rise, she then says, above differences in metaphysical or religious orientation. Hmmmm, I have heard that one before. They can be filled out in particular ways in each "locality." Their thickness gives "us" resources to draw upon in expressing and informing compassion for people suffering in other places. And their vagueness allows them to be particularized to those localities. So Nussbaum appreciates both the "universal" and "the particular."

Sounds pretty good, huh? But not, on reflection, good enough. There is far too little appreciation in Nussbaum's account of how much each rendering of the universal itself is shaped and conditioned by the specific cultural experiences from which it is crafted. Consider merely the first two items on her list of ten universal goods:

1) Being able to live to the end of a complete human life, as far as is possible; not dying prematurely, or before one's life is so reduced as to be not worth living.

2) Being able to have good health; to be adequately nourished; to have adequate shelter; having opportunities for sexual satisfaction; being able to move from place to place.[15]

Yes, these vague generalities make a claim on us. I embrace them. But as soon as three people anywhere discuss them a series of intense debates arise as to how they are to be interpreted and applied. And yet the list of universals is supposed to regulate those debates. Thus the situation today with respect to several issues encompassed by merely the first two items on the list:

• The right to doctor-assisted suicide

• The relation between sensuality and chastity

• The relation between marriage and sexuality

• The legitimacy of homosexuality

• The legitimacy of abortion

There are profound disagreements over those issues, often between people who endorse the language adopted by Nussbaum. And it is imperative to acknowledge that these differences occur *within* numerous localities and states as well as *across* them. Such debates often reflect philosophical/religious differences. Take the issue of dying. Epicurus, Augustine, Kant, and Nietzsche — to select merely four exemplary perspectives only within Europe broadly defined—disagree profoundly on the question of when and how to die. Augustine insists that we are obligated to wait until God takes us. Kant agrees. He holds all those who attempt suicide in contempt. Nietzsche, however, recommends that you prepare yourself now to end life at the point when it falls below a minimal threshold of consciousness and vitality. Augustine and Kant would thus resist doctor-assisted suicide out of respect for the grace and wisdom of the universal God; Epicurus and Nietzsche would support it to encourage people to fend off existential resentment against finitude and the absence of an intrinsic purpose so as to be better able to tap into the existential fund of compassion and generosity in this life. To probe the issue more closely would be to encounter further nuanced difference between Epicurus and Nietzsche, as well as between Augustine and Kant.

All these differences flow to a significant degree from metaphysical/ religious differences lodged within a universal that proves to be more jerry-rigged than it might appear at first glance. Moreover, neither Nussbaum nor I thought of doctor-assisted suicide as a contemporary possibility until a new social movement converted it into an issue for us. And this despite the fact that we both embrace the relevant universals. Such surprises will occur again. And again.

These sharp disagreements find ample expression in contemporary life, again, *within* localities and states as well as *across* them. As do similar disagreements with respect to the other issues noted above. When you fold Islam, Buddhism, and Hinduism into the picture, the intralocal and cross-state plurality are both enlarged.

Nussbaum wants a general, nonmetaphysical list of thick, vague universals because she finds it impossible to imagine how compassion could find expression across states unless you uncover such an overarching consensus. She thus regularly describes those who contest the *sufficiency* of thick universals as "relativists" or "subjectivists" who lack compassion. These types are figured as cold, amoral, playful beings. The compassionate Nussbaum in fact shows little empathy for what these eccentric critters are trying to accomplish. Her representations sound eerily close to those Augustine gave of those pagans who did not endorse his universal God.

I contend, first, that there are actually few relativists running around these days and, second, that compassion plays a significant role in most of the orientations Nussbaum disparages. Nietzsche makes the same point about compassion in *Beyond Good and Evil* when he says it is "compassion, in other words, against compassion,"[16] a compassion (in his case) toward the "creator" in us that resists giving full hegemony to the "creature" in us. Nor do many theorists who resist Nussbaum's single-entry model of the universal represent *themselves* to be relativists. Nietzsche, for instance, claims that the drive to ressentiment finds some expression in every culture. He seeks to inspire more people to resist its ugly and punitive orientation toward eccentric elements of life wherever it arises. That does not sound to me like someone who says let every country or locality do as it pleases. Derrida thinks deconstruction is an important strategy to apply to every text and cultural practice, because of the unethical tendency in the infrastructure of cultural life per se to conceal points of rational undecidability in its universal formulas and to make the concentric habits of cultural judgment look, well, more generous and compassionate than they are.

So I dissent from Nussbaum's representations of her opponents. But why is she drawn to these representations? It is pertinent to note that her texts disclose a powerful tendency *to identify territorial cultures as if they were concentric, national cultures surrounded by a set of thick, vague universals.* It seems to me, however, that most politically organized territories today contain powerful tendencies that exceed and compromise the concentric image through which Nussbaum constitutes culture.[17] Cultural lines of flow, connection, flight, and compassion are ec-centric as well as con-centric.

Would Nussbaum's moral compulsion to misrepresent her opponents become less intense if her own conception of territorial culture were less concentric? I think so. For if relativism means accepting whatever norms a nation or locality adopts, it makes most sense either to *be* one or to *accuse others of being so* if *you* picture politically organized territories of the world as concentric cultures. Relativism, either as sin or as virtue, is implicitly invested in a concentric image of territorial culture. The charge thus reveals more about the presumptions and ideals of those who toss it around than about its targets. Hence Nussbaum, Virilio, and several others. The concentric model of culture also helps to explain Nussbaum's impatient irritation with deconstruction and genealogy. For if you are governed by a concentric image, you will see little reason for strategies designed to bring out the way that very image suppresses, marginalizes, and conceals eccentric flows and connections. And it will make all the sense in the world to conclude that those who practice these arts lack compassion, for you yourself are tone-deaf to the eccentricities to which that receptivity and compassion are applied.[18]

Let's test these speculations. Consider Nussbaum's imagination of a place called "Textualité," a world on another planet where those in love with French deconstructionism, as Nussbaum understands it, have won the cultural war with thick universalists:

There are on Textualité many nations. Some are rich and some are very poor. Within most of the nations, there are also large inequalities that have perceptible effects on the health and mobility and educational level of the inhabitants. The people of Textualité do not see things as we see them. For they have really discarded — not just in theory but in the fabric of their daily lives — the Earthly tendencies of thought that link the perception of one's neighbor's pain to the memory of one's own and the perception of a stranger's pain to the experience of a neighbor's, all this through the general idea of the human being and human flourishing. To these people, strangers simply look very strange. They are seen as other forms of life who have nothing in common with their own lives.[19]

Nussbaum shows how empty and cruel such a world would be. I agree. But in doing so she continues to misrepresent a series of political philosophies already in circulation on Earth. For she projects onto Textualité the same concentric image of culture she unconsciously clamps onto this one. That investment finds expression in the interdeterminations between a world of "many nations," "the people of Textualité" (all of whom have lost the human capacity for compassion), "they," "strangers," and "forms of life." She thinks that if they do not share a thick conception of human flourishing they must appear as strangers to one another. This charge reveals an inability to come to terms with a variety of connections across difference in which people touch each other now in this way and now in that, and through which larger webs of alliance and loyalty are often forged. Her description of Textualité reflects her own implicit demand that thick universals and concentric culture be joined together. Textualité tells us more about Nussbaum than about the positions she criticizes. Nussbaum's concentric model of culture discourages her from coming to terms with the politics of becoming by which new identities flow into being and through which new connections and alliances are often forged. It also discourages her from exploring the ethics of those eccentric flows already in motion within and across territorial regimes.

Nussbaum does advise cosmopolites to pay attention to the "particularities" of foreign places. You compare your cultural assumptions to theirs to locate the element of *commonality* between them. Not a bad recommendation. But also insufficient. For often enough, *commonalities across cultures themselves urgently need to be subjected to critical scrutiny.* Previous conceptions of women, sexuality, race, and the obligation to ground a state in one religion carried considerable weight across several regimes at one time or another. Many treated them as parts of the thick universal. But each was eventually called into question at a later date by eccentric movements within and across those same regimes. And, moreover, when eccentric connections become consolidated, they might both resist resolution into concentric form and throw off that aura of denigration previously surrounding them in the concentric world they now complicate. Such things are apt to happen again. And again.

The *insufficiency* of the concentric image and thick universals must be challenged together. It is appropriate to put some ethical money on thick universals that have acquired cultural density in your regime, as you weigh the desire of people to be judged according to operative standards of desert, sexual normality, marriage practice, punishment, dying, parenting arrangements, faith, and so on. But if you put *too much* money on them you won't have much to go on when new, unexpected movements induce a sense of anxiety or panic into a chunk of your religious faith, your sexuality, your gender, your conception of reason, or the source of morality you honor. You won't have enough to go on as the acceleration of pace throws uncertainty into some operative dimensions of your way of life that have inadvertently become consolidated into the layered experience of thick universals. You will be inclined to treat the next surprise automatically as an affront to the proper authority of the universal.

Because we *are* empirically defined, to a significant degree, by the circles in which we move, *we need periodically to work on ourselves to de-universalize selective particularities that have become universalized in or by us.* And we are unlikely to know in advance exactly which operative universals will need the most work. So, again, it is not that the concentric image misrepresents territorial culture entirely or that thick universals must be scrapped. Far from it. But when insufficiently complicated by an appreciation of dense, eccentric flows that cross and disrupt these circles, the concentric image points you either to the bellicose particularism of the nation/ civilization (Huntington) or to the impatient universalism of concentric cosmopolitanism (Nussbaum).

Nussbaum weaves the images of slow time, concentric culture, thick universals, the eclipse of metaphysics, consensus, compassion, and respect for particularity into a picture of a world in which the acceleration of pace does not make a difference. While respecting the extranational aspiration that inspires her, I invoke, first, a rift in time made more visible by the acceleration of pace today; second, creative tension between concentric and eccentric connections in cultural life; third, a double-entry orientation to the universal (yet to be discussed); fourth, an element of contestability in any specific rendering of the universal; and fifth, a practice of compassion that includes critical responsiveness to new flows of identity and aspiration challenging the previous sense of sufficiency of concentric culture.[20]

Imagine a slow world elsewhere in the universe called Concentricus. There people live entirely in circles of belonging that radiate out from the unity of the individual, through the family, neighborhood, locality, region, territorial nation, and civilization to a dense ring of universals that forms a beautiful aura around the whole. Their compassion is bountiful as it flows up from lower to higher universals and down again to lower particulars. Theorists in Concentricus do debate whether the largest circle is the universal, the civilization, the nation, or the community, but other than that they are pretty much in harmony with one another. Delicate adjustments are made to the particularities of each locality, as these are created by variations in climate, technology, economic specialization, and so forth. But neither agonistic respect nor compassion is forthcoming for differences and eccentricities that do not fit the concentric scheme; nor is critical responsiveness extended to movements that seek to create space for new things to be in ways that challenge elements in *both* the settled character of the locality and the aura of the universal. Differences that exceed, compromise, extend, or break the web of concentric circles are authoritatively defined through the dismissive vocabularies of relativism, subjectivism, narcissism, nihilism, and perversity. For Concentricus does not recognize noncircular orders of being and becoming.

Fortunately, we do not quite live in this horrific world of one-dimensional compassion. But some movements marching under the complementary banners of particularism, localism, nationalism, civilizationalism, and universalism remain eager to create it.

Toward a New Matrix of Cosmopolitanism

Speed is not the only solvent of thick universals. Surprising events can also shock cultural sedimentations when things move at a fairly slow pace. Thus Bartolomé de Las Casas, the sixteenth-century Spanish priest who accompanied the Conquistadors to the New World, eventually shifted from a campaign to convert "the pagans" in the New World to Christianity to a quest to roll back the incredible destruction of Amerindian life engendered by the conversion imperative of Christianity. An agonizing reappraisal of the Christian universalism he brought with him to the New World enabled him to accomplish this amazing feat of self-redefinition.[21] One side of his faith, Christian *love*, moved him to modify the universal *doctrine* of Christianity under new and surprising circumstances. He came to terms anew, for instance, with the element of mystery in divinity; and he began to think of Christian and New World cosmologies as two diverse ways to engage the element of mystery. His Christian universalism, that is, became more hesitant and cautious, and this hesitancy allowed him to forge new connections with non-Christian faiths. That, at least, was his eventual reaction to the stunning shock to his faith engendered by the encounter with a New World populated by millions of people who did not recognize the universal God.

The acceleration of pace may increase the number of such shocks and surprises, even as it multiplies lines of contact and connection. Sometimes the surprise numbs its recipients, at least for a time. That is one of the dangers of an accelerated tempo of life. But when joined to a double-entry orientation to thick universals, the acceleration of pace can also inspire generous *possibilities* of thought, judgment, and connection otherwise unlikely to emerge.[22]

Today, for instance, the speed and global networks of communication make it a little less easy to avoid the question of the place of indigenous peoples in "settler societies." Vigorous movements by indigenous peoples in the United States, Canada, Australia, and New Zealand are magnified by the ability of these constituencies to combine their efforts and reach an audience beyond the states in which they are contained. For hegemonic constituencies, responsiveness to such movements involves agonizing reconsideration of the practices of sovereignty, territoriality, and nationhood that have informed them.[23] A similar set of cross-country pressures is discernible with respect to homosexuality. The activation of cross-national gay rights movements places internal and external pressure on a variety of states to reconsider the universalization and naturalization of heterosexuality. And since the naturalization of heterosexuality has been inscribed on several layers of being, including the visceral level, the cultivation of responsiveness to these movements involves work on the intersubjective layers of being by multimedia means such as films, speeches, marches, and demonstrations. You reenact some of the ways in which heterosexuality became naturalized to deprogram it as an implicit universal.

Perhaps some theorists depreciate the ambiguity and layered character of constitutive universals because they want morality to function smoothly without the agents of morality having to work critically on the shape of their own layered identities. They wish ethics were less disruptive to the stability of identity than it often must be. But the most fundamental obstacle to ethical mobilization is not, as Kantians and neo-Kantians often think, mustering the collective will to enact a thick universal already there. That is difficult enough. The most fateful ethical issues arise when unexpected conflicts emerge over the shape of thick universals themselves in ways that disturb visceral elements of identity in the parties involved. For these conflicts involve deep disagreements over the legitimate sources to appeal to in negotiating them. Genealogy, deconstruction, and political disturbance can be deployed to help call some elements in the settled interpretation of thick universals into question when such disagreements arise. These strategies also help to call into question the incontestability of the moral sources we provincials tend to treat as universal. Both of these effects are all to the good for ethics. But before productive work proceeds far, you may also need access to a regulative idea to offer positive inspiration and initial guidance. This is the point at which Kant's notion of a regulative idea might do productive work for non-Kantians. The distinction between a thick, constitutive universal and a regulative universal may already find some expression in Nussbaum's phrase "reason and *the love of humanity*," *if* the latter feeling is understood to conflict sometimes with the putative dictates of reason.

I support a double-entry orientation to the universal, then. If constitutive particulars often become consolidated in our habits, institutions, and practices *as if* they formed a set of thick universals, the very diffuseness of a regulative idea now becomes a compensatory virtue.[24] Kant's version of the regulative idea, however, needs some critical work, particularly his demand that it be the same regulative idea for everyone everywhere. In Kantian philosophy regulative reason functions as a diffuse, universal background idea, guiding, in different ways, speculative reason, practical reason, and aesthetic judgment. Regulative reason is unified, even as it manifests itself differently in each domain and even though we are incapable of formulating this idea in clear concepts. But the Kantian regulative idea presupposes a two-world metaphysic of the supersensible and the sensible. It thus embraces a profoundly contestable metaphysic during a time in which the global variety of religious/metaphysical perspectives is both visible and palpable.

Perhaps today in a world revolving faster than heretofore we can act *as if* a diversity of regulative ideals is both ineliminable and replete with promise. There are multiple regulative ideas in play, but, against the Kantian expectation and demand, it does seems unlikely that a single one will emerge as the diffuse source that all thoughtful pluropolites must draw upon. For some, the regulative idea might be responsibility to difference inspired by a monotheism of the Book; for others, contact with the nothingness of being that may inspire participants in Buddhism; and for yet others, the Kantian idea of reason. Each variant of cosmopolitanism secretes a distinctive regulative idea, then. If a general matrix is to become consolidated, several of these variations must find ways to enter into receptive negotiation. The task today is not to articulate one regulative idea that encompasses all others — the goal of Kantianism, religious ecumenism, and single-entry universalism. Nor is it to rise above metaphysical differences, as if that were an easy or possible thing to do. The task today is to inspire more participants in each religious and metaphysical tradition to come to terms receptively with its comparative contestability and to explore creative lines of connection to other orientations. That order, while tall enough, is no taller than the call to diversify Christianity within European states was at the inception of secularism. It sets a horizon toward which to move as time flies by.

The term *idea*, in my use, means a thought-imbued affect that enters into an ethical sensibility. A regulative idea is not something you invoke every time judgment is needed. It comes into play most actively when the necessity or morality of some elements in a thick universal already in circulation has been called into question. *It comes into play most dramatically during those numerous junctures when the forking of time is significant, ushering events, pressures, or constituencies into being imperfectly appreciated by established interpretations of the universal.* The contemporary acceleration of pace, and the larger differentials between zones of time, accelerate the occurrence of such strategic moments.

Let me, then, identify two regulative ideas that inspire nontheists such as me in such situations, to the extent I can. They are attachment to the earth and care for a protean diversity of being that is never actualized completely in any particular cultural setting. These thought-imbued sources of inspiration in turn are grounded in visceral gratitude for an abundance of being that precedes them. Such attachments and ideas, however, do not transcend the interests, desires, and identities of those moved by them; rather, they enter into these modalities, stretching them a little here and ennobling them a bit there. Such ideas are capable of inspiring a significant minority ethically; they are susceptible to further cultivation by artistic means; and they are invaluable to draw upon periodically when some elements in a constitutive universal heretofore occupying you has been called into question by a new fork in time. Moreover, these regulative ideas may help nontheists learn how to listen more closely to less earthy ethical orientations. For many devotees of one or another religion of the Book construe the most fundamental ideas in our perspective to be indispensable way stations in their own perspectives; while we consider the fundamental conceptions of divinity they endorse to be contestable projections we can respect as contestable possibilities without adopting them ourselves. Here we uncover, then, a potential line of selective *connection* that does not assume the form of an overarching *commonality*. There are numerous other such possibilities.

The idea-feelings in the regulative ideal I embrace are susceptible to cultivation if and when they already have some foothold in the sensibility informing your conduct. There is no cosmic guarantee that such a sensibility must find a foothold in everyone. Having a relatively fortunate childhood helps. Once it has acquired existential weight, the affect-imbued ideas in it can be activated and mobilized by particular events. You might, for instance, encounter unexpected suffering in others engendered by the specific interpretation of a thick universal you had heretofore accepted as part of the furniture of being. This has happened to millions of people many times over the past few decades in the domains of faith, race, income, sensuality, and gender roles.

Or you might find yourself gazing one day at a surprising image of the planet Earth. In 1968, *Apollo 8* sent back to earthlings a picture of a vivid azure planet suspended in the middle of the solar system, a stunning, bright sphere unlike any planet so far observed from the ground of the earth. This image, received as if from nowhere, underlines the fragility and uniqueness of the earth as well as its richness as a source of sustenance. Distributed to diverse places in the world, it provides a bountiful source of energy for cross-country ecological movements—a new perspective on the world enabled by speed.

By contrast to the Kantian postulate of a world intelligible in the last instance—even if humans are incapable of grasping that instance—the regulative ideas advanced here project a world containing incorrigible elements of opacity, unintelligibility, and unpredictability because it was neither created nor designed by a higher being. Such a regulative idea requires neither a "dogmatic" (as Kant would say) conception of God nor the "necessary" postulate of a moral God, although there are versions of both to which it can connect. It is grounded, let us say, in the earthy experience of groundless being in a world of abundance without higher design. Such regulative ideas move you closer to sources prospected by Epicurus, Lucretius, Spinoza, Hume, Nietzsche, and Deleuze than to those invoked by Augustine, Newton, and Kant. Again, I do not reject the latter faiths as possible sources of moral inspiration for others. I merely deny the logic of universality in which each is set.

It still remains perplexing to many Kantians, neo-Kantians, orthodox Christians, and single-entry universalists how some could be moved by such an earthy idea. And, it must be said, some of us remain perplexed as to why so many adults require either a transcendental command or the self-sufficiency of thick universals to energize and guide ethical life. The probable persistence of such reciprocal perplexity is a key issue to acknowledge and address in the new matrix of cosmopolitanism. It may be ineliminable.

Kant gives vent to such perplexity when he asks how Spinoza, who seemed moral to him, *could* consistently be so. Spinoza is a pivotal figure. This two-time heretic inside seventeenth-century Europe lived outside the protection of Christianity and Judaism, the only two organized religious communities of the time.

He is a good symbol of an eccentric in a concentrically ordered world. Spinoza, Kant says, is righteous, but is "persuaded there is no God," and "no future life." He is

> unselfish and wants only to bring about the good.... Yet his effort encounters limits: For while he can expect that nature will now and then cooperate contingently with the purpose of his that he feels so obligated and impelled to receive, he can never expect nature to harmonize with it in a way governed by laws and permanent rules (such as his inner maxims are and must be). Deceit, violence, and envy will always be rife around him, even though he himself is honest, peaceable and benevolent. Moreover... the other righteous people he meets... will stay subjected to these evils, always, until one vast tomb engulfs them... and hurls them, who managed to believe there were no final purpose in creation, back into the abyss of the purposeless chaos of matter from which they were taken.[25]

Kant resists the temptation to convict Spinoza of a "lack of compassion." He is to be appreciated for that, since Spinoza was widely condemned as an atheist in his day. But it does sound as though Spinoza—already convicted of heresy by the Jewish community in his hometown and commonly defined by Christian philosophers of the day as a Jewish philosopher—is now doomed to hell on earth by Kant because he does not endorse the Kantian postulate of a moral God. Let us set aside whether Kant correctly attributes to Spinoza the idea of nature as a "purposeless chaos of matter." The point is Kant's failure to explore how some might be *inspired* ethically by visceral and intellectual participation in a rich world held by them to be ungoverned by moral laws. Kant convicts such an orientation of a performative self-contradiction because he cannot imagine how the adventures, trials, and creative possibilities rendered vivid by such an immanent orientation could inspire a sense of responsibility to the world and the future in some. He thus de-moralizes an immanent source of ethical inspiration in others to curtail the pluralization of final moral sources in Europe. At the close of the paragraph in question, he insists that Spinoza "must, from a practical point of view... assume the existence of a *moral* author of the world, i.e., the existence of a God; and he can indeed make this assumption, since it is at least not intrinsically contradictory."[26] Let's call the universalization of this "practical point of view" transcendental blackmail. It amounts to saying, "Either you confess the apodictic recognition of morality as law and/or the thick universal I take to be essential or I will convict you of inconsistency or a lack of compassion." Such a strategy reeks of dogmatic cosmopolitanism. It is true, of course, that Spinoza also thinks his philosophy is true universally. But much more than Kant, he acknowledges robustly the need to come to terms affirmatively with the persistent plurality of final ethical sources actually embraced in the world.[27]

It may be impossible for parties on either side of the transcendental/immanent divide to appreciate *fully* the force of regulative ideas embraced by those on the other. Why so? Well, your ability to assess the inspirational power of my faith is limited by the fact that you are not yourself inhabited by it. Indeed, in a world marked by mystery and a persistent plurality of deep interpretations there is simply not enough time for mortals to inhabit experimentally every challenging possibility. If we lived forever, that difficulty might be attenuated. But we don't. Wherever mortals honor freedom, then, they might strive to come to terms ethically with the persistence of an irreducible plurality of regulative ideas. They might practice agonistic respect toward existential faiths that do not move them.

Kant walks to the edge of this perspective when he confesses that his idea of morality rests in the last instance on recognition rather than argument. But he converts his acknowledgment of the limits of argument into a demand that every reasonable person must recognize things as he does. And he secures that demand by leveling harsh charges against those inside and outside "the West" who do not do so.

But the jig is up. As the hope to secure a single regulative idea is shaken by a world spinning faster than heretofore, a small window of opportunity opens to negotiate a plural matrix of cosmopolitanisms. The possibilities of affirmative negotiation depend upon several parties relinquishing the provincial demand that all others subscribe to the transcendental, universal, immanent, or deliberative source of ethics they themselves confess. That ain't easy. Still, a start can be made in Euro-American regimes as Kantians, neo-Kantians, and Nussbaumites acknowledge the profound contestability of the conception of morality they confess most fervently, and as they adopt a modest stance toward those who do not confess it. By affirming without existential resentment the element of comparative contestability in the respective regulative ideas that move us, we contribute new energies to a plural matrix appropriate to the late-modern world. The possible consolidation of such a matrix involves cultivation of agonistic respect between parties who proceed from diverse sources. Indeed, the pursuit of agonistic respect across such lines of difference sets a threshold against which to measure the element of compassion in each. Unless, of course, one party dissolves the mysteries of being by proving that its thick universals, transcendental arguments, apodictic recognition, or discursive proof sets the sufficient frame in which everyone must participate. Don't hold your breath waiting.

To do so is to forfeit the time available to pursue a plural matrix grounded in respect for diverse responses to persisting mysteries of being.

The indispensability and deep contestability of alternative regulative ideas set two conditions of possibility for a new matrix of cosmopolitanism. To the extent that a variety of Christians, Jews, secularists, neo-Aristotelians, Islamists, Kantians, deep ecologists, Buddhists, and atheists cultivate such self-modesty in their respective existential faiths, the late-modern world becomes populated by more citizens coming to terms thoughtfully with contemporary issues unsusceptible to resolution by one country, one faith, or one philosophy.

Notes

1. The Body/Brain/Culture Network

1. Isabelle Stengers, *Power and Invention: Situating Science*, trans. Paul Bains (Minneapolis: University of Minnesota Press, 1997), 39. Much of what Stengers says about the circumstances of modern science is anticipated by Martin Heidegger in "The Age of the World Picture," in *The Question Concerning Technology*, trans. William Lovitt (New York: Harper & Row, 1977). This essay, written in 1935, poses the issues that Stengers pursues, but then responds to them in a different way.

2. The force of that history is felt even by those of us who want to refashion it. So in an article in *Australian Feminist Studies*, Elizabeth Wilson, who seeks to overcome this separation, says, "Within feminist work, a determination to refute biological reductionism has had the effect of excluding the biological from consideration altogether." Elizabeth Wilson, "Somatic Compliance: Feminism, Biology and Science," *Australian Feminist Studies* 14, no. 29 (1999): 8.

3. Antonio R. Damasio, *The Feeling of What Happens: Body and Emotion in the Making of Consciousness* (New York: Harcourt, Brace, 2000), 64–65.

4. V. S. Ramachandran, *Phantoms in the Brain: Probing the Mysteries of the Human Mind* (New York: William Morrow, 1998), 130.

5. Ibid., 47–48.

6. Spinoza distinguishes two attributes of substance, extension and thought, which are distinct but coordinated with each other. A change in one correlates with a change in the other without either causing the other. Stuart Hampshire translates Spinoza's rendering of two complementary attributes of substance into two irreducible human perspectives on the same activities, the perspective of lived experience and that of external observation of the body/brain states during those experiences. In his account a change in brain composition can have an effect on thinking and vice versa, even though thinking is not itself reducible to observed brain states. That is the version I endorse. As we shall see, such a perspective suggests the need for reconstituting established notions of causality in cultural life. I approach this topic in this study, particularly in chapters 2 and 4. See, for instance, Hampshire's introduction to *The Ethics*, trans. Edwin Curley (Oxford: Penguin, 1994).

7. Gerald M. Edelman and Giulio Tonino, *A Universe of Consciousness: How Matter Becomes Imagination* (New York: Basic Books, 2000), 83. This book was published too recently for me to incorporate it into this study. The authors' exploration of the rapid, complex "reentry combinations" between different subsystems of the brain is very pertinent. These reentry combinations engender consciousness. This book also brings out why we need to supplement the concept of efficient causality with what in the Spinoza tradition would be called "immanent causality." An immanent cause is one that emerges out of the intersection between external events and the system of reentrant combinations in a system like the body/brain network. It can usher something new into the world. Social scientists too often simplify causality, while interpretive theorists run away from it.

8. In a recent book, Jean-Pierre Changeux, a neuroscientist, and Paul Ricoeur, a philosopher and phenomenologist, debate the role of neuroscience in the study of thinking and ethics. Each announces himself at the outset as a Spinozist with respect to the mind/body problem, but differences soon emerge in their interpretations of that doctrine. Ricoeur deploys parallelism to protect thinking from technique, while Changeux treats it as precisely the philosophy that encourages such interventions. I agree with Changeux on this point, as will become clear in chapter 4. Although the authors try to bracket differences in "ontology," Ricoeur's desire to insulate the highest levels of being from neuroscience expresses one existential faith while Changeux expresses investment in another. Neither faith has been proven to date. And I doubt that such differences can be bracketed entirely, although how they are introduced is crucial. See Jean-Pierre Changeux and Paul Ricoeur, *What Makes Us Think? A Neuroscientist and a Philosopher Argue about Ethics, Human Nature, and the Brain* (Princeton, N.J.: Princeton University Press, 2000).

9. Damasio, *The Feeling of What Happens*, 62.

10. Ramachandran, *Phantoms in the Brain*, 130.

11. Ibid., 141.

12. Ibid., 26–27.

13. Ibid., 33.

14. Ibid., 35.

15. Ibid., 56.

16. See Laura Mulvey, "Visual Pleasure and Narrative Cinema," *Screen* 16, no. 3 (1975): 6–18; Tania Modleski, *The Women Who Knew Too Much: Hitchcock and Feminist Theory* (New York: Metheun, 1988), chap. 6.

17. In *Looking Awry: An Introduction to Jacques Lacan through Popular Culture* (Cambridge: MIT Press, 1992), Slavoj Zizek offers masterful readings of several Hitchcock films, including *Vertigo*. In the latter, he explains the attraction of the plot amid its apparent improbability "precisely" by "this impossible relationship between the fantasy figure and the 'empirical' woman who, quite by chance, finds herself occupying this fantasy place" (83). "The point of these observations," in turn, "is that the sublime quality of an object is not intrinsic but rather an effect of its position in the fantasy space" (84). I find Zizek's account persuasive, up to a point. The dissent arises *if* the fantasy becomes treated as both an all-consuming and unmodifiable feature of desire. On my reading, Hitchcock's tactic to plant a subliminal doubt in Scottie about the falling body suggests both that

additional lures are needed to draw him into the search for Madeleine and that the fantasy itself, if and as it arises, might be susceptible to modification by tactical work. Both points apply to viewers of the film, too, some of whom are less invested in the fantasy than others. Some men and women, for instance, are closer in temperament to Midge—the down-to-earth designer of undergarments for women—than to either Scottie or Madeleine. It is not Zizek's interpretation, then, that I contest, but the aura of certainty and incorrigibility that surrounds it. That issue, in turn, is linked to the question of how film techniques work on us and what difference our appropriations of them can make to the type or strength of the fantasies in which we participate. Freud himself, as we shall see, worked hard to delimit legitimate techniques of self-modification. I seek to expand their *range*, without claiming too much for their *efficacy*. Zizek and I may well diverge at this point. Finally, Zizek gives no sign that he acknowledges the deep contestability of the most basic assumptions of Lacanian theory. I will argue that this acknowledgment forms a critical virtue of theory itself. Finally, he often notes how theorists such as Deleuze and Foucault cannot "explain" *x*, or offer an adequate "account" of it, suggesting that he has not addressed their claim that the very quest for consummate explanation reflects a contestable image of nature, thinking, and culture, one they do not embrace. On this point, too, I concur with them.

18. Robert Bresson, *Notes on the Cinematographer*, trans. Jonathan Griffin (London: Quartet, 1986), 124.

19. In *The Enchantment of Modern Life: Attachments, Crossings, and Ethics* (Princeton, N.J.: Princeton University Press, 2001), Jane Bennett examines several reductionist readings of the aestheticization of politics and makes the case for a positive relation between enchantment and ethics.

20. For a very thoughtful study that examines comparatively the ontological dimension in several political theories, including mine, exploring comparatively how this dimension infiltrates into ethical and political priorities, see Stephen K. White, *Sustaining Affirmation: The Strengths of Weak Ontology in Political Theory* (Princeton, N.J.: Princeton University Press, 2000).

21. "The free will finds itself immediately confronted by differences which arise from the circumstance that freedom is its inward function and aim, and is in relation to an external and already existing subsisting objectivity, which splits up into different heads: viz. anthropological data . . . , external things of nature which exist in consciousness, and the ties of relation between individual wills." George Hegel, *Hegel's Philosophy of Mind*, trans. William Wallace (Oxford: Clarendon, 1971), no. 483, p. 241. Hegel folds the objective dimension of culture into a inestimable and cannot be criticized). Therefore they are *necessary* allies, so that if they are to be fought they can only be fought and called into question together" (153).

6. Nonequilibrium "may in fact be taken as the very basis of the definition of a biological system." Ilya Prigogine and Isabelle Stengers, *Order Out of Chaos: Man's New Dialogue with Nature* (New York: Bantam, 1984), 13.

7. Ilya Prigogine, with Isabelle Stengers, *The End of Certainty: Time, Chaos, and the New Laws of Nature* (New York: Free Press, 1997), 14, 72.

8. Ibid., 189. Elsewhere, Prigogine puts the point this way: even in chaotic phenomena like turbulence, "a strange tumult reigns, the complete opposite of indifferent disorder." Ilya Prigogine and Isabelle Stengers, "Postface: Dynamics from Leibniz to Lucretius," in Michel Serres, *Hermes: Literature, Science, Philosophy* (Baltimore: Johns Hopkins University Press, 1982), 153.

9. Prigogine, *The End of Certainty*, 16. Here is a formulation by Nietzsche that is remarkably close to that of Prigogine: "That the world is not striving toward a stable condition is the only thing that has been proved. Consequently, one must conceive its climactic conditions in such a way that it is not a condition of equilibrium." *The Will to Power*, no. 639, p. 341.

10. Immanuel Kant, preface to the 2d ed., *Critique of Pure Reason*, 2d ed., trans J. M. Dent (New York: Everyman's Library, 1954), 13–14.

11. Prigogine and Stengers, *Order Out of Chaos*, 13.

12. Ibid., 187.

13. The notion of reversible and determinist trajectories "does not belong exclusively to classical dynamics. It is found in relativity and in quantum mechanics" as well. For example, in the model of the atom wherein "each orbit is characterized by a well-determined energy level in which electrons are in steady, eternal, and invariable movement.... The orbits are defined as being without interaction with each other or with the world." This is the case even though other aspects of quantum mechanics are at odds with this Leibnizian model: electrons are also pictured as able to "jump from one orbit to another.... It is here that quantum mechanics ... does not define the determinist and reversible description as being complete." Prigogine and Stengers, "Postface," 146.

14. Stengers, *Power and Invention*, 10–11.

15. Nietzsche, *The Gay Science*, no. 112, p. 173.

16. Prigogine and Stengers, *Order Out of Chaos*, 187.

17. Stengers, *Power and Invention*, 39.

18. Alan Sokal and Jean Bricmont, *Fashionable Nonsense: Postmodern Intellectuals' Abuse of Science* (New York: Picador, 1998), 15 n. 14.

19. Prigogine and Stengers, *Order Out of Chaos*, 181.

20. Quoted in Stengers, *Power and Invention*, 40.

21. See Henri Bergson, *Creative Evolution*, trans. Arthur Mitchell (New York: Dover, 1998); Stephen J. Gould, *Evolution and the History of Life* (New York: Basic Books, 1999).

22. Keith Ansell Pearson, *Viroid Life: Perspectives on Nietzsche and the Transhuman Condition* (New York: Routledge, 1997), 132.

23. A suggestive exploration of the culture of birds in relation to human culture is developed in Gilles Deleuze and Félix Guattari, "1837: Of the Refrain," in *A Thousand Plateaus: Capitalism and Schizophrenia*, trans. Brian Massumi (Minneapolis: University of Minnesota Press, 1987).

24. This is an area of considerable dispute in neurophysiology today. Daniel Dennett, reviewing the available evidence in *Consciousness Explained* (Boston: Little, Brown, 1991), supports the idea. Andy Clark, in *Being There: Putting Brain, Body, and World Together Again* (Cambridge: MIT Press, 1999), contests it. The example alluded to in the text comes from new research that has not yet been critically examined by other investigators. The results were attained by a team of neuroscientists at the University of Washington studying dyslexic children. They are summarized in Eric Nagourney, "Exploring Dyslexia and Brain Energy," *New York Times*, June 6, 2000.

25. Maurice Merleau-Ponty, *Phenomenology of Perception*, trans. Colin Smith (London: Routledge, 1962), 189.

26. Nietzsche, *The Gay Science*, no. 333, p. 262.

27. Friedrich Nietzsche, *Twilight of the Idols*, trans. R. J. Hollingdale (New York: Penguin, 1968), 82–83.

28. Nietzsche does and must work hard to reconfigure our reading of these two modalities as well.

29. William James, *Principles of Psychology*, vol. 1 (New York: Dover, 1890), 288.

30. Nietzsche, *The Will to Power*, no. 477, pp. 263–64.

31. Shaviro, *The Cinematic Body*, 255, 256.

32. For an excellent study that places a god where I locate the nonideational outside of thought, see Charles Taylor, *Sources of the Self: The Making of Modern Identity* (Cambridge: Harvard University Press, 1989). Taylor appeals to divine grace in the penultimate sentence of the book, where he resists the idea that a certain alienation is our "inevitable lot." "It is a hope that I see implicit in

Judeo-Christian theism (however terrible the record of its adherents in history), and in its central promise of a divine affirmation of the human, more total than humans can ever attain unaided" (521). I respond to Taylor's idea of a divine intelligence to which human thought seeks to become attuned in "Where the Word Breaks Off," in *Politics and Ambiguity* (Madison: University of Wisconsin Press, 1987).

33. Martin Heidegger, *On the Way to Language*, trans. Peter D. Hertz (New York: Harper & Row, 1971).

34. I make the positive case for this ethical orientation as one among others to be negotiated in a positive ethos of engagement in "An Ethos of Engagement," in *Why I Am Not a Secularist* (Minneapolis: University of Minnesota Press, 1999), 137–61.

35. In *Being There*, Andy Clark explores how language provides an indispensable "scaffolding" for refined thinking. He shows thereby how thinking extends beyond the brain of a thinker into a public world. In that book, and particularly in his chapter 10, Clark supports the themes I am exploring. His exposé of how non-representational theories overplay their hand is particularly useful, for he shows how the expressive and representational images, once both are refined, can be rendered compatible. Clark, however, may underplay how discursive practices fold back upon selves and constituencies, helping to modify elements in their bodies and brains.

36. For an exploration of the connection between the expressive and self-organizational dimensions of language in Augustine, see William E. Connolly, *The Augustinian Imperative: A Reflection on the Politics of Morality* (Newbury Park, Calif.: Sage, 1993). I pose the issue in chapter 2 of that volume: "Words, for Augustine, provide the fuel of confession. Words do not simply represent a world of determinate things. Nor do they simply create (or constitute) things according to the dictates of cultural convention.... Words, strained through the soul of those who speak them and hear them, can be media of perversion or of conversion.... Divine words inscribed in scripture, when they are confessed to the one true god, are the most powerful media of conversion, healing, and moralization available to humanity" (43–44). Of course divine grace is even more powerful. My sense is that some secular theorists of language shy away from its expressive and compositional dimensions because they fear that attention to these very dimensions will give too much power to religious forces. In doing so, however, they lose sight of important connections among thinking, language, and freedom.

37. The most significant places this amendment is pursued are in Gilles Deleuze, "The Image of Thought," in *Difference and Repetition*, trans. Paul Patton (New York: Columbia University Press, 1994); and Gilles

Deleuze and Félix Guattari, "Micropolitics and Segmentarity," *A Thousand Plateaus*.

38. Nietzsche, *Twilight of the Idols*, no. 47, p. 101. The text by Antonio Damasio is *Descartes' Error*. Damasio is superb at presenting examples of people who have lost some or part of their affective capacities through selective brain damage and then articulating the effects this has on the quality and timbre of thought. Although calculative thinking can proceed without much affect, he concludes, lack of affect imposes severe limits on pure reason. If Damasio's excellent research were joined to the model of nature advanced by Nietzsche and by Prigogine and Stengers, who knows what profound things would emerge? Damasio is already tempted a bit in this direction. Perhaps this is a suitable place to draw attention again to Brian Massumi's superb essay "The Autonomy of Affect."

4. Techniques of Thought and Micropolitics

1. Lucretius, *De Rerum Natura*, in *The Epicurean Philosophers*, ed. John Gaskin, trans. C. Bailey, R. D. Hicks, and J. C. A. Gaskin (London: J. M. Dent, 1995), 126, 161. The editor worries about the physiology of Lucretius. It is "old-fashioned by the standards of Alexandrian science even when he wrote. Fortunately the philosophical argument is not disturbed by reading 'brain' ... for 'middle region of the breast.'" (161 n).

2. Tor Nørretranders, *The User Illusion: Cutting Consciousness Down to Size*, trans. Jonathan Sydenham (New York: Viking, 1998), 255.

3. Rafael Nuñez, "Reclaiming Mind, Body and Cognition," in *Reclaiming Cognition: The Primacy of Action, Intention and Emotion*, ed. Rafael Nuñez and Walter J. Freeman (Exeter: Imprint Academic, 1999), 59. Several essays in this volume struggle with the question of how to reconceive causality in a body/brain/culture matrix marked by innumerable relays and feedback loops. The key, I think, is to translate efficient causality into immanent causality. The latter involves, first, the relation between external events and internal circuits of self-organization and, second, a process of infusion or composition by which body/brain processes become organized into new patterns.

4. Nørretranders, *The User Illusion*, 170.

5. Reported in Matthew W. Browne, "Who Needs Jokes? Brain Has a Ticklish Spot," *New York Times*, March 10, 1998, D1.

6. As Nørretranders points out in *The User Illusion*, the "half-second delay" is actually an average. Nørretranders appreciates that you might object that some reaction times are "a lot shorter than 0.5 second. It does not take a half a second to snatch your fingers away when you burn them! So how can it take half a second to move of your own free will? ... Well, it can because reactions are *not* conscious. ... Our reaction time is much shorter than the time it takes to initiate a conscious action" (221). We move here, as we shall see, into the quick, crude reaction time of the amygdala that precedes feeling and consciousness.

7. Ibid., 164. This phrase occurs when Nørretranders is contesting the sufficiency of those computer models of the mind that seek to formulate the rules that govern conscious thinking. For a superb exploration of the "missing half second" that prompts some of my thinking, see Massumi, "The Autonomy of Affect."

8. An earlier, schematized discussion of how the half-second delay is subjected to different interpretations in the traditions of Kant and immanent naturalism can be found in my "Brain Waves, Transcendental Fields, and Techniques of Thought," *Radical Philosophy* (March/April 1999): 19–26. That essay foreshadows the engagement with technique in this one.

9. Immanuel Kant, *Critique of Pure Reason*, ed. and trans. Vasilis Politis (London: J. M. Dent, 1993), 145.

10. Immanuel Kant, *The Critique of Practical Reason*, trans. Lewis White Beck (New York: Macmillan, 1993), 49.

11. There is another contemporary reading of Kant that translates his complex revision of the two-world metaphysic into an early version of the "two-aspect" model. Whereas Peter Strawson, Stuart Hampshire, and Gilles Deleuze support the two-world interpretation of Kant (and then try to revise it in the direction of an immanent materialism), Paul Redding explores the work of philosophers who develop the two-aspect reading in *The Logic of Affect* (Melbourne: Melbourne University Press, 1999). This reading draws Kant closer to some of the recent work on thought in neuroscience. I think that reading, which its proponents concede has to truncate the Kantian model of judgment, is easiest to defend if you restrict your attention to the first *Critique* and ignore the relation of the second and third to it. For Kant himself says that he is trying, first, to create room for religious faith and, second, to show how pure practical reason *expresses* morality as law apodictically. And those two tasks require the postulate of the super-sensible. Why use Kant to support the two-aspect theory when you can draw on Epicurus, Spinoza, Nietzsche, Freud, Deleuze, Hampshire, and Damasio to do so? It is tempting to some, I imagine, because several of these latter thinkers play up the dissonances between layers and the element of wildness in thinking in ways that pull them away from the juridical model of thought in Kant. Whichever way you turn on these questions, however, Redding builds an excellent case that mechanical models of materialism were deepened and challenged by eighteenth- and nineteenth-century idealist

philosophies (Kant, Schelling, Hegel) that explored the unconscious and intersubjective conditions of possibility for conscious thought.

12. Kant, *The Critique of Practical Reason*, 99; emphasis added.

13. In November 2000, the Center for the Critical Analysis of Contemporary Culture at Rutgers University organized a daylong discussion between Charles Taylor and me on these questions. We concurred on the idea that faith in the grace of God and nontheistic gratitude for being are two ethical sources grounded in differences of faith unlikely to be resolved by definitive means. The ethical question became how to negotiate relations between bearers of such diverse orientations.

14. Stuart Hampshire, "A Kind of Materialism," in *Freedom of Mind* (Princeton, N.J.: Princeton University Press, 1971), 211.

15. Ibid., 211–12.

16. Ibid., 213.

17. Spinoza's parallelism has a fascinating complexity. For him the parallelism between thought and extension means that a change in one is matched by a corresponding change in the other, even though there is no causal connection across these lines. This means you can improve the capacity of the body by improving thinking and improve the capacity of the mind by acting upon the body. Unfortunately, Spinoza does not focus on the second domain in the *Ethics*, saying in part V, "Now we are not concerned here ... with the science of tending the body so that it can be perfected. ... Here ... I shall be dealing only with the power of mind or reason." Baruch Spinoza, *Ethics: Treatise on the Emendation of the Intellect and Selected Letters*, trans. Samuel Shirley (Indianapolis: Hackett, 1992), 201.

18. Hampshire, "A Kind of Materialism," 218.

19. LeDoux, *The Emotional Brain*, 280.

20. Ibid., 240.

21. Varela et al., *The Embodied Mind*.

22. Ibid., 86.

23. Ibid., 139–40.

24. Ibid., 86.

25. Gilles Deleuze, *Difference and Repetition*, trans. Paul Patton (New York: Columbia University Press, 1994), 25.

26. Ibid., 139; emphasis added.

27. Ibid. The above quotes point to a line of difference between Deleuze and Hampshire. The lines of connection are even more important. They are further suggested by the fact that Hampshire wrote one sympathetic book on Spinoza and Deleuze wrote two.

28. Walter Benjamin, "The Work of Art in the Age of Mechanical Reproduction," in *Illuminations*, ed. Hannah Arendt (New York: Schocken, 1955), 235.

29. Deleuze, *Difference and Repetition*, 50.

30. Deleuze's image invites comparison to that developed by Hannah Arendt in *The Life of the Mind* (New York: Harvest, 1971). There Arendt explores how thinking involves a relation of "two in one" and also how thinking occurs in an unsettled "gap" between past and future. The main difference between them, perhaps, is that Deleuze also accepts a philosophy of nature that breaks with a linear conception of time, and he also seeks to fold that conception of nature into the logic of thinking itself. More about this in chapter 6, where we engage "the rift in time" more closely.

31. Deleuze, *Cinema 2*, 107–8.

32. Ibid., 107, 207.

33. Quoted in Buster Olney, "Between Pitches (Twist, Tap), a Game within the Game," *New York Times*, August 22, 1999, 3E.

34. In *The Terms of Political Discourse* (Boston: Heath, 1974; Princeton, N.J.: Princeton University Press, 1984), I introduced such terms as *misticket* to illustrate how conceptual innovations in an established network of practices help to promote and consolidate political change. I continue to hold to the ideas of essentially contested concepts and the close relation between conceptual revision and political change adumbrated in that book. The major revision I make today is not on what might be called the horizontal register of inter-subjectivity, but on the vertical layering of thinking and culture. Thinking works on both registers simultaneously. Proto-thoughts are linguistic in one sense of the term, but because they arise out of the lower brain regions even while having a cultural, intersubjective dimension, they are not so in a refined or complex way. I resist the (predictable) effort to reduce the lower layers of thinking and judgment to brute instinct or pure subjectivity.

35. Hampshire, "A Kind of Materialism," 225.

36. Such a suggestion may reflect the unlayered conception of sensibility that emerges out of the Kantian tradition. If you deny the supersensible, however, it becomes possible to develop a richer, layered conception of the sensible and the infrasensible. This is approximately what Nietzsche has in mind when he says things like "The body is more profound than the soul."

37. Deleuze pursues "belief in this world" in *Cinema 2*. Here "belief" falls below the epistemological register, where you devise tests to ascertain whether a belief is true or false. That first register of belief is important. But conviction on the second register involves cultivation of

the sense that life with mortality is worth it, that the experience of nonlinear time can be tolerable or gratifying, that the fugitive complexity of the body is enchanting even amid its dispositions to injury, suffering, sickness, and death. Deleuze finds both theistic and nontheistic directors who promote this experience. He prefers the latter himself, but respects the former. Here is one expression of the idea: "What is certain is that believing is no longer belief in another world, or in a transformed world. It is only, it is simply, believing in the body. It is giving discourse to the body, and for this purpose, reaching the body before discourses, before words, before things are named" (172–73). Dreyer, Rossellini, Artaud, and Bresson are the artists he salutes on these pages.

38. I discuss this issue in "A Critique of Pure Politics," in *Why I Am Not a Secularist*, 163–87.

39. See Varela et al., *The Embodied Mind*, particularly chaps. 10 and 11.

40. As Asad says, in medieval monastic life, "liturgy is not a species of enacted symbolism to be classified separately from activities defined as technical but is a practice among others essential to the acquisition of Christian virtues." Talal Asad, *Genealogies of Religion: Discipline and Reasons of Power in Christianity and Islam* (Baltimore: Johns Hopkins University Press, 1993), 63.

41. Michel Foucault, "On the Genealogy of Ethics: An Overview of Work in Progress," in *The Foucault Reader*, ed. Paul Rabinow (New York: Pantheon, 1984), 369. The confined role given to argument in this conception of ethics actually tracks the Kantian claim that morality as law is not something known through argument but is recognized apodictically. This then is the point at which argument stops and something beyond it begins in Kantian morality. To translate the Kantian transcendental into an immanent field is to rewrite, rather than simply reject, Kant's view about the limits of argument in ethics. For an essay that responds to neo-Kantians who read Foucault reductively, see Jane Bennett, " 'How Is It, Then, That We Still Remain Barbarians?': Schiller, Foucault and the Aestheticization of Ethics," *Political Theory* 24 (November 1996): 653–72.

42. The need to step out of the flow periodically is developed in Jane Bennett, *Thoreau's Nature: Ethics, Politics, and the Wild* (Lauham, Md.: Rowman & Littlefield, 1994). For a discussion of the impetus to ethics from material sources, see Bennett's *The Enchantment of Modern Life*.

43. James Carey, "Political Ritual on Television: Episodes in the History of Shame, Degradation and Excommunication," in *Media, Ritual and Identity*, ed. Tamar Liebes and James Curran (New York: Routledge, 1998), 57.

5. Memory Traces, Mystical States, and Deep Pluralism

1. Sigmund Freud, *Moses and Monotheism*, trans. Katherine Jones (New York: Vintage, 1939), 89–90.

2. Ibid., 39.

3. Jan Assmann, *Moses the Egyptian: The Memory of Egypt in Western Monotheism* (Cambridge: Harvard University Press, 1997). The quotation is from line 65 of "The Great Hymn," reprinted on pp. 172–77. Assmann reviews the long minority history in the West in which the relation between Egypt and Judaism is subject to review, reconsideration, and assessment. He doesn't reach a strong conclusion on whether Moses was an Egyptian. And he shows how Freud misreads the Ikhanaton faith on the issue of forming images of the divinity. Two major contributions of Assmann's book are its exploration of the origins and effects of "counter-religions" on the faiths that preceded them and its review of how often "Moses" has been invoked in European history to reconsider the relation between monotheism and polytheistic orientations.

4. During a panel at the 1999 APSA convention at which Bonnie Honig and I both gave papers on *Moses and Monotheism*, she opted for the idea that the historical accuracy of the story is unimportant for it to do its work. Her thought was that both parties agree that Moses was raised as an Egyptian, and that fact is more important than his biological heritage. I agree that the biological heritage of Moses is unimportant. But, for Freud's story to work, you must invest a lot in the phrase "raised as an Egyptian." For Freud that means that Moses deeply imbibed the faith of Ikhanaton, and that he then labored intensively to give it to the Hebrew people after his father's death and the renunciation of that faith in Egypt in favor of a return to multiple gods.

5. Freud, *Moses and Monotheism*, 55, 79.

6. Ibid., 63.

7. "The Mosaic religion had been a 'Father religion.' Christianity became a 'Son religion.' The old God, the Father, took second place; Christ, the Son stood in his stead, just as in those dark times every son had longed to do. Paul, by developing the Jewish religion further, became its destroyer. His success was certainly mainly due to the fact that through the idea of salvation he laid the ghost of the feeling of guilt. It was also due to his giving up the idea of the chosen people and its visible sign—circumcision. That is how the new religion would become all-embracing, universal. Although this step might have been determined by Paul's revengefulness on account of the opposition which his innovation found among the Jews." Ibid., 112.

8. Ibid., 117.

9. Ibid., 127.

10. Joseph LeDoux, as I read him, would agree with Freud's idea of the trace but would probably call into question the long-term inheritance of traces of a primal killing of the father. See LeDoux, *The Emotional Brain*. A lot of anthropologists would call into question the universal character of the horde Freud projects into the future, without, in most cases, coming to terms with the idea of a trace. Anthropologists such as Talal Asad and Ann Stoler, however, seem to me to be drawn to some version of this latter idea while resisting the idea of a universal model of the horde in prehistoric human life.

11. Freud, *Moses and Monotheism*, 129–30.

12. "This state of affairs is made more difficult, it is true, by the present attitude of biological science, which rejects the idea of acquired qualities being transmitted to descendants. I admit, in all modesty, that in spite of this I cannot picture biological development proceeding without taking this factor into account." Ibid., 127–28.

13. The connection *and* difference between Freud and James is suggested in the following formulation by Gerald Bruns: " 'Let us then propose,' James says in his conclusion to *Varieties*, 'as an hypothesis, that whatever it may be on its *farther* side, the more with which in religious experience we feel ourselves connected is on its *hither* side the subconscious continuation of our conscious life.' (*V*, 512) The point not to be missed, however, is that the difference between hither and yon proves to be indeterminate." Gerald L. Bruns, "Loose Talk about Religion from William James," in *Tragic Thoughts at the End of Philosophy* (Evanston, Ill.: Northwestern University Press, 1999), 37. Bruns thinks that "loose talk" is the best kind here.

14. Here is Freud in his most confident and belligerent mode: "This does not mean that I lack conviction in the correctness of my conclusions. That conviction I acquired a quarter of a century ago, when I wrote my book on *Totem and Taboo* (in 1912), and it has only grown stronger since. From then on I have never doubted that religious phenomena are to be understood only on the model of neurotic symptoms of the individual, which are so familiar to us, as a return of long forgotten important happenings in the primeval history of the human family, that they owe their obsessive character to that very origin and therefore derive their effect on mankind from the historical truth they contain." *Moses and Monotheism*, 71.

15. William James, *The Varieties of Religious Experience* (New York: Penguin, 1902), 242.

16. Ramachandran, *Phantoms in the Brain*, 179.

17. Ibid., 186. In another set of experiments, Buddhist meditators were asked to signal with blinking eyes when they were in a state of lucid dreaming. (The eye muscles were chosen because "all other muscle movements are blocked" in this state.) Each time the signal was given, electroencephalographic sensors showed REM activity, the brain activity occurring when dreaming is active. See "Lucid Dreaming," in *Sleeping, Dreaming and Dying: An Exploration of Consciousness with the Dalai Lama*, ed. Francisco J. Varela (Boston: Wisdom, 1997). These pieces of evidence are subject to multiple interpretations, but they are suggestive. A larger interest explored in *Sleeping, Dreaming and Dying* is what happens when neuroscientists and Buddhist practitioners are brought together so that each group can pose questions to the other.

18. Damasio, *The Feeling of What Happens*, 62. Damasio goes on in this section to present the case of a woman whose amygdala on both sides of the brain was calcified. She understood intellectually about danger, but she was actually extremely trusting in her conversations and work life. It would be unwise to draw from a stray statement here or there that Damasio is a defender of a modern version of phrenology. He is not, and argues specifically against it. The different brain nodules, operating at different speeds and capacities, participate in complex networks. And any particular experience draws on relays and feedback loops in this network.

19. James, *The Varieties of Religious Experience*, 422–23.

20. Freud, *Moses and Monotheism*, 61.

21. Ibid., 109.

22. Ibid., 144.

23. Mikkel Borch-Jacobsen, *The Emotional Tie: Psychoanalysis, Mimesis, and Affect*, trans. Douglas Brick (Stanford, Calif.: Stanford University Press, 1992), 54.

24. Thoughtful discussions of irrational cuts are found in Deleuze, *Cinema 2*; and David Rodowick, *Gilles Deleuze's Time Machine* (Durham, N.C.: Duke University Press, 1997). Michael J. Shapiro, in "Toward a Politics of Now-Time," *Theory & Event* 2, no. 2 (1998) (http://muse.jhu.edu/journals/theory_&_event/toc/archive.html #2.2), explores the political geography of film technique and narrative in a very helpful way. See, too, a study that weaves the politics of ordinary life and the narrative techniques of several films into a fascinating pastiche in Thomas Dumm, *The Politics of the Ordinary* (New York: New York University Press, 1999).

25. It is possible to read *The Apostle* simply as the climb to authority by a white male figure who draws sustenance from African American life while draining authority from it. That is one thing going on. And the suggestion that it is the main thing has been made to me when I have presented the material in this chapter as a paper. The thing to avoid, in my view, is a critical presentation of this fact that treats it to be so powerful that it overwhelms everything else. The film's creative presentations

of how techniques and micropolitics work in down-and-out settings are also important. That's one of the reasons I introduce *The Return of the Apostle*. New work *is* needed on Sonny, but there are things about him that make it credible to imagine such work to be possible. The reductive reading misses much in the first film too. Sonny is a down-and-out guy, even as he becomes an authoritative male figure. And the racial crossing has considerable vitality and potentiality. What I resist most, then, is the type of reading that reduces Sonny to the authoritative male role in the putative name of criticizing such a monopoly, but then *itself* secretes presumptions about the ubiquity of the master role in a way that makes it impossible to devise strategies to break through it.

26. Vermes draws upon the Book of Common Prayer of the Church of England to draw out the differences between Jesus as Jew and the Pauline Jesus. The lines quoted are the first three lines of that prayer. Vermes says, "Today, as in past centuries, the believing Christian's main New Testament source of faith lies, not so much in Mark, Matthew, and Luke and the still sufficiently earthly Jesus, as in the centuries of speculation by the church on the theological Gospel of John with its eternal word become flesh, and perhaps even more in the letters of Paul with their drama of death, atonement and resurrection." Geza Vermes, *The Religion of Jesus the Jew* (Minneapolis: Fortress, 1993), 210.

27. "PENTECOST. From the Greek pentekonta ('fifty'). For the Jews an observance coming fifty days after the Passover and commemorating Moses' reception of the Law on Mt. Sinai. For Christians the Day of the Pentecost, coming on the seventh Sunday after Easter, commemorates the outpouring of the Holy Spirit." "PENTECOSTAL SECTS. A group of fundamentalist sects, centered in the United States, whose distinguishing mark is that act of 'speaking in tongues' associated with the Day of the Pentecost." *Dictionary of Philosophy and Religion* (Atlantic Highlands, N.J.: Humanities Press, 1980).

28. The longer formulation is this: "I can scarcely believe ... that men can be induced to examine this view without prejudice, so strongly are they convinced that at the mere bidding of the mind the body can now be set in motion, now be brought to rest, and can perform any number of actions which depend solely on the will of the mind and the exercise of thought. However, nobody has as yet determined the limits of the body's capabilities.... For nobody as yet knows the structure of the body so accurately as to explain all its functions." *Spinoza Ethics*, pt. III, P2, Scholium, p. 105.

29. At around this point, the question is posed, "But if you encounter, as you will, fundamentalists who insist the divine laws they obey are true and obligatory for everyone, what do you do?" The first point is not to let that question stop creative exploration of how to develop micropolitics appropriate to pluralism. Those who attribute fundamentalism to others might also take a look at the possible element of fundamentalism in their own position. In my experience the dogmatic element in some versions of secularism is apparent to many religious monists, and that dogmatism helps to intensify the character of their responses. Second, if and as you emphasize the element of contestability in your own fundamental faith, while exposing it in others as well, you may open a door to reciprocal engagement that would otherwise be closed. But if and as such invitations are consistently refused, and if you have pursued efforts to work on your own relational perspectives, it then becomes wise to forge coalitions through which to resist the forceful imposition of a single faith upon all of public life. The challenge is to do so in a way that does not draw you too close to the dogmatism you seek to oppose. There are no guarantees here.

6. Democracy and Time

1. Sheldon Wolin, "What Time Is It?" *Theory & Event* 1, no. 1 (1997) (http://muse.jhu.edu/journals/theory_&_event/toc/archive.html #1.1), 1.

2. Ibid., 2.

3. Ibid., 3.

4. Nietzsche, *Thus Spoke Zarathustra*, 157–58.

5. Hannah Arendt, *The Life of the Mind*, vol. 1, *Thinking* (New York: Harcourt Brace, 1971), 205.

6. Sheldon Wolin, "Fugitive Democracy," in *Democracy and Difference: Contesting the Boundaries of the Political*, ed. Seyla Benhabib (Princeton, N.J.: Princeton University Press, 1996), 43.

7. Michael Best and I explore changes in the general infrastructure of consumption that could move a state from the difficult task of generalizing exclusive goods to providing tax, subsidy, and infrastructural support for inclusive goods in *The Politicized Economy*, 2d ed. (Boston: Heath, 1982). That study of political economy would need to be updated to mesh with the idea of democratic pluralism developed here. But the account of the role that the replacement of exclusive goods by inclusive goods would play in a democratic political economy is still relevant.

8. William E. Connolly, *Political Theory and Modernity* (Oxford: Blackwell, 1988), 175.

9. Nietzsche, *Twilight of the Idols*, 93–94.

10. Nietzsche, *The Gay Science*, 303. The quotations to follow all come from no. 356, pp. 302–4.

11. Nietzsche, *The Will to Power*, 35.

12. Ibid., 38–39.

13. Nietzsche, *The Gay Science*, II, no. 76, p. 130.

14. Ibid., II, no. 76, p. 131.

15. Exemplary in this respect is William Bennett. See William E. Connolly, "Freelancing the Nation," in *Why I Am Not a Secularist*, 97–113.

16. Paul Patton admirably explores the relation of the actor to the artist, and, indeed, of affect to both, in "Nietzsche and the Problem of the Actor," in *Why Nietzsche Still? Reflections on Drama, Culture, Politics*, ed. Alan D. Schrift (Berkeley: University of California Press, 2000), 170–83. Brian Massumi and Paul Patton discuss allied issues in "Reagan and the Problem of the Actor" and "Response to Brian Massumi, 'The Bleed: Where Body Meets Image,'" in *Rethinking Borders*, ed. John C. Welchman (Minneapolis: University of Minnesota Press, 1996), 41–50.

17. Nietzsche, *The Gay Science*, IV, no. 319, p. 253.

18. Nietzsche, *Thus Spoke Zarathustra*, 203.

19. Nietzsche, *Twilight of the Idols*, 43–44. Nietzsche explicitly supports a politics in which enmity between believers and nonbelievers becomes "much more prudent, much more thoughtful, much more *forbearing*."

20. Nietzsche, *The Gay Science*, IV, no. 354, pp. 298–99.

21. These formulations are found, respectively, in Friedrich Nietzsche, *The AntiChrist*, trans. R. J. Hollingdale (New York: Vintage, 1968), 151; *Twilight of the Idols*, 82; and *The Gay Science*, 274.

22. I explore such techniques with respect to the issue of draining resentment from one's orientation to criminal conviction and punishment in *The Ethos of Pluralization*, chap. 2, and with respect to the question of doctor-assisted suicide in "The Will, Capital Punishment, and Cultural War," *Why I Am Not a Secularist*, 115–36.

23. Research carried out by Robert Stickgold of Harvard and Carlyle Smith of Trent University, as reported in Sandra Blakeslee, "For Better Learning, Researchers Endorse 'Sleep on It' Adage," *New York Times*, March 7, 2000, sec. 3, p. 8.

24. Nietzsche, *The Gay Science*, IV, no. 290, p. 232.

25. See B. A. Wallace, "The Buddhist Tradition of *Samatha*," in *The View from Within: First Person Approaches to the Study of Consciousness*, ed. Francisco J. Varela and Jonathan Shear (Lawrence, Kans.: Imprint Academic, 1999), 186.

26. Damasio, *Descartes' Error*, 150–51.

27. Nietzsche, *The Gay Science*, IV, no. 290, p. 233.

28. Friedrich Nietzsche, *Daybreak: Thoughts on the Prejudices of Morality*, trans. R. J. Hollingdale

(Cambridge: Cambridge Unversity Press, 1982), no. 103, p. 60.

29. Friedrich Nietzsche, *Human, All Too Human: A Book for Free Spirits*, trans. R. J. Hollingdale (Cambridge: Cambridge University Press, 1986), 383.

7. Eccentric Flows and Cosmopolitan Culture

1. The first three quotations come from Paul Virilio, *Speed and Politics*, trans. Mark Polizzotti (New York: Semiotext(e), 1986), 100, 78, 140–41. The next two come from *The Virilio Reader*, ed. James Der Derian (Oxford: Blackwell, 1998), 140, 189. And the last comes from *Speed and Politics*, 142. I am indebted to the excellent introduction to Virilio offered by James Der Derian and to his interview with Virilio.

2. "But in the moral religion (and of the public religions which have ever existed, The Christian alone is moral) it is a basic principle that each must do as much as lies in his power to become a better man, and that only when he has not buried his inborn talent (Luke XIX, 12–16), but has made use of his original predisposition to good in order to become a better man, can he hope that what is not within his power will be supplied through cooperation from above." Immanuel Kant, *Religion within the Limits of Reason Alone*, trans. Theodore Greene and Hoyt Hudson (New York: Harper Torchbooks, 1960), 48.

3. Kant, *The Critique of Practical Reason*, 48–49; emphasis added.

4. Indeed, if Kant rejected practical reason, and the "idealism" it sanctions, that would place his conception of theoretical reason under pressure, with corollary effects on the "realist" side of this thinking. For practical reason provides the "purest" expression of reason, and it therefore provides the best index of the regulative idea of reason governing theoretical reason, practical reason, and aesthetic judgment alike. For a thoughtful account of the central role that the regulative idea of reason plays in the Kantian system, see Susan Nieman, *The Unity of Reason: Rereading Kant* (New York: Oxford University Press, 1994).

5. Immanuel Kant, "Idea for a Universal History with a Cosmopolitan Intent," in *Immanuel Kant: Perpetual Peace and Other Essays*, ed. Ted Humphrey (Indianapolis: Hackett, 1983), 30. The larger quotation brings out the ways in which Kant's practical presumption of the possibility of cosmopolitanism constrains the empirical judgment he would otherwise make about the course of the world: "If we stray from that fundamental principle [that 'all of a creature's natural capacities are destined to develop completely and in conformity with their end'] we no longer have a lawful but an aimlessly playing nature and hopeless chance takes the place of reason's guiding thread."

6. Immanuel Kant, "On the Proverb: That May Be True in Theory But Is of No Practical Use," in *Perpetual Peace*, 86.

7. Ibid., 87.

8. Ibid.

9. I explore the tangled relations between the Kantian two-world metaphysic of morality and attempts by Rawls and Habermas to replicate significant aspects of it without adopting that metaphysic in *Why I Am Not a Secularist*.

10. The relation between the typical image of the nation and Huntington's image of Western civilization is brought out through the consideration of both in relation to David Campbell's *National Deconstruction: Violence, Identity, and Justice in Bosnia* (Minneapolis: University of Minnesota Press, 1998). Campbell shows how contending demands to create a nation out of the plurality of Yugoslavia engendered ethnic cleansing, population deportations, and massacres. Huntington, on the other hand, contends that the attempt to foster such plurality is the problem, because you can't mix "civilizations" in the same state. The implications this has for aboriginal peoples and ethnic minorities in a large variety of territorial states is pernicious. See in particular chapters 6 and 7 of the Campbell study.

11. Samuel Huntington, *The Clash of Civilizations and the Remaking of World Order* (New York: Simon & Schuster, 1996), 156. A comparison between Kant and Huntington that speaks to other issues can be found in William E. Connolly, "The New Cult of Civilizational Superiority," *Theory & Event* 2, no. 4 (1998) (http://muse.jhu.edu/journals/theory_&_event/toc/archive.html #2.4). The essays by Michael J. Shapiro ("Samuel Huntington's Moral Geography") and Sandra Buckley ("Remaking the World Order") in the symposium in which this piece occurs are also very relevant to the relation between speed and the politics of civilization.

12. For an excellent account of ecological "terrapolitanism," see Daniel Deudney, "Global Village Sovereignty: Intergenerational Sovereign Publics, Federal-Republican Earth Constitutions, and Planetary Identities," in *The Greening of Sovereignty in World Politics*, ed. Karen Liftin (Cambridge: MIT Press, 1998).

13. Huntington loves to reduce cosmopolitan connections above the intracivilizational level to snobbish gatherings of effete intellectuals and journalists. But, to cite just one example, the conference organized in Australia in 1996 by Paul Patton and Duncan Ivison on aboriginal rights in the United States, Australia, New Zealand, and Canada drew aboriginal leaders from all four countries, as well as an assortment of scholars from each. And it quickly became clear to the rest of us that the aboriginal leaders are in close cross-country contact with each other. For two books that cross and compromise lines Huntington draws so thickly, see Saskia Sassen, *Losing Control? Sovereignty in an Age of Globalization* (New York: Columbia University Press, 1996); and Michael Shapiro, *Violent Cartographies: Mapping Cultures of War* (Minneapolis: University of Minnesota Press, 1997). An unpublished paper by Stacie Goddard of Columbia University, "Of Boundaries and Societies: Population and International Relations Theory," also speaks to these issues very effectively.

14. Martha C. Nussbaum, *For Love of Country: Debating the Limits of Patriotism* (Boston: Beacon, 1996), 7, 8, 9, 13, 15.

15. Martha C. Nussbaum, "Human Functioning and Social Justice: In Defense of Aristotelian Essentialism," *Political Theory* 20 (May 1992): 222.

16. Friedrich Nietzsche, *Beyond Good and Evil*, trans. Marianne Cowan (Chicago: Henry Regnery, 1955), 151–52. In the paragraph from which this formulation is taken, Nietzsche expresses a hardness toward those who respect only the "creature" in humanity (as opposed to the "creator") that I do not endorse in the way he articulates it. My relation to Nietzsche is something like Nussbaum's relation to Aristotle. She draws extensively from the latter while resisting his orientation to slaves and women. I trust that it is not unreasonable to ask thick universalists to give the same respect toward selective indebtedness to Nietzsche that she solicits in the case of Aristotle. The point of the quote is to show that Nussbaum's "binary" distinction between the exercise of compassion and its lack is overdrawn.

17. I will shortly consider a quotation that reflects this presumption. There are others. And there are also some that pull Nussbaum away from such a focus. Here is one that both opens up the possibility of learning from other cultures and encloses that learning in a conception of culture all too concentric in character for me. "For we want to allow the possibility that we will learn from our encounters with other human societies to recognize things about ourselves that we had not seen before, or even to change in certain ways, according more importance to something we had considered peripheral." Nussbaum, "Human Functioning," 216. Yes, but if you start with a reading that plays up the interdependence and tension between the concentric and the eccentric in the life of a state (more than do "we," "our encounters," "ourselves," and "other human societies"), you are in a better position to appreciate how minorities in one state might forge significant connections with minorities or majorities in other states, commanding the attention of authorities in both.

18. This may help to explain the caustic and crude summary of Judith Butler's perspective advanced by the compassionate Nussbaum in a 1999 article in which she ends up insisting that Butler's philosophy "consorts with

evil." Martha C. Nussbaum, "The Professor of Parody: The Hip Defeatism of Judith Butler," *New Republic*, February 22, 1999, 37–45. From reading Nussbaum's piece you would not know that Butler had previously responded critically and politely to Nussbaum's universalism with a double-entry model that has some affinities to the one I pursue. The main difference is that Butler does not there endorse a regulative idea against which to test thick universals under new and unexpected conditions. See Judith Butler, "Universality in Culture," in Nussbaum, *For Love of Country*, 45–52. For a conversation between Judith Butler and me that explores the role of technique and the complexity of the universal, see "Politics, Power and Ethics: A Discussion between Judith Butler and William Connolly," *Theory & Event* 4, no. 2 (2000) (http://muse.jhu.edu/journals/theory_&_event/v004/4.2butler.html).

19. Nussbaum, "Human Functioning," 241.

20. For an essay that explores the strengths and weaknesses of my conception of "critical responsiveness" in relation to two other notions, see Stephen K. White, "Three Conceptions of the Political: The Real World of Late-Modern Democracy," in *Democracy and Vision: Sheldon Wolin and the Vicissitudes of the Political*, ed. Aryeh Botwinick and William E. Connolly (Princeton, N.J.: Princeton University Press, 2001). A relativist, Nussbaum says, is someone who thinks that "the only available standard to value is some local group or individual." "Human Functioning," 242. I agree. That is why I resist the idea that Nietzsche, Derrida, Foucault, Butler, and I are relativists. But what does it mean to say a perspective might be "contestable"? Is that another word for the same thing? Far from it. To say a basic perspective is contestable is to say that it advances presumptions and claims that can be supported but have not yet received, and are not likely to receive in the foreseeable future, such definitive support that they rule out of court every other possible perspective. To be a relativist is to discourage dialogue and debate across cultures, theories, perspectives. To adopt the theme of deep contestability is to encourage it, for the alternative perspective might make surprising claims upon you, or bring out elements in your perspective that you now see need reformulation or revision, and so on. To affirm the contestability of the interpretation you honor the most, and to do so without existential resentment, is to seek to find ways to promote agonistic respect across these differences, while engaging the challenges the other positions pose to your existential faith. The latter promotes intra- and cross-cultural exchanges; the former discourages it. Too radical a commitment to thick universals exerts the same sort of pressure that relativism does, although Nussbaum, to her credit, seeks to soften these tendencies. She could do so even more if she were to fold more revisions into the concentric model of culture.

21. An excellent account of the struggle of Las Casas appears in Tzevetan Todorov, *The Conquest of America: The Question of the Other*, trans. Richard Howard (New York: Harper & Row, 1985). I explore the implications of the Las Casas conversion for contemporary global politics in "Global Political Discourse," in *Identity\Difference: Democratic Negotiations of Political Paradox* (Ithaca, N.Y.: Cornell University Press, 1991).

22. I say possibilities, not probabilities. A key role of theory is to probe positive possibilities that might otherwise be overlooked and that, indeed, may be unrecognized because they have been generated by new circumstances of being. The next thing to do is to inspire the pursuit of those possibilities that are most desirable. Paying too much attention to "probabilities" undercuts these two efforts. For, most of the time, the recognized register of probabilities consists of things that are already part of established practice. Those who pursued Christianity, secularism, feminism, gay rights, and so forth at the key moments of their emergence from below the register of established practice were not probabilists of the sort annointed by most social scientists. They were acting to bring something new into the world even more than they were watching to see what was already there. And each time such a project succeeds, in a large or small

way, it provides another piece of evidence, for those who will look, against the ontology of much of contemporary social science. Possibilities are for visionaries and activists; probabilities are for spectators and consultants.

23. For an account that takes several valuable steps in the needed direction, see James Tully, *Strange Multiplicity: Constitutionalism in an Age of Diversity* (Cambridge: Cambridge University Press, 1995).

24. On this issue, see the introduction by Bruce Robbins in Pheng Cheah and Bruce Robbins, eds., *Cosmopolitics: Thinking and Feeling beyond the Nation* (Minneapolis: University of Minnesota Press, 1998); and Peter Euben, "The Polis, Globalization, and the Citizenship of Place," in *Democracy and Vision: Sheldon Wolin and the Vicissitudes of the Political*, ed. Aryeh Botwinick and William E. Connolly (Princeton, N.J.: Princeton University Press, 2001).

25. Immanuel Kant, *Critique of Judgment*, trans. Werner S. Pluhar (Indianapolis: Hackett, 1987), II, no. 87, p. 342.

26. Ibid.

27. I discuss this issue in "Spinoza and Us," *Political Theory* (August 2001): 583–95.

Index

affect: and ethics, 107, 133; and language, 64–76; and thinking, 9, 64–78, 91, 95, 97, 170; ubiquity of, 76–78; and virtual memory, 28, 33–37

agonistic respect, 108, 111, 147, 160, 164, 171, 200

amygdala: and body/brain processes, 8, 27, 90, 91, 104, 127, 206, 212

anxiety, 109, 146, 148, 166, 169

Apostle, The: and deep pluralism, 136–37; and irrational cuts, 134; reductive readings of, 212; and technique, 133–37

Arendt, Hannah: and Deleuze, 210; on gap between past and future, 146–47, 210

arts of the self: Augustine on, 208; Bennett on, 210; Deleuze on, 107, 108; Foucault on, 107, 108, 210; Hampshire on, 107; Kant on, 85, 88; and micropolitics, 108, 113; Nietzsche on, 77, 107, 163–66, 169–74

Asad, Talal: on symbolism and technique, 107

Assmann, Jan: on Moses and monotheism, 211

atheism. *See* nontheistic gratitude for being

Augustine: and language, 73, 74, 208; on paradox of time, 44

becoming: in nature, 53–58, 66; Nietzsche on, 53–55; politics of, 72, 129, 130, 145, 159, 171, 179, 186–87, 192, 194

Being John Malkovitch: and complexity of perception, 29–30

Benjamin, Walter: on cinematic technique, 95

Bennett, Jane: and arts of the self, 210; and enchantment, 204

Bergson, Henri: and cinema, 41; and Einstein, 60; and James, 205; on memory and perception, 16, 26–30, 41, 167; and Nietzsche, 77; on the virtual, 96; body: the body/brain/culture network, 1–21, 36, 63, 75, 90, 92–93, 112

Borch-Jacobsen, Mikkel: on Freud, 131–32

brain, the. *See* neuroscience

Bresson, Robert: on hostility to art, 17

Bruns, Gerald: on James, 211

Buckley, Sandra: on speed and politics, 214

Buddhism, 93, 96, 124, 170

Butler, Judith: and universalism, 215

Campbell, David: on deconstructing the nation, 214

capitalism, 143, 148, 149–53, 163

causality: efficient, 57, 203, 208; immanent, 57, 203–4, 208; and neuroscience, 82; Nietzsche on, 57–58, 67; Prigogine and Stengers on, 57–58

Changeux, Jean-Pierre: on parallelism, 204

Christianity: and anti-Semitism, 119–24; developments in, 172; and Kant, 84, 107, 180–85, 214; and New World, 194–95; and public ethics, 115; and the Right, 161; and spiritual exercises, 133–37

cinema: effects of, xii, 2, 13; and effects on infraconscious perception, 13–16, 25, 67–68, 95; and fantasy, 204; and memory, 15, 93–99; and techniques of self, 96, 168–69; and thinking, 93–99

William E. Connolly teaches political theory at The Johns Hopkins University, where he is professor and chair in the political science department. In 1999 he was awarded the Benjamin Lippincott Award for *The Terms of Political Discourse*, an award given for "a work of exceptional quality...still considered significant after a time span of fifteen years." His recent publications include *The Ethos of Pluralization*, *Why I Am Not a Secularist*, and a new expanded edition of *Identity\Difference*, all published by the University of Minnesota Press.